BETTING THE HOUSE

BETTING THE HOUSE

THE INSIDE STORY OF THE 2017 ELECTION

TIM ROSS and TOM McTAGUE

Biteback Publishing

First published in Great Britain in 2017 by
Biteback Publishing Ltd
Westminster Tower
3 Albert Embankment
London SE1 7SP
Copyright © Tim Ross and Tom McTague 2017

ISBN 978-1-78590-295-6

10 9 8 7 6 5 4 3 2 1

A CIP catalogue record for this book is available from the British Library.

Set in Sabon

Printed and bound in Great Britain by
CPI Group (UK) Ltd, Croydon CR0 4YY

MIX
Paper from
responsible sources
FSC® C020471

CONTENTS

ACKNOWLEDGEMENTS

This book was a huge logistical challenge that would have been impossible without the goodwill, hard work and generosity of many people. The authors would like to thank the team at Biteback for their patience and hard work – especially Iain Dale, James Stephens, Olivia Beattie and Bernadette Marron. The expertise of Frank Prenesti and Kate Devlin was vital during the redrafting process. Thanks also to Simon Walters, Glen Owen and Brendan Carlin at the *Mail on Sunday* for their work during the serialisation.

Tim Ross would like to thank: my editors and colleagues at Bloomberg, especially John Fraher, Emma Ross-Thomas, Flavia Krause-Jackson, Simon Kennedy, Heather Harris, Eddie Buckle, Alan Crawford, Robert Hutton, Thomas Penny, Svenja O'Donnell, Alex Morales and Charlotte Ryan. Apologies are due to Cincinnati CC and Three Line Whip for my absences. The greatest debt by far is to my family – especially my parents for their constant encouragement and invaluable insights. Thanks also to the Stockwells for ongoing help and patience with book-related demands. Most of all, I owe this book to my wife, Amy, who made numerous essential suggestions on the text, and kept two boys and a husband going for far longer than was fair.

Tom McTague would like to thank: my colleagues at Politico, particularly Matt Kaminski, who gave me the time off when he didn't have to, but also Kate Day, Charlie Cooper and Annabelle Dickson, who took the strain during a busy summer. As ever, I am grateful to my parents for their help, which this time even extended to offering their flat as a temporary work den. Most of all, however, I'd like to thank my wife, Louise, and son, Leo, who have had to do without me for longer than is fair and whose support, love and understanding have kept me going. I could not have done it without you both. A final shout-out to my family and friends, particularly to Joe, Penny, Kate and Jules, to whom I've been an absent bore; the TIGs for being missing in action; and to Dan next-door, whose creativity and generosity I wish I'd tapped earlier.

Countless protagonists, including senior Cabinet ministers, shadow Cabinet ministers, MPs, campaign strategists, party officials and others who wished to remain anonymous were generous with their time and information. Without their contributions, the story told in these pages would not exist and we thank them all. Among those happy to be quoted, the authors would like to thank Jonathan Ashworth, Paul Butters, Andrew Cooper, Sir Lynton Crosby, Craig Elder, Nigel Farage, Damian Green, Ben Gummer, Andrew Gwynne, Jon Lansman, Andrew Marr, Jim Messina, Katie Perrior, Niall Sookoo, Will Tanner, Sam Tarry, Nick Timothy and Chris Wilkins.

INTRODUCTION

At 4.30 a.m. on election night, Theresa May arrived back at Conservative headquarters with the country in chaos. Ministers were losing their seats. Labour was running rampant. The pound was in freefall.

She hurried past the party workers slumped in chairs in the campaign war room and into a small private office to consult her aides. Gone was her dream of reshaping Britain at the head of a landslide-winning Conservative government. In its place, one desperate thought remained: stop Labour.

'We have got to make sure Jeremy Corbyn is not the Prime Minister,' an emotional May blurted to her stunned team. Some around May believed she might quit, devastated by her failed campaign. But the desire to prevent a hardline socialist taking over Downing Street was motivation enough. 'I must stay,' she said.[1]

In the space of six and a half hours, May's political mission had been transformed; her credibility and authority shredded, her chances of surviving the next twenty-four hours slim. Even if she did make it through to the weekend, May looked likely to be gone soon after.

As for Corbyn, when the exit poll was announced on TV at 10 p.m., he was serving vegetarian tortillas to friends at his home in Islington. They were swapping bets on Labour's likely share of the vote, an election party game. These were not the actions of a man who expected to have to contemplate walking into No. 10 a few hours later.

*   *   *

For the third time in three years, after David Cameron's majority in 2015 and the EU referendum of 2016, a national vote shocked Britain. Instead of the landslide they were hoping for and expecting, the Conservatives lost their majority altogether. May finished with just 318 seats, while Corbyn's Labour Party defied the commentators and most of the pollsters to win thirty more seats than he had before, finishing with 262. The implications of the hung parliament were profound. May was forced to agree £1 billion to Northern Ireland to secure the support of the Democratic Unionist Party in a 'confidence and supply' alliance.

Furious Tory MPs demanded the heads of May's two powerful chiefs of staff, Nick Timothy and Fiona Hill. They were gone within hours. The Liberal Democrats' Tim Farron and UKIP's Paul Nuttall also quit as leaders of their parties in the aftermath of the election. Tory leadership rivals including David Davis and Boris Johnson were rumoured to be 'on manoeuvres'. As for May, she survived the summer and has claimed she wants to lead the Tories into the next election in 2022. After the disaster of 2017, few of her colleagues believe she will be given the chance.

Aside from the individual casualties, the political impact of the snap election was huge. May called the vote to strengthen her hand ahead of Brexit negotiations. She sought a mandate for her vision of a so-called hard Brexit – but her party lost the mandate to do anything in government alone. Labour stood on an ambiguous but 'softer' Brexit platform, promising to put 'jobs first' and talking up the single market, and won support. Since the election, Labour's backing for the EU single market and customs union has grown, and the Prime Minister has accepted that Britain will maintain a 'status quo' transition period lasting two years. What Brexit will really mean is less clear than before.

May's programme of social and economic reforms – from reintroducing grammar schools to overhauling social care – was also left in turmoil. Getting anything controversial through a hung parliament is a major undertaking, involving knife-edge votes late at night, backroom deals between party whips and rebel MPs, and concessions to awkward peers in the House of Lords. In the words of a senior Whitehall mandarin, it's a mess.

* * *

This book is an attempt to understand what led Theresa May to gamble her career and the country's future on a snap election in the spring of 2017 – and why her bet backfired. How did the Conservative campaign go so badly awry given the crop of hugely experienced election consultants and political strategists who were working in the party's war room? How could a Tory machine that won a higher share of the vote than even Margaret Thatcher still lose its majority? What were the forces driving the unexpected and largely unnoticed groundswell of support for Jeremy Corbyn and his radical Labour platform? Why did none of the political parties truly see what was happening? What influence did the character of the leaders have on their campaigns? Did the surprise nature of the election change the contest? And how did two terrorist attacks affect the result?

In order to answer some of these questions, this book relies on the evidence from more than 100 interviews, emails, text messages, memos, private polling reports, target seat data lists and other material from original sources. The authors have heard from individuals involved at all levels in the campaign, from the very top of politics to party workers out canvassing on the streets during the election. Most of the sources still work in politics and have requested to speak anonymously in order to give their candid opinions and recollections. In the book, the term 'private interview' is used to attribute quotations and information derived from formal but anonymised interviews with sources. References listed as 'private information' relate to other material for which the confidential sources cannot be given. Reconstructions of conversations are based on accounts directly from the participants themselves, or from eye-witnesses. A number of the most senior figures involved have agreed to speak and their words are reflected in named interviews throughout the book.

Passions run high in political life, and the conversations that are the subject of this book frequently involve the use of coarse language by the protagonists. The authors have chosen to retain their original language where it is important to the narrative.

The 2017 election effectively ended multi-party

politics and heralded a resurgence of the old two-party system at Westminster. This book therefore deals primarily with the battle for No. 10, fought between Theresa May and Jeremy Corbyn. The successes of the two major parties mirror the failures of their smaller rivals, in particular the dramatic decline in support for the UK Independence Party and the Liberal Democrats' inability to recover lost ground.

*   *   *

The first part of the book tells the story of how Theresa May came to be persuaded to gamble on a snap election, describing some of the key characters in her team, and how Corbyn's Labour Party was set up to respond. Part Two examines the scrambled strategies that the main parties deployed, looking at their rival ground campaigns as well as the so-called air war in the media and the digital battle, which was a critical part of the contest. Part Three covers campaign events, including the rival manifestos, and the two terrorist attacks, in Manchester and London, which halted the election twice. Finally, Part Four deals with the drama of the election itself.

*   *   *

Given the shock outcome, it would be easy to see Labour's campaign as a success and the Tory operation as a failure. The truth is much more complex. Although they felt like they lost, the Conservatives remain in government and won more seats and votes than Labour with 42.4 per cent of the vote. Since the election, May, derided as robotic and lampooned for her failed gamble, has shown resilience and a determination to do her duty by her party and her country.

While Corbyn's supporters are jubilant and he is stronger as leader, Labour are still fifty-six seats behind the Tories and have lost their third election in a row. The party has already started campaigning for the next one, but to win, it must be able to maintain the enthusiasm of its supporters, stay united through the divisive process of Brexit, and persuade enough older voters that Corbyn is the right man to be Prime Minister.

This book is not just about analysing electoral processes, tactics, trends and results. It is also a human story. Character played a crucial role in shaping the contest. Politicians – and voters – take their democracy seriously. They care about the arguments fought over during campaigns and how the main actors conduct themselves. Whatever the faults of candidates and their advisers, these political professionals are almost always committed to worthy ideals. The characters in this story are real; most are honest, intelligent, hard-working individuals, trying, often with limited success, to tangle with difficult questions facing the country.

When the 2017 snap election was called and power was transferred to the people, politicians faced a choice too. It was a choice that defined careers and shaped the country: to play it safe, or to bet the house.

PART ONE

THE SNAP

CHAPTER 1

MAYISM

THERESA

'She'll be like Margaret Thatcher, she'll be brilliant.' Geoffrey Boycott was the picture of certainty. The former England cricketer, bloody-minded Yorkshireman and blunt-speaking media pundit believed that Theresa May was the next Iron Lady, and the right woman to run Britain. 'She's got the Prime Minister's job at a very tough juncture in our history,' he told a group of travelling British political reporters who bumped into him in the foyer of New Delhi's vast Taj Palace Hotel in November 2016. 'She's strong. Life is about integrity and principles – it should be. We want politicians like that, with integrity, with principles, with honesty.'

Boycott was in town ahead of the first Test match between India and England, starting the following week. By coincidence, May, a lifelong cricket fan, was in the same hotel for a summit. It was her first trade mission to India. Her goal was to prepare the ground for stronger commercial ties between the two nations when India's former colonial masters finally left the European Union.

It was not a happy trip. New Delhi was choking. The

worst smog for nearly twenty years closed hundreds of schools and forced the city's authorities to ban cars from the roads. The air was so thick with pollution that clouds of it filled the marble- and gold-trimmed ground floor of the Taj Palace. During her three-day visit, May achieved little other than a cordial chat about cricket with her host, Indian PM Narendra Modi. There was no clarity on how Britain and India would be able to reinforce their post-Brexit trading links, and she received a public dressing down from Modi over her refusal to allow more Indian students to enrol in British universities.

The gloomy backdrop made Boycott's praise a highlight for May. She invited him to a party at the British High Commissioner's residence that evening for some mutual appreciation. May had a poster of the former opening batsman on her bedroom wall when she was growing up. Asked once why the curmudgeonly Boycott, famous for his lack of flashy stroke-play, had been her childhood hero, she apparently said she admired his staying power and his ability to break down opponents through his sheer determination not to make a mistake.

Whether Boycott told May to her face that she would be as good as Thatcher is not known. May herself dislikes the comparison, though that never prevented others from making it. In his final session of Prime Minister's Questions in the Commons in July 2016, David Cameron couldn't resist gloating at the Tories' superior record on promoting women, despite the lengths his opponents went to in the quest for female voters, which included Harriet Harman touring the country in a fuchsia-coloured minibus. He told the Labour leader Jeremy Corbyn: 'When it comes to women Prime Ministers, pretty soon

I am pleased to say it's going to be two-nil, and not a pink bus in sight.'

In the months before she called the snap election of 2017, the Prime Minister seemed to her colleagues to be every bit as politically invincible as the Iron Lady. Some male Tory MPs, huddled in private conversations in Westminster bars, even took to referring to her as 'Mummy'.

NASTY PARTY

When it comes to her style of politics, Theresa May is certainly more Geoff Boycott than Ian Botham, Boycott's flamboyant England teammate: she dislikes media attention and revelled in former Chancellor Ken Clarke's description of her as a 'bloody difficult woman'. Famously private, May made a virtue of her reputation in Westminster for being a dour dining guest and a minister who doesn't wear her heart on her – admittedly designer – sleeve. 'I know I'm not a showy politician. I don't tour the television studios. I don't gossip about people over lunch. I don't go drinking in Parliament's bars,' she said as she launched her leadership campaign on 30 June 2016. 'I just get on with the job in front of me.'

May's career has been steady rather than spectacular, built on perseverance, painstaking professional attention to detail, and a natural aversion to unnecessary risk. The daughter of a vicar, she realised she wanted to become an MP at the age of twelve. Soon afterwards, she began stuffing envelopes for her local Conservative association and has been a loyal servant of the party ever since.

Aged seventeen, Theresa Brasier, as she then was, arrived at Oxford on the day of the 1974 election, already a Conservative Party member. As she embarked on a geography degree, she told her tutorial partner Alicia Collinson – the future wife of Tory Cabinet minister Damian Green – that she wanted to become Prime Minister one day. It was at a student disco that Benazir Bhutto, the future Prime Minister of Pakistan, introduced her to another budding young Tory, Philip May. The couple fell in love and have been together ever since. To their friends and Oxford contemporaries – who included Green, now First Secretary of State, and Michael Crick, *Channel 4 News*'s political correspondent – Philip seemed the more likely to enter politics full time, having been elected president of the Oxford Union in 1979. But Theresa decided to stand as a councillor in Merton, south London, and represented the Wimbledon Park ward from 1986 to 1994. She entered Parliament in 1997, winning the new seat of Maidenhead, and by 1999 was already a member of the shadow Cabinet. It was around this time that May seems to have first told her husband of the intensity of her ambition to become PM.

May's most memorable contribution as a shadow Cabinet minister was during her tenure as Conservative Party chairman. In a famously uncompromising address to the Tory conference in Bournemouth in 2002, May declared her own side needed to modernise, to embrace the world as it is, rather than as it used to be. With Tony Blair fresh from a second landslide victory a year earlier, May warned a stunned and silent party faithful that they were still seen by too many voters as 'the nasty party' which was not interested in the welfare of the many.

There's a lot we need to do in this party of ours. Our base is too narrow and so, occasionally, are our sympathies. You know what some people call us – the nasty party. I know that's unfair. You know that's unfair. But it's the people out there we need to convince – and we can only do that by avoiding behaviour and attitudes that play into the hands of our opponents.

While she might have been right, the unflattering epithet instantly stuck. Labour could hardly believe their luck. Even now, Labour MPs readily reach for May's 'nasty party' description as a shorthand for why the Tories cannot be trusted to care for public services such as the NHS, or to look after the interests of children growing up in poverty, or to support people with dementia. It was a comment that would come back to haunt May again when her 2017 election campaign began to unravel. The allegation was that policies such as reforms to the funding of elderly care, ending universal free school lunches and cutting the winter fuel allowance re-toxified the Tory brand.

BLOODY DIFFICULT

When David Cameron led the Tories back into power in an unlikely coalition with the Liberal Democrats in 2010, he made May Home Secretary and she quickly gained a reputation as the most stubborn and unbiddable Tory in the Cabinet. While she earned the grudging respect of some colleagues, including the Lib Dem Deputy Prime Minister, Nick Clegg, Cameron grew frustrated with the Home Office's refusal to do as he asked.

In July 2015, two months after unexpectedly winning a majority, the Tory government confronted a crisis at the border with France. Thousands of migrants repeatedly tried to storm the French entrance to the Channel Tunnel to gain entry to Britain, forcing the tunnel to be closed and causing chaos on the roads. One migrant died, 10,000 lorries were backed up on the roads either side of the Channel and tens of thousands of holidaymakers suffered delays and disruption.

Cameron was out of the country on a trip to Singapore, leaving May in charge of the response in London. According to a senior figure in Cameron's team from the time, May repeatedly refused to call a meeting of the government's emergency Cobra committee to coordinate the crisis plan. She apparently did not think it was necessary. Officials told May that it was essential to convene a meeting of the Cobra committee in order to reassure the public that the government was taking every step it could to bring the chaos to an end. But May would not agree, even as calls grew for the British Army to be sent to France to stop the disorder. As one official recalls: 'She just wouldn't do it. In the end, we had to ring up Cameron and get him to force her to call a Cobra meeting.'

May could also be frosty with other Cabinet ministers, according to colleagues who served with her in government. It was something of a ritual before Cabinet meetings for ministers in Cameron's top team to meet early inside No. 10, where they would be served tea, coffee and bacon sandwiches. While most ministers would be swapping small talk, the unclubbable Home Secretary would not engage.

* * *

There were reasons for May to keep her counsel. As a young woman, she had lost both her parents by the age of twenty-five. Intensely private by nature, she is known to confide in only a handful of people, chief among them, her husband, Philip. The couple don't have children. May has revealed that this is a source of sadness to her but has resolutely refused to say more about it.

In 2013, she disclosed that she had Type 1 diabetes and has to inject herself with insulin four or five times a day. May and her team have made a conscious effort to keep her in good health. She was largely kept away from Conservative Party campaign headquarters during the 2017 election because the building, full of Tory staffers working in close proximity, was regarded as too much of a health risk by the Prime Minister's senior strategists. Like many political leaders, May loves to work out. Unlike Cameron, Osborne and Boris Johnson, however, she is reluctant to be filmed jogging around a park, opting instead for Saturday morning sessions in the gym, away from the cameras.

SUDOKU

By temperament, May prefers hard work to idle gossip. Her officials at the Home Office and later in Downing Street were always impressed with her work ethic. She would often stay late in the office, or take ministerial red boxes home to work on, and be up again early, with all her papers signed.

But in a world saturated with social media and rolling news, it is not enough for a leading politician simply to do the job and shun all attempts to capture something personal. It is a cast-iron law of Westminster that every party leader – and all candidates who aspire one day to become one – must give the public some insight into their private lives. Despite the best efforts of her media advisers, May, consciously or not, has resisted most journalists' attempts to get under her skin and find out what makes her tick.

Interviewers sent to paint a portrait of May have resorted to describing her shoes, her trousers, her furniture, and even her favourite dishes to cook for her husband in an attempt to colour in the sketchy outline of a politician who by her own admission is not 'showy'. On one occasion, in preparation for such an interview, May's advisers asked her to think hard for any other hobbies she might be able to share with the public, any interests or particular passions that would help convince people she led a rich and interesting life outside work. 'Well, I do really like Sudoku,' the Prime Minister replied. Horrified Tory aides regarded such an admission as potentially devastating, the kind of detail that could trigger a tsunami of ridicule, and begged her not to mention her fondness for Japanese number puzzles ever again.

'She's shy, she's private, she doesn't show her feelings in the open,' says Katie Perrior, May's former communications director in No. 10. 'She feels her role in life, what she was born to do, was to find the fix to problems and that's all people want from her. She cannot understand that they want more. It doesn't compute.'

Reporters would want to ask the PM how she felt

about losing her parents at a young age, or about not having children. An exasperated May would ask her aides, 'What do they want from me? Why do they want me to say this stuff?' One of her senior media handlers told her the public wanted to know 'that you hurt the way they hurt, that you cry the way they cry'. There was little point. 'It's just a shell. You can't ever get through it. People interview her and say, "It's a nightmare,"' says one aide.

Away from the public eye, however, May's team insist she is a different woman, with a cheeky – and sometimes risqué – sense of humour. 'She is a wonderful, brilliant, funny and sensible person to be around,' says one No. 10 staffer. 'She is lovely – always very grateful for your efforts, and is an impressively hard worker,' says another. Former aides attest to May's lack of pomposity, a down-to-earth quality often missing in top-rank politicians. 'I found her to be the opposite of the brittle, calculating politician of endless newspaper articles: she was a polite, thoughtful and thoroughly decent woman,' according to former speechwriter Alasdair Palmer. 'She never lost her temper or shouted, and she never pulled rank (which she was of course entitled to do). She treated me as an equal, which, in the hierarchy of the Home Office, I obviously was not.'[2]

Soon after entering Downing Street, May told an interviewer that she grew up with dogs at home, and described how Larry, the No. 10 cat, kept his distance from her. Some of her advisers proposed privately that the Prime Minister should get a puppy. While May said she would love to bring an adorable chocolate-coloured Labrador puppy into No. 10, as her aides were suggesting, she worried she would not have the time to care for her new pet. Who would take it for walks and look after it when she was on official trips overseas, she wondered. The Prime Minister's response to the idea sheds light on her reflective nature and her sense of personal responsibility.

It is one of the ironies of the 2017 election campaign that so much focus should be placed on May as a single, presidential candidate, with the Conservative Party's branding deliberately airbrushed from much of the publicity material. In reality, the Tory Party has been a constant in May's life since childhood – and with it her sense of public duty to party and country. These values have always animated her politics far more than any desire to form a personality cult. The conflict between the electioneering hype and the reality of the candidate was rarely more obvious than at the launch of the Tory manifesto in Halifax on 18 May, when the BBC's Nick Watt asked her if the fateful tome represented the bible of Mayism. 'There is no Mayism – I know you journalists like to write about it,' the Prime Minister said, shaking her head in frustration. 'There is good, solid Conservatism which puts the interests of the country and the interests of ordinary working people at the heart of everything we do in government.'

While unbendingly faithful to the cause, May does not regard her Conservatism as theologically fixed. She is flexible, pragmatic and keener on finding answers than clinging to political dogma that will throw up new problems. 'Theresa is quite a distinctive type of politician,' says Will Tanner, who worked with May as a senior policy adviser in the Home Office and No. 10.

She isn't driven by abstract principles and ideologies – she cares about what works in the interests of the people she serves. She also isn't very driven by publicity and self-promotion, which is relatively unusual in the parliamentary party. People play up her religious beliefs and so on, but she is motivated by what I would describe more as a Victorian sense of duty. And she's very down to earth. She's always cautious about what decisions will mean for real people. And she's willing to bend what would normally be quite strong ideological lines in order to get to solutions. She's just driven by outcomes rather than abstract principles.

SUBMARINE

During the tumultuous European Union referendum campaign of 2016, May was largely silent. To David Cameron's frustration, she refused to give more than a lukewarm endorsement of EU membership and declined to repeat his hard-hitting warnings that UK security would be radically eroded outside the bloc. Her sole contribution of note was a speech in which she hedged her bets to such a degree that she managed to annoy both Remainers and Leavers. May argued that EU membership was 'on balance' a better idea than Brexit. But she was not enthusiastic.

'I do not want to stand here and insult people's intelligence by claiming that everything about the EU is perfect, that membership of the EU is wholly good, nor do I believe those that say the sky will fall in if we vote to leave,' she told an audience at the Institute of

Mechanical Engineers in London. 'The reality is that there are costs and benefits of our membership and, looking to the years and decades ahead, there are risks and opportunities too.'

This was it and it was pretty thin. For Cameron and his chief spin doctor, Craig Oliver, May's half-hearted campaign for Remain was deeply disappointing. Some in Cameron's Downing Street dubbed her 'submarine May', even speculating that she was an 'enemy agent' deliberately trying to sabotage the PM, according to an account of the time from Oliver.

LEADERSHIP

On 24 June 2016, defeated and depressed, Cameron announced his resignation. The country needed 'fresh leadership' to carry through the will of the people who had narrowly – but clearly – voted to leave the EU. The race to succeed him was short, brutal and characterised by the staggering readiness of leading contenders to quit or self-implode.

With Cameron's closest ally, Chancellor George Osborne, previously seen as a favourite, deciding not to stand, the leadership contest was initially seen as a straight fight between Boris Johnson, who led the Leave campaign, and May. The Home Secretary devoted some of her initial launch speech to discrediting the former London mayor's record. But she need not have bothered. Boris pulled out of the race after his campaign chief Michael Gove announced he would be standing against him because he believed Johnson was incapable of leading the country. Gove himself was eliminated in a vote of MPs after horrifying colleagues by stabbing his friend so spectacularly in the front.

The final two candidates whose names were to be put to the party membership for a ballot were May and Andrea Leadsom, another leading light from the Brexit campaign. Yet here, too, May was lucky. Her rival quit the contest before it even got going. Leadsom was too mortified to continue after suggesting to *The Times* that she would make a better Prime Minister because she was a mother and understood the world in a different way to the childless Theresa May.

A head-to-head campaign expected to last two months was over in just six days. On 13 July, Cameron received a standing ovation from the Commons at his final PMQs, met the Queen at Buckingham Palace and resigned. Minutes later, May's car left Parliament for the short journey along the Mall to the Palace, where Her Majesty invited her to form a government.

Yet the ease with which May attained the premiership came at a cost. She had not been given the chance to make her own case to the party or the country. She had no real mandate from her own grassroots members, never mind the wider electorate. Just one year into a majority Conservative government, May had reached the summit of power, only to find waiting for her the baggage of Brexit and her predecessor's manifesto to deliver. Yet, she repeatedly ruled out calling an election earlier than scheduled in 2020. 'There is an immediate need for political certainty and economic confidence following the referendum,' she said. 'So that means no second referendum and no general election before 2020.'

May's lack of a personal mandate meant she found it difficult to stamp her identity on the government's agenda and in some cases seemed to make it more difficult for her to get her job done. A full leadership contest 'would have given her much more authority', according to Tanner, who served as deputy head of May's No. 10 Policy Unit.

'I think if Boris had continued to run in that leadership campaign, she'd still have won,' says Tanner. 'She was the person that the party wanted, post-David. An authentic leader with a strong foundation in the grassroots of the party. And for that reason, I think if she'd run against George, she would [also] have won.'

There was perhaps another implication for the election campaign that followed. By the time she had decided to reverse her position on an early election, May still had not been tested as a frontline campaigner on the national stage. Nobody in her own team, or anywhere else, really knew whether she would be any good under the scrutiny that comes with a long, attritional battle for votes, played out in the full glare of the nation's news and social media.

Looking back on the 2017 election, one Cabinet minister ruefully observes: 'Theresa is a much better Prime Minister than she is a campaigner.' Another Tory puts it less kindly: 'She's better at the marriage than the wedding.'

CHAPTER 2

THE CHIEFS

FI

Fiona Hill was ready to party. It was 2 November 2016, and the Tories' weekly magazine of choice, *The Spectator*, was holding its annual political awards. Famously lavish, the champagne reception and dinner was the first glittering ceremony of London's winter season of political soirées.

It was a big moment for Theresa May. The awards were also a test for May's two most trusted aides, Nick Timothy and Fiona Hill, on whom she depended for advice and guidance in matters of government. That evening, she needed them to help her deliver an entertaining speech and navigate the perilous social assembly of newspaper columnists, television presenters, political rivals and editors with charm and style.

Hill returned to No. 10 early in the evening after changing into a glamorous party dress, looking like a million dollars, according to a colleague. She was in a good mood; May was still in her honeymoon period as the new Prime Minister and Hill appeared to be looking forward to letting her hair down with friends.[3]

At that point, however, her colleagues did not know what was to unfold. They had no inkling that Hill would use the occasion to angrily confront one of the country's most famous journalists in front of the Prime Minister, in a tirade that left party guests stunned.

Timothy, meanwhile, barked an order to a colleague to help draft May's speech as quickly as possible, 'and make it funny', he advised.[4] Katie Perrior, May's director of communications, who reported to Hill and Timothy, came up with the idea that the Prime Minister should use the occasion to poke gentle fun at George Osborne, the man she had summarily fired five months previously as Chancellor. Osborne was due to be presenting May with the award for Politician of the Year, in recognition of her triumph in the Tory leadership contest.

Perrior's idea, conjured up at short notice, was for May to take the stage and pass Osborne a hard hat and a hi-vis jacket. Then she would say to Osborne – who made touring building sites dressed in full protective gear a signature image of his chancellorship – 'George, without those I didn't recognise you.'

May decided to go one step further, and put the jacket and helmet on herself before taking the stage, to laughter from the tables of guests. 'That was something she wanted to do. She hid it in her bag and wore it under her coat and it was very funny,' Perrior recalls.[5]

So far, so good. But when it came to May's speech, the jokes fell a bit more heavily. She settled a series of scores, suggesting Boris Johnson, her Foreign Secretary, a former *Spectator* editor and potential leadership rival, was like a dog who might one day need to be put down. She reserved her most brutal comments for her predecessor's director of communications, Sir Craig Oliver, whom David Cameron had knighted in his final honours list as Prime Minister.

In his memoir on the Brexit referendum, Oliver described how the result left him feeling physically sick.
May took up the story:

> I'm particularly pleased to see that Craig Oliver... sorry,
> Sir Craig, is here tonight. In his book he said that when
> he heard the result of the referendum, he walked out of
> the office and as he walked into Whitehall started retch
> ing violently.
>
> I have to say that I think we all understand that feel
> ing; most of us experienced it too when we saw his name
> on the resignations honours list.

To Perrior and other observers, this was unnecessarily
brutal. The UK Prime Minister shouldn't have stooped
to the level of insulting a former aide to the man she'd
replaced as premier. 'She didn't need to do that. It wasn't
very prime ministerial,' says Perrior.

*   *   *

After the meal, the BBC's Nick Robinson sauntered over
to Hill, who was two seats away from May. Robinson
and Hill had fallen out two years previously, over his
report on a government leak scandal that eventually
cost Hill her job. She had been upset at the time because
Robinson had named her and her partner in his news
report, but the journalist thought it would be polite to
exchange pleasantries rather than avoid each other.

He was mistaken.

When Robinson approached Hill, she erupted. 'You made my mother cry,' she said.

As Hill berated the BBC man, he protested, 'I was just saying "hello". This isn't really the time or place for this.'[6]

Robinson made his excuses and moved on to talk to someone else. Later in the night, the pair bumped into each other again as they made their way out towards the cloakrooms – and Hill let fly another burst of anger.

The incident shocked Robinson, a former political editor who now presents the *Today* programme, the BBC's flagship morning radio show, which has been required daily listening in Westminster for decades. He told other guests how inappropriate he felt Hill had been to attack him in the most public of settings, in front of his peers, colleagues and even the Prime Minister herself. One witness says: 'It was extraordinary. The thing that amazed me about her behaviour was that it was so reckless.'[7]

What struck others, however, was that the Prime Minister simply ignored the whole scene as it unfolded a few feet away. 'The Prime Minister doesn't say anything when Fiona goes off on one,' Perrior says. 'She just has a look which says, "It's not good, all of this, is it, but, well, here we are." It was quite clear. I thought it was a relationship where she knew exactly what Fiona's faults were but she cared about Fiona – and Fiona cared about her.'[8]

*   *   *

Fiona Hill's first full day working in No. 10 as the Prime Minister's co-chief of staff was also her forty-third birthday. Her new job was a crowning achievement in an impressive career spanning media and politics, a career in which she'd earned the respect – and fear – of her colleagues and opponents alike. Born in Greenock, on the west coast of Scotland, and educated at a state school in Port Glasgow, Hill cut her teeth as a reporter on *The Scotsman* and the *Daily Record* newspapers, where, as the new girl, she had to cover subjects ranging from fashion to football. According to colleagues from the time, one of her best qualities was her tenacity – she was always there. Immaculate and stylishly dressed, she would hang around the office, looking for interesting work to do.[9]

Hill quit the print media to work for Sky News, where she was able to combine her sharp news judgement with effective organisational skills and an ability to stay calm under intense pressure, according to colleagues. She left journalism and was in and out of the Tory Party's press office during its time in opposition, working first for shadow Health Secretary Andrew Lansley and then for Chris Grayling, who served as shadow Home Secretary before the 2010 election. When David Cameron made May Home Secretary in the 2010 coalition with the Liberal Democrats, Hill joined May in the department as a political special adviser, along with Nick Timothy. Between them, Hill and Timothy became indispensable to May; trusted and powerful, often fierce and always loyal, they ruled the Home Office on behalf of the woman they called 'the boss'.

Initially, Hill's expertise was in media management, given her background as a journalist. She was tasked with taking charge of May's personal image (both women love flamboyant kitten heels) and fighting to keep her out of trouble with the media. During this time, Hill and Timothy cultivated a strong relationship with the *Daily Mail*, arguably the most powerful national newspaper in Britain, which had a reputation for extinguishing promising ministerial careers and was obsessed with a campaign against rising immigration. As Home Secretary, controlling the border, cutting net migration to the Tory target of the 'tens of thousands' and deporting 'foreign criminals' were among May's chief responsibilities. These chimed perfectly with the *Mail*'s agenda. The fact that May remained in her job for so long – she was the second longest-serving Home Secretary in UK history – is in no small part due to Timothy and Hill's media management skills, especially given her poor record of repeatedly missing the government's target to cut migration.

Yet Hill wasn't just a spin doctor. She is also credited with bringing her highly rated political instincts to bear on key policies, and worked especially closely with May on developing the Modern Slavery Act, a law the Tory leader now sees as one of her greatest achievements.

In 2014, Hill's impulse to go on the attack in order to protect her boss backfired so badly that she was forced out of her job. It was this crisis that led her to fall out with Nick Robinson. The trigger was a row that the Home Office had with Michael Gove, then the Education Secretary, over tackling extremism in schools. Gove secretly briefed the media that the Home Office was failing to 'drain the swamp' of extremists. He criticised Charles Farr, May's counter-terrorism adviser – who was in a relationship with Hill at the time. A furious Hill then found a way to retaliate. The Home Office website published a private letter that May had sent to Gove suggesting his department had failed to stop alleged extremists from taking over state schools in Birmingham.

Such letters between Cabinet colleagues are usually highly confidential, so the Home Office's decision to publish it online at 12.24 a.m. caused uproar. Cameron launched an inquiry. The investigation, which the Cabinet Secretary Sir Jeremy Heywood led, revealed Gove as the source for the original briefing and blamed Hill for the counter-attack, in which an unnamed individual said the Department for Education's failure to get a grip on child protection 'scares me'. Cameron forced Gove to apologise for his actions and later demoted him from Education Secretary to Chief Whip at the next reshuffle. Hill, however, was forced to resign – despite May's strenuous efforts to retain her trusted ally.[10] Relations between Hill and Cameron's team were said to be so toxic that she was not afforded a second chance.

Hill's departure delighted those in the media and the Tory Party who counted themselves among her enemies – but it proved not to be a permanent exile. She remained in touch with May over the next two years, while working for the conservative think tank the Centre for Social Justice and for a lobbying and communications firm. When David Cameron quit hours after losing the EU referendum in June 2016, Hill raced back to May's side for the leadership contest that followed. She ran the Home Secretary's campaign for No. 10 with the same ruthlessness and tenacity that she had always brought to her work, and with the same partner who formed the other half of May's Praetorian Guard: Nick Timothy.

NICK

Twelve months before the leadership contest, Nick Timothy had been out of work. When David Cameron unexpectedly won a majority in the 2015 election, Timothy decided he was not going to return to the Home Office for another five-year stint as Theresa May's special adviser. He had worked full-time on the local campaign in South Thanet, in the ultimately successful – but controversial – Tory campaign to stop UK Independence Party leader Nigel Farage winning his first Commons seat.[11] After five years as a special adviser in the Home Office, and at still only thirty-five, he wanted to move on to something new.

He spent his time catching up with friends he had not seen in the hectic run-up to the election, and planning a different kind of career, combining writing and work for a charity. In the end, he chose to take up the role of director of the New Schools Network, an independent charity that helps groups set up free schools under the education reforms that were the brainchild of Michael Gove.

Timothy was careful not to cut ties with May. Cameron was at the height of his powers after winning the first Tory majority for twenty-three years, but he had already made it clear that he would not seek to lead the party into the next election, scheduled for 2020. While Timothy would joke to friends that there was 'no vacancy' for his old boss to fill, he was clear that should one arise, he would be back at May's side to fight her campaign in an instant.

Timothy remained a source of informal advice for

May during the months that followed his departure from government. When the Home Secretary had to prepare her keynote speech to the Conservative Party's annual conference in Manchester, it was Timothy who helped her to write it, even though he had no official role in her team. He even travelled up to help her prepare in person.

In her speech, May set out her hardest position to date on curbing mass immigration. Numbers were too high and unsustainable, she said, as she proposed a series of measures to reduce asylum applications. Usually supportive business groups accused her of 'pandering to anti-immigration sentiment', while refugee campaigners described her comments as 'chilling'.

As he paced the streets of Manchester in the October rain afterwards, another subject was on Timothy's mind: the seemingly unstoppable rise of one of May's biggest Cabinet rivals, George Osborne. Since the election, the Chancellor had been feted as the political genius behind the most successful Tory campaign in a generation. He was seen as Cameron's anointed heir and widely regarded as the Prime Minister in waiting. But Osborne had clashed repeatedly with May – and Timothy – over questions of security and immigration. Privately, Timothy held the Chancellor in contempt. Osborne opposed May's tough stand on controlling the numbers of foreign students and, much to Timothy's horror, was relaxed about allowing Chinese state-owned companies to invest in critical UK infrastructure, such as the plan for a new nuclear power station at Hinkley Point in Somerset. Timothy believed such an approach amounted to selling Britain's national security to a potentially hostile foreign state.

Osborne's reputation suffered a series of blows in the months after conference. First his plan to cut tax credits crashed into opposition in the House of Lords, and then Iain Duncan Smith quit as Work and Pensions Secretary in a row over the Budget's plan to cut welfare. Nick Timothy was amused to see how little support the Chancellor seemed to have among backbench MPs when few were willing to come to his defence. As Osborne's star faded, space opened up for other leadership candidates to shine.

*   *   *

Timothy is the son of a steelworker and a school secretary and as an Aston Villa fan is proud of his Birmingham roots. Raised in a working-class area of the city, his formative political experience came in 1992. John Major, another working-class boy, was leading the Conservative Party and seemed destined for defeat at the hands of Neil Kinnock's Labour. For Timothy, only months into his career at King Edward VI Aston grammar school, such an outcome represented an existential threat:

> I knew that if Labour won the election, my school would be closed down and the opportunity I had been given would be taken away. Thanks to the Tories, that did not happen and I became the first member of my family to go to university.
>
> 1992 was the year the Conservatives asked the electorate: 'What does the Conservative Party offer a working-class kid from Brixton?' The working-class kid, of course, was John Major and the answer was that they

made him Prime Minister. I knew what the Conservative Party had to offer me that year, and as a twelve-year-old, I learned early that Labour, in the pursuit of equality, only hold people back, but it is the Conservatives who help you to go as far as your potential allows.

That, to me, is the fundamental difference between the two parties, and it is why I have been a Conservative ever since.[12]

Timothy took a first-class degree in politics at Sheffield before finding his way, via a spell volunteering, into a job with the Conservative Research Department, the traditional nursery for future Cabinet ministers and party stars. While in Tory Central Office, as the party's headquarters were known at the time, Timothy met May and became her full-time researcher while she was shadow Transport Secretary in 2002.

By the time May entered government in 2010, the pair were already friends as well as colleagues. Although he survived when Hill was forced to quit over the row with Michael Gove, Timothy was no more popular with Cameron's set.

In 2014, Timothy and Stephen Parkinson, another aide to May, were struck off the list of approved Tory candidates for the coming general election – allegedly because they refused to campaign in a by-election. Timothy blamed Downing Street for the snub.

In the year between the 2015 election and the 2016 EU referendum, Timothy's freedom from the constraints of government allowed him the space to develop and set out his own political views. In a series of articles for the influential Tory website ConservativeHome.com and the *Telegraph*, he gave a hint, at least, of the direction May would take government policy in when she won the leadership.

In these articles and interviews, Timothy discussed ending the ban on grammar schools,[13] curbing benefits for pensioners, and the national security implications of allowing the Chinese to buy up critical British infrastructure. His columns were varied in content and tone: some were passionate, some angry, others contained humour. Most of Timothy's pieces contained within them a clear and distinct sense of his own beliefs, as well as a strong commitment to a particular strain of Conservative thinking.

BREXIT

Despite supporting Brexit, Timothy railed against the conduct of the two sides during the EU referendum and called for a fundamental rethink of the way political campaigns operate. The lies, cynical communication techniques and reduction of the debate to false choices left him feeling 'frustrated, disappointed and worried about the future'. 'The referendum campaign is bringing to the surface everything that is wrong about our politics,' he said, as he criticised 'the Political Rules of Engagement'. These include changing the subject of debate by any means necessary, if it is easier than changing voters' minds through persuasion; reducing everything to 'a binary choice', no matter how complex the issues; and sacrificing truth and accuracy for influence over the electorate. 'Even if you have told a whopper, it doesn't matter so long as everybody is talking about it,' he says.

> In fact, the rules say that the more your opponents try to dispute the accuracy of your claims, the happier you should be – because they're drawing attention to your issue of choice.
>
> I do not mean to sound weak or lily-livered about the rough and tumble of political campaigning. I have worked on and run enough campaigns to know that they should offer a tough and relentless examination of the propositions made by the rival sides. But the reality of the way this campaign is being fought – and how our politics are becoming in general – is corrosive to the quality of our democracy and trust in government. And it is patently very damaging to the Conservative Party.
>
> It is of course too late now to drain the poison from this campaign, but when the referendum is over – whatever the result – we are going to need to do something to change these Political Rules of Engagement. We need only look across the Atlantic to the United States – where the political culture is even more cynical and the rules even more firmly entrenched – to see where we risk heading.[14]

Much to Timothy's professed annoyance, these articles were treated with something close to scriptural reverence when he entered No. 10, leading the media to focus on him as 'the thinker' who was sometimes labelled 'May's brain'. The views of the Prime Minister herself, and of her other chief of staff, Fiona Hill, were apparently discounted.

In one article, Timothy called for a new form of Tory modernisation. The party shouldn't choose the Easterhouse modernisation, espoused by Iain Duncan Smith, the former Tory leader, which focused on the poorest inhabitants of the infamous Glasgow housing estate. Nor should the party pursue the socially liberal 'Soho modernisation' beloved of Osborne and Cameron. Instead, the Conservatives should ask themselves what they have to offer a boy from Erdington, the working-class district of Birmingham where he grew up.

Then, he set out what must now – after the election disaster that he oversaw – seem an even more bitter truth. 'The most serious weakness that the Conservatives have', he wrote, 'is the perception that we simply do not give a toss about ordinary people.'[15] But by focusing on people who have modest means, who distrust radical policies and have conservative instincts, the Tories can do the right thing for society and win votes, Timothy argued.

> With this approach, of course we would still help the very poor and of course we would fight injustices based on gender, race and sexuality, but the Party would adopt a relentless focus on governing in the interests of ordinary, working people. They are the people whose lives are most affected – for better and worse – by politics. They can't choose to send their kids to a private school when the schools around them are terrible. They can't opt out of the NHS if they find themselves in a dirty hospital or at the end of a long waiting list. They are the ones who find themselves out of work, on reduced hours, or with never-ending pay freezes when the economy goes wrong. They find themselves unable to afford

the mortgage when interest rates go up. They have to go without when their taxes rise. They are the people for whom debates about tax credits are not about spreadsheets, headlines or dividing lines but about whether mum can go back to work or not.[16]

When it came to devising a Brexit policy, Timothy more than anyone can claim responsibility for transforming Theresa May from a reluctant Remainer to a passionate Leave supporter. He co-wrote her landmark Brexit speech, which she delivered in front of European ambassadors at Lancaster House one cold, bright day in January 2017. In it, May set out her vision for a clean break from the EU. Without leaving the single market, she said, Britain would not be leaving the EU at all. Without leaving the customs union, the UK would lose all the opportunities that a new world of global trade could offer. Her mission – Timothy's mission – was to honour the anger that 52 per cent of voters had expressed at the referendum the previous June: controlling immigration took priority over the economy. Timothy, more than anyone, made the Tory Party the party of hard Brexit. It was a decision that had a far-reaching impact on the election six months later.

By Timothy's own account, he, Hill and May are close and enjoy each other's company. 'We all liked working with one another and I think we worked well together and we're all friends,' he says. 'Of course we're tight.'[17]

In the crude and sometimes cruel way that politicians indulge in pseudo-psychological gossip about each other, some ministers see in Nick and Fiona the children that Theresa and Philip May never had. One senior figure in the 2017 election campaign sees it differently: 'I think they are more influential than that. I'm close to my kids, but my kids don't tell me what to say. They are more like parents, actually. It's unusual.'

When May became Prime Minister on 13 July 2016, the speech she made outside No. 10 was drafted by her new chief of staff. In it, she set out the same values he had articulated a few months earlier. Even the rhetorical structures of his style are clear to see.

The mission to make Britain a country that works for everyone means more than fighting these injustices. If you're from an ordinary working class family, life is much harder than many people in Westminster realise. You have a job but you don't always have job security. You have your own home, but you worry about paying a mortgage. You can just about manage but you worry about the cost of living and getting your kids into a good school.

If you're one of those families, if you're just managing, I want to address you directly.

I know you're working around the clock, I know you're doing your best, and I know that sometimes life can be a struggle. The government I lead will be driven not by the interests of the privileged few, but by yours.

We will do everything we can to give you more control over your lives. When we take the big calls, we'll think not of the powerful, but you. When we pass new laws, we'll listen not to the mighty but to you. When it comes to taxes, we'll prioritise not the wealthy, but you. When it comes to opportunity, we won't entrench the advantages of the fortunate few. We will do everything

we can to help anybody, whatever your background, to
go as far as your talents will take you.[18]

Here was Mayism. And its father was Nick Timothy.

NO. 10

Once the glossy black door of No. 10 had closed behind
them on 13 July 2016, May, Timothy and Hill began
reshaping the Tory government in their image. The
Cabinet reshuffle was dramatic and brutal. Within minutes, May sacked George Osborne and replaced him
at the Treasury with Philip Hammond. Out, too, went
Osborne loyalist Nicky Morgan and Hill's arch foe,
Michael Gove. Back from the political graveyard came
Liam Fox, David Davis – and Boris Johnson. These three
Brexiteers owed their second chances, and therefore
their loyalty, to May.

The shake-up was total. It was hard not to read May's
revolution as a deliberate cull of the Cameroons. In the
days and weeks that followed, the machinery of government was torn up, a new Brexit department and a
Department for International Trade created, and civil
servants and ministerial advisers were required to clear
all their plans through Downing Street. Inside No. 10,
officials were required to clear all their work through
'the chiefs', as Timothy and Hill became known.

As for the strategy of communicating with the wider
world, there was to be a clampdown, with control wielded solely by May's two aides. 'In as much as they had a

playbook, it was to find the Craig Oliver playbook and write the word "not" in it a lot,' one Tory says.

May's team grew. Out went Cameron's Policy Unit and in came Will Tanner, from the Home Office and John Godfrey, from Legal & General, where he was corporate affairs director. In place of Sir Craig Oliver, whose post-Brexit queasiness so amused the new PM, Katie Perrior was hired to be director of communications. Lizzie Loudon, Iain Duncan Smith's former special adviser, who had worked for Vote Leave in the referendum, joined No. 10 as May's press secretary, while Liz Sanderson took charge of the PM's profile as head of features, focusing less on day-to-day news management and more on promoting May's image in magazines and newspapers.

Other key figures in May's inner circle arrived. Joanna Penn, known as 'JoJo', a former Harvard scholar, joined as deputy chief of staff. Alex Dawson and Stephen Parkinson, two longstanding May loyalists, were also brought in, while Chris Wilkins, a Welsh Tory, became director of strategy and gained a place alongside Timothy in crafting all the Prime Minister's most important speeches. Among the MPs, May's former university friend Damian Green got his first Cabinet job as Work and Pensions Secretary. Ben Gummer, the son of former Tory minister John Gummer, gained the trust of the chiefs (and therefore the PM) in his role as Cabinet Office minister, and became a key figure in their circle.

For a time, it seemed the new team could do no wrong. Yet, bit by bit, complaints began to surface in the bars and cafés of Westminster that May's regime was too controlling. Where were all the announcements?

What did she want to achieve? Why was it impossible to get a slot in the Downing Street media 'grid' for a busy and ambitious minister to give an interview or make a speech?

Officials working with May's team in Downing Street had to reconcile the fact that they were in the seat of power, doing the job of their dreams, with a regime that frequently bordered on dysfunctional. 'It was completely amazing to be in there, but it was a really toxic atmosphere,' one former No. 10 staffer says.

Perrior in particular faced a difficult time. She found herself repeatedly overruled by Hill, who was reluctant to relinquish the levers of media management, even to an experienced communications professional such as Perrior. Hill once sent her a text in which she said: 'One day you'll make a great director of communications.' It was already her title.

It wasn't just Perrior getting a rough ride – so too were some ministers inside the Cabinet. 'I told about a third of the Cabinet – all men – to stop thinking Theresa May doesn't like you, that she thinks you're shit and everyone in No. 10 is working against you,' says Perrior.[19] 'I told them, "That's bullshit. It's not you." But when you are in your own personal bubble, you truly think they hate you, there's some reason you're shit and they're coming for you. You don't realise someone else is being treated the same.'

By Christmas 2016, resentment within government at the influence of Hill and Timothy had reached a crescendo, not helped by the official disclosure that they were each earning £140,000, almost as much as a Cabinet minister. Complaints came from across Whitehall,

with ministers and their advisers lining up to attack the
reign of terror that the 'control freak' chiefs of staff were
orchestrating at the top of government. One minister
warned privately that May was becoming isolated and
the behaviour of the chiefs, who were fiercely protective
of their own relationship with the PM, was cutting her
off. Even ministers loyal to May were now reluctant to
tell her their true views, for fear that Hill or Timothy
would take the career-ending decision to write them off
thenceforth as an enemy, the minister said.

Philip Hammond, the Chancellor, was once even
forced to ask an official he trusted inside No. 10 whether
a circulating rumour was true: did the PM's circle really
refer to the Chancellor of the Exchequer in his absence as
a 'c***'? Senior Tories who worked in No. 10 and later
on the election campaign attest that they did hear this
extreme language being used to describe Hammond.[20]
How Hammond heard the news, and how he took it,
is unknown. Such levels of disrespect astonished some
of those present. Timothy insists: 'It is fairly well known
that Philip [Hammond] and I did not get on but I have
no recollection of this language being used at all.'

Inside No. 10, there was even a room that was apparently set aside for the chiefs to rebuke officials and
sometimes ministers who had fallen short. Adjacent to
the historic Cabinet Room, and close to May's own office,
lay what was known as Room B. It was also known
as 'the Bollocking Room'. The name dates back to an
occasion when David Cameron disciplined Timothy and
Hill there. In this room, anyone judged to have made
a mistake would be taken and given a dressing down,
according to some who worked in No. 10. Occasionally,

people would be summoned from across Whitehall and made to wait and sweat for hours in there, only for the chiefs of staff eventually to cancel the meeting. According to one No. 10 staffer, Timothy would even say, 'Meet me in the Bollocking Room in five minutes.'

*   *   *

It was not just ministers and aides who suffered. Helen Bower, the respected civil servant who had served as the Prime Minister's official spokesman to both Cameron and May, quit No. 10 for a job in the Foreign Office. Bower has kept her counsel about her time in No. 10, but according to those who worked with her, she experienced a difficult time.

One incident stands out. It was 8 December. Perrior was walking back to No. 10 from Buckingham Palace, where she had been having her regular monthly catch-up meeting with royal aides. Boris Johnson, the Foreign Secretary, with whom she had worked closely in the past, rang in a blind fury. 'You've issued a line, it's outrageous,' he said. 'I haven't issued any line, let me find out what's going on,' Perrior replied. The previous night, *The Guardian* had quoted comments from Johnson made the week before, in which he accused Saudi Arabia of abusing Islam for political advantages and 'puppeteering and playing proxy wars' in the region. It was an embarrassing breach of convention from the Foreign Secretary, made worse because it came to light just as the Prime Minister returned from a two-day visit to Saudi Arabia.

What happened next, according to one account, was

that Hill asked Helen Bower to issue a blunt rebuke to
Johnson at the regular morning media briefing for political lobby reporters in Westminster, telling them that he
was not speaking for the government. Bower, the Prime
Minister's impartial civil service spokesman, raised concerns with Hill that to do so would be seen for what
it was – a blatant slap-down of the Foreign Secretary,
whose job it is to represent the government's views
around the world. Hill persisted, and Bower was forced
to comply. Hill was not the only senior figure in No. 10
pushing for a strong line to be taken against Johnson.
Senior political aides and civil servants with foreign
policy expertise were also angry with him. But May had
delegated control over many media matters to Hill and
Timothy, whose expertise she relied on and trusted.[21]

Saudi Arabia 'is a vital partner' for the UK in the
region, especially on counter-terrorism, Bower told the
assembled press at the lobby briefing. Asked if May had
any sympathy with Johnson's concerns about Saudi,
Bower replied: 'Those are the Foreign Secretary's views,
they are not the government's views on Saudi and its
role in the region.'

When the briefing finished, the prime ministerial slap-
down of the Foreign Secretary burst onto news bulletins,
websites and Twitter. Perrior recalls:

> When I got back to No. 10, I said, 'I've got the For-
> eign Secretary doing his nut at me, what has happened?'
> and Helen said, 'I told her this would happen.' I was
> despatched to go and try and calm him down. He was
> furious. It was hugely damaging to him. Our job in com-
> munications is to shut that story down.[22]

STAND-UP COMEDY

Most worryingly for their colleagues, there was a sense that Hill and to a lesser degree Timothy appeared to revel in their reputation for being abrasive and unpredictable, which made some people's lives a misery.

The culture of drinking after work was a feature of life for May's political team, just as it was for many others working in Westminster, where the bars are plentiful and the hours anti-social. If you were a part of the chiefs' club, you would be invited out to a nearby pub such as the Westminster Arms, or the Clarence, or a hotel like the Corinthia or St Ermin's. Rounds of drinks would be bought, gossip would be exchanged and you would feel special. But if you fell out with Hill or Timothy, you would quickly feel unwelcome. 'The last time I felt like that I was twelve and at school,' one former colleague says. The fact that the two most powerful unelected officials in the country were frequently socialising with colleagues raised eyebrows with some but seemed to offer a way in to those on the outside.

Katie Perrior felt relations with Hill were so bad that she would eventually have to quit. The decision was mortifying. She had given up a job she loved, and co-ownership of the company she founded, in order to work with May's fledgling administration in No. 10. She was determined to try anything she could think of to make the relationship work. She bought Hill a gift and left it on her desk, but the gesture went unremarked for three days. Then, in February, she arranged to meet Hill for a drink and a bite of dinner in the Clarence pub, just across Whitehall from Downing Street. While Perrior waited, Hill, clearly a busy woman, did not turn up.[23]

RED BOXES

A minister's red briefcase – known as the 'red box' – contains papers for them to review and sign overnight or over a weekend. The documents will typically include policy submissions; briefings on a wide range of subjects; proposals from Cabinet colleagues; letters to check and sign; draft speeches and replies to Parliamentary Questions to approve; and minutes from Cabinet meetings.

In May's Downing Street, the chiefs would demand to review the documents before they went into the PM's red box for her to work on overnight. While this was not unusual for a No. 10 chief of staff, Hill and Timothy took the practice to a new level, according to their colleagues. They would comment on documents that ministers and senior officials sent to the Prime Minister in a more systematic way than Downing Street insiders had seen before, especially when the subject related to domestic policy and issues the chiefs felt were central to May's political mission.[24] The intensity of the chiefs' involvement in the detail put some civil servants' noses out of joint, according to reports.[25] In order to help manage the growing mountain of paperwork, Hill and Timothy were given two private secretaries and a diary assistant.

Officials recall – and Timothy confirms – that if the chiefs were unconvinced by one of May's decisions on a red box submission, they would seek to reopen the debate about the item in question, either in a conversation alone with the Prime Minister or during the regular afternoon meeting of senior No. 10 staff. While there is nothing sinister about this, it demonstrates the degree of influence that the two chiefs of staff had over the policy-making process in May's government.

Under the government code covering the work of political special advisers – such as Hill and Timothy – the chiefs were allowed to 'review and comment on – but not suppress or supplant – advice being prepared for ministers by civil servants'.[26] One senior official says the chiefs never crossed this line and always allowed civil servants' advice to be put to the PM, even if they disagreed with it.[27] Official guidance says ministers 'are required to' consider fairly the advice from the impartial civil service and others, 'but should themselves make all significant policy decisions'.[28]

Some of those who worked with her believe May effectively subcontracted large amounts of decision-making to Timothy and Hill. A number of Downing Street insiders confirm that May was more willing to delegate some decisions to her chiefs than David Cameron had been, but they insist she remained firmly in charge of 'core policy and strategy'.

*   *   *

'You'll never get a fag paper between me, the Prime Minister and Nick.' This was one of Hill's favourite lines, according to people who worked with her. She was passionate, committed to protecting her boss, and, according to her colleagues, could sometimes be 'volcanic', showing flashes of frustration if work was unsatisfactory.[29] There was an agreement between the two chiefs that they would not publicly criticise each other or be seen to differ on anything, in front of lower-ranking members of staff. They appeared to extend this approach to the entire government and civil service. The tight-knit nature of their relationship, and their proximity to May, created an air of mystery around how exactly particular choices were made at the top. 'We would not witness the final crunch on decisions so we didn't know how much of it was Nick and Fi telling her what to do and how much of it was her saying, "This is what I want." You never quite know who is calling the shots,' according to one individual who worked with the chiefs.[30]

May herself seemed to be a nervous character, someone wary of making big calls. She was disinclined to challenge the more outlandish examples of her aides' behaviour. Hill in particular was not popular with some Cabinet ministers, who complained she was too controlling and would not respond to messages. One said he had not seen worse behaviour from a senior aide in twenty-five years.[31]

Another Cabinet minister was more forgiving of the chiefs' motivations and behaviour.

> I think they acted with the right motives but I don't think anybody realised, I'm not sure even the Prime Minister realised what a barrier they had become to access to her. They were dedicated, loyal servants to the Prime Minister and unfortunately it went wrong, but it was not out of malice, it was not out of vindictiveness. It was a fierce loyalty and desire to protect her, and sometimes it got a bit too fierce.[32]

THREESOME

'Those guys were an asset to her. They gave her things that she probably couldn't have got from very many people.' Will Tanner, who worked in the Home Office with May and moved to become deputy head of the No. 10 Policy Unit, is convinced. For all their foibles and faults, the chiefs were a critical part of the Prime Minister's success. 'Nick is, whatever his faults, a thoughtful observer of trends in British politics and a person with interesting answers to some of those problems. Fiona is an extremely effective communicator, even if she sometimes rubs people up the wrong way – and they got her through some very tough times.'[33]

One Tory official explains that May relies on Timothy to do the ideological heavy lifting and Hill for media management. May will take advice, 'once she trusts you' the official says. 'She trusted Nick to provide intellectual ballast and coherence and political strategy, which I think she probably wasn't that interested in, or didn't feel well qualified to provide. She trusted Fi on communications and to have relationships with journalists where she didn't want to.' But what did May herself bring to the table? She was 'the figurehead' providing the leadership at the top 'and making the really tough calls that only she can make'.[34]

Senior officials who remain loyal to the two chiefs say that while they were not 'angels' in the office, their demanding behaviour, intense loyalty and degree of influence were not unprecedented or in any way inappropriate. It is, nevertheless, remarkable how many questions remain among senior Tories who have worked closely with Hill, Timothy and May about the close nature of their working relationship. It is clear that Hill's combative personal style made enemies. Some of them have spoken out about what they regard as unfair treatment. She herself has declined repeatedly to be interviewed, or to respond to written requests for comments on specific allegations. Hill's reluctance to engage on these matters inevitably makes it more difficult to understand and convey her side of the story.

Even allies and friends of Hill and Timothy remain mystified about what really went on, and whether the influence the chiefs wielded over May, however well intentioned, was sensible. It certainly was not common. Why were they so reluctant to allow others to see how they operated? Did the PM encourage their pugnacious behaviour? More to the point, was the Prime Minister derelict in her duty by giving these people so much scope?

It was as if May, at times, deemed herself unfit to rule alone, and relied on the counsel of her two chiefs of staff, as well as her husband. Given how closely she worked with the chiefs, it seems unlikely that May was unaware of some of the difficulties – or at least the complaints – their inner circle generated. May was said to have lacked confidence in her own judgement, according to multiple sources, including ministers who remain supportive of her.

A Tory veteran who is close to the PM says: 'The threesome is quite an unusual political model. Most politicians have a tight team but it's almost as if they were actually an entity. Some people said it was like they were joint Prime Ministers. I've never seen anything quite like it.'[35]

Another senior party source who watched the three of them together says: 'I've never seen such a tight unit – they were her crutch. It was symbiotic. My assessment is actually she did subcontract everything to Nick and Fi. She was afraid to take a decision. She's not a bad person, she's just different.'

Whatever else can be said of her, Hill was a passionate and loyal ally and adviser to May, who was totally committed to her role. Timothy was also deeply committed to May as a friend, as much as to their shared political project. According to Perrior, 'Nick and Fiona loved her – too much in some respects. They really did care for her and she really did care for them. I think Nick and Fi thought we wanted a bit of that, and I never did.'

According to Timothy, all this talk is exaggerated:

The way we work together is a massively overdone thing. Of course we're tight. And of course we kept some things quite tight but so does any other senior politician or chief executive, or whatever. But there are loads of people with whom we've worked quite closely in different positions who were part of the thing and were very trusted members of the team – it was open.[36]

Timothy names Chris Wilkins, who was May's strategy director, JoJo Penn, her deputy chief of staff, Ben Gummer, the Cabinet Office minister, and Sir Jeremy Heywood, the Cabinet Secretary, as examples. He also dismisses the idea that May was only capable of making decisions after discussing issues in private with Hill and Timothy. 'That's just not true,' he says.

> There will obviously be occasions when you have a discussion with somebody, and then you go away and look at the evidence or talk to other people and think through what's feasible. But anybody who has been in any meetings with her as PM or Home Secretary knows that she takes decisions in open formats all the time.
>
> I think it's overdone – and it's overdone because it's the age-old thing, when people want to criticise the leader but don't feel they can criticise the leader, so they criticise the people close to the leader. That's what happens.[37]

CHAPTER 3

INHERITANCE

BUDGET BLUES

Ben Gummer slipped into No. 10 and took his seat at the far corner of the Cabinet table. It was the morning of Wednesday 8 March and as a new Cabinet minister, the 39-year-old was about to experience first-hand one of the major set-piece events in any top-flight politician's life: Budget Day from inside Downing Street.

Twenty-two years Gummer's senior, Philip Hammond was also preparing to make his Budget debut to Parliament. The Chancellor was to brief the Cabinet on the contents of the statement he would be making to the Commons later that day. With the Prime Minister due to trigger Brexit by invoking Article 50 of the EU treaty before the end of the month, the decision had been taken to make it a low-key fiscal event, with no fireworks or big giveaways. Hammond wanted to ensure he had 'gas in the tank' to cope with any bumps on the road to Brexit.

Nevertheless, for Gummer, it was an exciting moment and he felt privileged to be there, having been a Cabinet member for less than a year. Ministers who are of a lower rank must wait with the rest of the world for the Chancellor to deliver his statement in Parliament at 12.30 p.m., but the Cabinet receives a confidential briefing on the headlines a few hours early. On a day laden with two centuries of tradition, ministers customarily show their appreciation when the Chancellor has finished by banging on the famous coffin-shaped table that Conservative Prime Minister Harold Macmillan introduced to the Cabinet Room.

Hammond began by setting the context for his Budget – Brexit negotiations. Then he outlined a few of the slimmed-down measures he was ready to announce. One in particular piqued Gummer's interest. National Insurance contributions were in need of an overhaul because the current system gave an unfair advantage to people who classed themselves as self-employed, the Chancellor said. The result of the reform would be to increase fairness in the tax system, he argued.

As Minister for the Cabinet Office, Gummer was responsible for overseeing the implementation of the Conservatives' 2015 election manifesto. Among the highest-profile election pledges that David Cameron's Tory Party had made before winning its unexpected majority was a 'tax lock' promise not to raise VAT, income tax – or National Insurance. Gummer sensed that something could be tricky in Hammond's plan to raise NI contributions for the self-employed.[38] The meeting broke up and ministers picked their way through the thundery showers to head to the Commons. Gummer went away planning to look up the details later. He could not have known quite how spectacularly the measure would rebound on the government. By the time the Chancellor presented the case to the Cabinet that Wednesday morning, it was far too late to change course.

A tsunami of criticism followed Hammond's announcement. Tory MPs decried the policy as a tax on entrepreneurship and a grotesque and blatant breach of voters' trust. How would they be able to look their constituents in the eye after breaking a manifesto pledge, MPs asked.

A week later, at 8 a.m. on 15 March, Hammond met May and agreed to reverse the centrepiece of his Budget. The PM told him that his defence – that the Tories had already protected National Insurance contributions for other workers in an earlier reform – would not hold water. Minutes later, Hammond announced his U-turn in a letter to MPs. At an awkward Prime Minister's Questions afterwards, May did her best to argue that some reform of National Insurance would be needed because the system was not fair, with millions of self-employed people enjoying lower tax bills than their peers in other jobs.

Despite May's diplomacy in public, the episode provoked a spectacular private briefing war between No. 10 and the Treasury, which was so bitter that it almost pushed Hammond to the point of resigning.[39] A source close to Hammond was quoted in the press describing May's aides as being 'economically illiterate'. Nick Timothy took it highly personally and, according to several witnesses, was 'incandescent' with anger.[40] Some ministers blamed Gummer, the keeper of the manifesto pledges, for the failure to stop Hammond's plan, but in reality he found out far too late. The Budget process was so secretive that only two private secretaries in No. 10 were allowed to see the detail of spending commitments before the rest of the world, according to one source.

'There is this silly game that goes on every year, has done under whoever, where the Treasury drip-feeds information, and bounces stuff in at the last minute,' the source says.[41] Other Tories blamed Hammond personally for failing to see the political danger of his technocratic interpretation of the Cameron manifesto.

When the arguments simmered down, the protagonists were left with one inescapable fact: they were handcuffed to a programme for government that they believed was no longer fit for purpose. Nor was it the first time the government had encountered such trouble. It began to dawn on May's team that every fiscal event since the 2015 election had featured a hitch, thanks to the Tories' precarious working majority of just seventeen. Hammond's predecessor, George Osborne, was forced in his 2015 Autumn Statement to drop his plan to cut tax credits after it ran into a road block in the House of Lords and a rebellion from his own side. Then Iain Duncan Smith resigned in protest at Osborne's policy of fresh welfare spending cuts, set out in the Budget of 2016.

'I think Hammond's Budget was the moment that people really started to think, actually, if we are going to do anything we want to do, we might need to win our own mandate, on our own manifesto,' says Chris Wilkins, Downing Street director of strategy under May.[42]

SEEING REDS

Relations between No. 10 and Philip Hammond, the man Nick Timothy, Fiona Hill and Theresa May had picked to be Chancellor, were already strained. He was said to have told aides that Timothy, who believed the state had a legitimate role intervening in markets that were not working, was more of a 'socialist' than a real Conservative.[43] Hammond was especially irate about Timothy's agenda for reforms to the way businesses run themselves. Corporate governance is an area that Hammond regards as within his remit in the Treasury, rather than a matter for No. 10. Yet under Timothy's plan, shareholders would be given a binding annual vote on executive pay rates, and workers would get a place on company boards.

The plan was intended to encourage businesses to be more responsible on the issue of excessive or 'fat cat' boardroom pay levels and to keep the gap between boardroom and shop-floor wages in check.

But Hammond saw red. He protested to the UK's most senior civil servant, the Cabinet Secretary Sir Jeremy Heywood. One No. 10 source recalls: 'Hammond complained to Heywood about Nick's corporate governance reforms. He was angry, saying, "There's no mandate for this, it's not Conservative, Nick Timothy is trying to take control,"' the aide says.[44]

On Brexit, too, the pair clashed repeatedly. Hammond is the Cabinet's most vocal supporter of a so-called soft Brexit, having supported Remain in the referendum and continued to worry about the impact on the economy of withdrawing from the EU. Timothy, however, was a staunch Leave supporter in the referendum, and the chief author of May's vision for taking Britain out of the EU single market and customs union. It was Timothy's view that controlling immigration was more urgent than averting an economic hit arising from the end of single

market membership. May repeated the argument in her
January 2017 speech at Lancaster House in London.[45]

YOU CHOOSE

The Chancellor was not alone in his resistance to Timothy's agenda. According to a senior Downing Street
official, even allies and strong supporters of May like
Greg Clark struggled to give her what she wanted, despite their good intentions. Clark, the Business Secretary,
insisted that he liked Timothy's plan for a modern industrial strategy. The policy was to boost the economies
of the regions that had been flagging and actively use
the power of government to drive growth in promising
industrial and business sectors. The trouble was it did
not seem like a very Tory idea. Clark, along with others
on the liberal economic wing of the party, instinctively
felt that it was not the government's job to 'pick win-
ners' – such decisions should really be left to the market.
One adviser says:

> Greg Clark intellectually likes the idea of an industrial
> strategy but when it comes to it, to have an industrial
> strategy does mean to some extent having to choose.
> Greg didn't like the idea that he would choose particular
> sectors that we might invest more money in, or particu-
> lar parts of the country we thought might need boosts in
> a variety of different ways.

Similarly, Education Secretary Justine Greening 'took a
long time to get on board with the idea that Theresa

really wanted the reintroduction of grammar schools. She just didn't seem to believe it.'[46]

May, Timothy and Hill were ambitious, but increasingly frustrated by the circumstances in which they found themselves. They had a plan they wanted to enact, and it was the broad vision of social reform the new PM set out in Downing Street on the day she took office.

Some of May's team of political aides in Downing Street came to believe that she would have benefited from having to fight harder to win the Conservative crown. It became a favourite taunt of opposition MPs that May had no mandate from voters – even to lead her own party. 'It could be a bit of a struggle getting some Cabinet ministers to understand what Theresa wanted in policy terms from their departments and they could be reticent about engaging on the things she was particularly passionate about,' according to Will Tanner, who was deputy head of the No. 10 Policy Unit. 'That was partly because Theresa hadn't had a long leadership campaign in which she could very clearly set out the things she stood for and gain the support of the party to do those things, so it emboldened detractors but it also led to people misunderstanding Theresa.' Tanner says a longer leadership contest would have forced May to spell out her vision more clearly to her own party, as well as giving her a clearer mandate to lead it. 'I think it would have given her much more authority,' he says.[47]

*   *   *

Even if the party had better understood May's own vision for government, she would still have been forced to adhere to the programme set out by her predecessor. Given the history of rivalries between Cameron's team and May's, it's hardly surprising that her new administration resented being bound by his earlier promises. One former senior aide to May recalls: 'Nick always wanted an election. He operated as if he was effectively the Prime Minister. He hated David Cameron's manifesto and he wanted his own.'[48]

Others point out that not even Cameron expected to be in a position to implement his manifesto in 2015, when all the pollsters were predicting another hung parliament. Both Cameron and Nick Clegg, Liberal Democrat leader at the time, had an understanding that they would be ready to discuss a second coalition, bartering away elements of their respective manifestos if necessary.

'Basically, the Cameron team never intended that manifesto to hold because they always expected to have to negotiate half of it away, so we were stuck with it,' says Chris Wilkins.[49] 'That was a bit of a millstone. There were things that she wanted to achieve which actually we saw were going to be difficult to achieve without her own mandate.'

EUROPE

Notwithstanding the 2015 Tory manifesto, the most significant legacy that Cameron bequeathed to May was, of course, Brexit. Here, Nick Timothy was clear: May had the right plan but she needed the endorsement of the electorate to persuade Parliament to agree. 'There was just this realisation that maybe we needed to change things to get this stuff through,' Timothy says.

There were three Brexit monkeys that May's team couldn't shake off their backs: the Lords, the Commons and the Europeans.

The House of Lords has long been a source of annoyance to governments of all stripes. As a revising chamber, its job is to improve and alter legislation sent across Parliament from the House of Commons. The Tories did not have a majority in the Lords, so nothing was certain to pass unaltered unless it was clearly set out in the manifesto on which the party was elected. Known as the Salisbury Convention, this practice means that the Lords will give way to the elected government on questions which seem to have won the clear support of the electorate.

However, May discovered to her cost that the Lords would not quietly accede to her proposals for a 'hard Brexit' which ripped the UK out of the single market. There was no mandate for that, peers repeatedly argued. Inside No. 10, Nick Timothy conceded the point. While he felt May's plan for a clean break with the other twenty-seven EU member states was the best policy, it had not been on the ballot paper at the referendum. The Lords even attempted to amend the Article 50 Bill, the basic piece of law that would give effect to the referendum result. May had not wanted to give legislators such an opportunity, but she was forced to bring the Bill before Parliament after losing a battle in the Supreme Court. Nothing about implementing the 2016 vote for Brexit was turning out to be easy.

As for the elected House, the Tories had only a slender majority. May's Brexit vision came under attack from rebel MPs, including former Chancellor George Osborne

and ex-Education Secretary Nicky Morgan, both of
whom she had sacked during her first twenty-four hours
in No. 10. One former minister close to May explains:

> Your parliamentary party is less whippable than it used
> to be. In the 1970s, if you stepped out of line, the Chief
> Whip would ring up the chairman of your association
> and you'd be in serious trouble. It was a different atmos-
> phere. Even stuff which was in our manifesto we were
> finding difficult.

May had been struck by the hostility of Labour MPs,
openly jeering on the day she sent the letter triggering
Article 50 to European Union President Donald Tusk.[50]
All May was doing was giving effect to the will of the
people to take Britain out of the EU. A day later, Tom
Brake, a Liberal Democrat MP, said May's plan to use
her executive authority to convert EU law into British
statute on Brexit Day amounted to a 'shameless power
grab' that 'would have made Henry VIII blush'. May's
team insisted such measures were needed to avoid a legal
vacuum on the day the UK leaves the EU but Brake went
on: 'If needed, we will grind the government's agenda to
a standstill, unless proper and rigorous safeguards are
given.'

These arguments were taking place before May or her
Brexit Secretary, the pugnacious David Davis, had even
left British soil to begin negotiating with the European
Commission in Brussels. The PM and her aides were in
no doubt that the Europeans were ready to make Britain pay for its decision to break away. In addition to
an uncompromising approach to any future trade deal,

with warnings that it would inevitably be worse than EU membership, Brussels was drawing up a one-off exit bill estimated to be up to €100 billion.

Davis worried about the short timetable for the Brexit talks, which would need to be concluded before 29 March 2019, when the UK would automatically crash out of the EU even without a deal. This left a tight window of just over a year to negotiate first the UK's exit terms (including bartering over that potentially huge fee) and then a contract for the ambitious new free trade agreement May wanted to secure.

Critically, the greatest pressure would be on Britain – and in particular on May – because the talks would be reaching their intense conclusion in spring 2019 just as politics in Westminster was turning its attention to another general election, scheduled for 2020. This added political burden would be unhelpful, to say the least, Davis told May. Philip Hammond agreed and between them, they began working to convince the Prime Minister that a snap vote could help. Separately, Timothy, Hill, Chris Wilkins and JoJo Penn all began discussing the government's difficulties and the unavoidable argument in favour of an early poll. Timothy explains:

> The conduct of the other parties in the Commons and the Lords meant that the Brexit process was going to be really hard. We hoped to be able to get a mandate for the Brexit plan, which would help with the Lords, but we would also hopefully have a bigger majority, which would help in the Commons.
>
> We didn't only want to be a Brexit ministry. We had a social and economic reform programme, which we

could have done bits of, but we also needed a mandate to do some of it. The electoral timetable was a problem because the conclusion of Brexit talks in 2019 and the election in 2020 gave the Europeans an advantage to some degree. So changing the election timetable was quite a significant factor. Those were all good reasons.[51]

CHAPTER 4

CORBYN'S COMRADES

Jeremy Corbyn did not want to be leader of the Labour Party, let alone Prime Minister.

On Monday 15 June 2015, a month after Ed Miliband had led his party to a devastating defeat in the general election, Labour needed a saviour. It was the job of the party's diminished and demoralised band of MPs to decide who would be in the leadership contest that followed. They had six days to choose which candidates should be allowed to progress to the next stage, a national campaign followed by a ballot of the party's grassroots members. With fifteen minutes until the deadline for nominations, Corbyn – the token representative of the party's far left – was three short of the thirty-five MPs he needed to get onto the ballot paper. It was only thanks to a final flurry of nominations from sympathetic MPs that he made the cut.

'You had better make fucking sure I don't win,' Corbyn said to one of his closest allies when he heard the news. The backbench Member of Parliament for Islington North was terrified at the possibility, however slim, that he might have to lead a national political party at the end of a long summer of campaigning. Labour MPs agreed with him. They did not want Corbyn to be their chief any more than he did, but they felt including him

on the ballot would 'widen the debate' in the party and
put to rest the idea that his form of socialism could be
the answer to their electoral misery. Within two years,
turning sixty-eight, Corbyn would be leading Labour in
a snap general election campaign against a Tory Party
touching 50 per cent in the polls.

*   *   *

'He did have a bit of a panic,' recalls his friend and leadership campaign manager Jon Lansman. 'You have to
remember, when he said "yes" to be the candidate, he
did not expect to be on the ballot paper.'[52]

Corbyn had not even been the Labour left's first
choice. Ian Lavery, his future general election campaign
coordinator, had been the preferred candidate of the
small rump of Labour MPs in Parliament known as the
socialist campaign group, but ruled himself out when he
backed an early frontrunner, the shadow Health Secretary Andy Burnham. Lansman, Corbyn's fellow traveller
on the left, had even announced his support for another
frontbencher, Jon Trickett, only for Trickett to say he did
not want the job either.

The socialist grouping of MPs and activists eventually alighted on Corbyn because he was the last option
available who stood a chance of winning the thirty-five
nominations from MPs to get on the ballot paper. The
logic for their choice was critical. 'The reason we latched
onto Jeremy was because Jeremy had no enemies,' says
Lansman. 'He is a decent person.'

Political ambition has never trumped personal de-
cency for Corbyn. In some ways, he is a classic English

eccentric, a political obsessive who loves to spend time on his allotment, tending to his tomatoes and making jam. He does not drink alcohol and has been a vegetarian for almost half a century because, while working on a pig farm aged twenty, he became 'attached to the pigs'. Corbyn's team say he is unfailingly polite. Almost every morning in Parliament, he will personally leave his office and head into the cafeteria to buy a round of teas and coffees for his colleagues. When travelling up and down the country on trains, he will – repeatedly and insistently – offer to share his food with his companions. 'It's usually a cheese sandwich for Jeremy, sometimes with pickle,' says one. 'He always tries to give you half of his sandwich – always. He just likes sharing. That's the way he is – he's always looking for opportunities to share.'

As the token socialist on the ballot paper, Corbyn proved attractive to activists on the Labour left. Here was a man everyone liked. He was decent, principled, unthreatening. He was authentically himself.

Corbyn's character and his left-wing politics, his divergence from the mainstream, clean-cut professionalised class of political leaders, formed the basis of his campaign in the summer of 2015. It proved to be a uniquely compelling offer, the exact tonic that a demoralised left craved to pull them out of their despair at the election result that delivered neither the hung parliament nor the Labour government they had expected and hoped for, but a shocking majority for David Cameron, who looked set to rule for the next five years. Everywhere he went, Corbyn drew crowds, including many young people and left-wing activists who had backed movements such as Stop the War and the Campaign for Nuclear Disarmament. As this summer of love for the left continued, Corbyn's team had to book ever larger venues. In the final days of the leadership contest, 'Jezza' was treated like a rock star by his adoring fans. Cameron licked his lips. Was it really possible that this most uncharismatic, shambling socialist in his sixties could be chosen to face the all-conquering Tory king across the despatch box at Prime Minister's Questions? 'He can't actually win, can he?' the Prime Minister asked friends in July 2015, barely able to contain his delight.

But who is Jeremy Corbyn? What is it about him that apparently connects with ordinary men and women around the country? Who are the loyal disciples who first saw something in Corbyn that almost nobody else did? And who are the technical advisers, political aides and party operators who have so successfully transformed Corbyn's character into a powerful national campaign?

COMRADE JEZZA

On 27 June 2016, the Labour leader was locked in a crisis meeting with 200 of his own MPs. The atmosphere inside the packed and airless room in Parliament was hostile and hardening. One after another, Labour MPs stood up and told Corbyn to quit. 'You're not fit to be Prime Minister and you have got to resign,' said one. 'You're not just letting the party down, but the whole country,' another warned.[53] Corbyn sat in silence. Labour MPs were convinced their leader was an electoral liability and blamed his lacklustre efforts in the referendum campaign for the Brexit vote days before. They felt they had no option. They resolved to move a vote of no confidence in Corbyn, triggering a formal leadership election.

To understand Jeremy Corbyn, it is instructive to examine how he handled this extraordinary revolt, which was without doubt the biggest crisis of his leadership. In the vote of no confidence that followed the meeting, 172 MPs called on Corbyn to go. Only forty backed him. Faced with overwhelming opposition, and such open contempt, most politicians would have bowed to the apparent inevitability of their departure. Yet despite lacking the support of 80 per cent of his parliamentary party, Corbyn refused to quit.

It was a matter of principle. He had won an overwhelming 59.5 per cent of the vote from the 422,664 Labour Party members and supporters who took part in the 2015 leadership contest. A couple of hundred MPs who wanted him gone could not outweigh numbers like those. Corbyn believed he had a duty to respect the result of that leadership election, to do his best to deliver the changes he had promised – and that meant he had to stay in his place. The episode uncovers the core of Corbyn's character as a politician. On points of principle, he is simply unshakable. He will not compromise.

For Corbyn, then as now, political authority does not derive from Parliament but from 'the people'. His commitment to this belief goes to the heart of the wider movement of Corbynism. Despite being an MP for more than thirty years, in his heart, Corbyn is less a parliamentarian than a tribune. He sees his role as being to campaign, corral and protest. He has done it all his life and would not stop just because he had become leader of Her Majesty's loyal opposition.

Conservatives have long known of Corbyn's populist instincts. As far back as 1987 they held him up in party political broadcasts as an example of the so-called hard left still active in the Labour Party. In a video recorded during that year, one of Corbyn's fiery declarations flashed up on screen. 'Defeat of the Tory government will be brought about by a series of disputes of which Parliament is only a part.' Thirty years later, he still believed it.

CORBYN'S CAUSES

According to those who have known him longest, Corbyn's inner strength comes from his conviction that, while it may take decades, he is always proved right in the end. 'Remember, this is a man who marched through London on Pride marches as a straight man in the 1980s,' says Niall Sookoo, a close family friend who moved from Unite to be his campaign chief for the general election. 'He is someone who fought for racial and sexual equality when we were all being dismissed as loony lefties. All that stuff is mainstream now. You can see how that gives him enormous self-confidence.'[54]

Gay rights was just one of a satchel full of unfashionable causes that Corbyn carried with him on his lonely march as a backbench MP, in defiance of the mainstream political opinions of the time. Others included reaching a settlement with republicans in Northern Ireland at the height of the Troubles, opposing the 2003 war against

Saddam Hussein in Iraq – and any other war, for that matter – and campaigning against nuclear weapons.

Corbyn's public displays of unity with Sinn Féin throughout the IRA's bombing campaign in the 1980s caused particular disquiet among his parliamentary colleagues. The Labour leader has insisted he was simply working to achieve peace. To some, this marks him out as a Walter Mitty-style fantasist; he had no formal role in the peace process. But to Corbyn's supporters it is another example of his foresightedness. He was simply advocating talking to the IRA before Margaret Thatcher opened back channels in 1990. Either way, Corbyn's views are resolutely held and remain consistent – they do not change with the political weather.

'That's part of his appeal,' a Labour strategist close to Corbyn says. 'He wasn't an ambitious greasy-pole guy. People know that people like Bernie [Sanders – the US politician] and Jeremy have been saying this stuff for a long time. They are not just saying it to win votes.'[55] Corbyn's friends and allies cannot name a single issue on which he has changed his mind since the 1970s. Even during the European Union referendum, in which Corbyn agreed to campaign for Remain, there were severe doubts about whether he had truly relinquished his decades of deeply held Euroscepticism. According to one of his oldest friends: 'Jeremy likes the company of those he agrees with.'[56]

Such rigidity, which could seem closed-minded, translates into an overall impression of a man who is consistent and authentic. This image lies at the heart of Corbyn's national appeal, particularly among young voters. One of the most popular videos of the Labour

Party leader, viewed 5.3 million times on Facebook, is called 'Jeremy Corbyn Through The Ages'. It was produced by Channel 4 and shows him saying what he believes over and over again throughout his political career. 'If you believe in something, you should say it,' he says in one clip taken from 1999. 'If you don't believe it, you shouldn't say it. There are principles involved here. If I stand for election as a Labour candidate, as a socialist, people know what they are voting for.' That he never changes his mind is attractive to voters sceptical about politicians who they feel will say anything to get elected. Corbyn's consistency makes him trustworthy. It also marked a point of contrast with Theresa May, when she was forced into a U-turn on a central manifesto pledge halfway through the 2017 election campaign.

ORGANIC LABOUR

Corbyn's outlook, according to his closest friends, is grounded not in political dogma but in the sense that he has identified what is right and will not be diverted from it. 'He is not really ideological,' says Lansman, who has known him since the 1980s. 'He is certainly less ideological than John [McDonnell]. But he's also less compromising.' Fundamentally, Corbyn's politics are rooted in a sense of political morality, not economics. 'It is ethical, that is the best way to describe it,' says Lansman.[57] Corbynism isn't 'Old Labour' or 'hard left'. It is Fair Trade Labour, Stop the War Labour or, perhaps, Organic Labour.

The most extreme example of Corbyn's ethical

fundamentalism came in the education of his children. In 1999, the then Labour backbencher split with his second wife, Chilean national Claudia Bracchitta, after he refused to sanction sending his son Benjamin to a grammar school even though the local comprehensive was on Ofsted's failing list for the third year running.

Corbyn refused to bend on his principles and the pair split up after twelve years of marriage. His wife released a statement leaving no doubt as to why they had split. 'My children's education is my absolute priority,' she said in a statement.

> This situation left me with no alternative but to accept a place at Queen Elizabeth boys' school [in Barnet]. The decision was made by myself alone and without the consent of my husband. The difficulties of making decisions under these circumstances have played an important role in bringing about a regrettable marital break-up.[58]

Corbyn lost the battle of his son's schooling but stayed true to his principles. He sacrificed a marriage to avoid the charge of hypocrisy. For a generation of voters who feel cheated by a political class that brought them the Iraq War and annual university tuition fees of £9,000, such examples mark him out as ultimately trustworthy.

It is this ethical purity that makes Corbyn a perfect figurehead for younger voters who expect their leaders to conform to their standards. With the new supremacy of online activism, political parties that fall short of these values can now be boycotted just like a company caught using sweatshop workers. Seen in this light, Corbyn's supporters are political consumers, not simply ground troops following orders from the centre of the Labour Party. 'This isn't an army,' Lansman says of Corbyn's supporters. 'They don't have a tribal loyalty. They are loyal to the cause. It's the politics which drives them, not tribal loyalty. Corbyn's victory actually signifies the death of tribal loyalty.'[59]

SOUTHSIDE

'Just because you're paranoid doesn't mean they aren't after you,' writes Joseph Heller in *Catch-22*. This summed up the wary approach Corbyn's aides took to the rest of the party. They had good reason to feel under threat, of course, but it was not just MPs they eyed suspiciously. 'Southside' – the name given to the building that housed Labour HQ on Victoria Street, central London – was a bastion of anti-Corbyn resistance working surreptitiously with MPs to undermine his leadership, in their eyes.

When damaging leaks appeared in the press before and during the campaign, Corbyn's aides blamed Southside. Lifelong Labour staffers were not trusted because of connections to MPs opposed to Corbyn. Ties to his deputy Tom Watson were a particularly toxic stain. Even the party's general secretary Iain McNicol was not fully trusted by some in the leader's office.

The mutual suspicion meant Corbyn hired advisers from outside the party whenever he could. Seumas Milne was brought in from *The Guardian* as communications director and Karie Murphy, a close ally of Unite general secretary Len McCluskey, became chief of staff.

Others also joined, but never from Southside. James Schneider from Momentum and Matt Zarb-Cousin from the Campaign for Fairer Gambling were drafted in to deal with the media. Even Sinn Féin's long-time London chief, Jayne Fisher, was brought on board ahead of party insiders.

The atmosphere of distrust continued into the 2017 election campaign, with key meetings of the leader's team often held at Unite's London HQ rather than in Labour's offices. Senior campaign officials at Southside were given 'shadows' who were proven to be loyal to Corbyn in the leader's office. Corbyn's aides also believe high-ranking members of staff at headquarters had already signed up to work on post-election leadership campaigns for the so-called moderate Labour MPs Chuka Umunna and Yvette Cooper.

The suspicion ran so deeply that Corbyn's core team were amused to discover that their passes to Southside were deactivated on 9 June – the day after the election. 'They thought the nightmare would end, didn't they?' says one key Corbyn lieutenant. Officials at Southside insist it was simply an administrative mix-up, but the leader's allies are not so sure.

SEUMAS

The barely suppressed hostility between Labour HQ and Corbyn's office has raised the bar for loyalty in the leader's team. Officials working in Corbyn's inner circle must be personally trustworthy and – if possible – politically aligned with his vision. Nobody in the Labour hierarchy is closer to Corbyn, in personal or political terms, than his director of communications and strategy, Seumas Milne. Their strong connection makes Milne the most powerful figure on the party's staff. The pair, who have known each other for decades, speak and text 'all the time', colleagues say, and agree on almost everything. Those who clash with Milne do not last long.

Neale Coleman was a respected figure at Westminster and beyond. He had helped oversee the 2012 Olympics from City Hall and had taken a job as Corbyn's head of policy. But in January 2016 he quit, amid rumours of disagreements with Milne. Others have followed. Simon Fletcher, a key aide, walked out in February 2017 as Corbyn's campaigns director. At the time, Fletcher had been reporting to Labour HQ but his replacement reported directly to Milne instead, consolidating the latter's power. In Corbyn's office, 'Seumas is undeniably the most important figure,' according to one source close to the Labour leader.

A former *Guardian* comment editor, Milne is a friend, confidant and ideological soulmate of Corbyn's. He is the radical intellect behind Corbynism. Born in 1958 and educated at Winchester and Oxford, Milne is a straightforward, lifelong socialist. A defender of the Soviet Union and communist East Germany, he is arguably more intellectually committed to his politics than the ethically driven Corbyn.

Milne does not look or sound like your classic revolutionary. He is often seen sipping an espresso in Portcullis House, the modern atrium annexed to the Palace of Westminster that is a favourite spot for politicians, aides and journalists to meet. He rarely appears anything less than entirely at ease in his surroundings. He is well spoken, confident and charming when he wants to be. Some have detected a certain aloofness and an air of intent.

As a schoolboy at Winchester College, one of England's most prestigious boarding schools, he stood for election as a Maoist. 'If a Maoist government was elected, foreign debts would be renounced, as after the Russian Revolution, and we would withdraw from NATO and the EEC,' Milne declared. 'Military spending would be cut and all troops would be recalled.' Milne's politics have not changed dramatically in the decades since. At Oxford, he became involved with left-wing politics, specifically the 'broad left' movement. This was a pro-Soviet group, which advocated cooperation between Labour and the Communist Party.

After university, Milne went to work for *The Economist* magazine before finding his home at *The Guardian*, where he notoriously gave Al-Qaeda terrorist leader Osama bin Laden a byline. In a series of incendiary columns, Milne sparked controversy by claiming the murder of Fusilier Lee Rigby by Islamist terrorists in 2013 'wasn't terrorism in the normal sense' because the soldier had fought in Afghanistan. Two days after the 9/11 attacks, Milne wrote that Americans were 'reaping a dragons' teeth harvest they themselves sowed'.

Milne is a firebrand in print, but not in the office. That is left to someone else.

STREET FIGHTING

Karie Murphy had not long been appointed chief of staff to the Labour leader when Jeremy Corbyn met one of his close advisers at an event in Scotland, where he had been campaigning for a few days. The Labour leader asked his adviser how Murphy was settling into life in his parliamentary office back in London. 'I said it's great,' the aide recalls. 'Karie has got two positions: she will either take you off at the knees or take you off at the head. Jeremy said: "That's absolutely right."'

Corbyn is not interested in office politics, but he is canny enough to know he needs people around him who are effective in the darker practices of Westminster life. In the rough trade of political dealing, naturally diffident leaders such as Corbyn – and Theresa May – need street fighters, as well as philosophers, on their side. Just as May made use of the tough and sometimes abrasive Fiona Hill, so Corbyn relies on Murphy to do what is necessary for the cause. She runs Corbyn's office, appoints shadow ministerial advisers and hires key staff.

Murphy is not as political as Milne; her values are left-wing but that is not what sets her apart in the leader's office. Murphy is interested in power: principally, the location of power within the Labour Party. 'She just really likes fighting,' says a former colleague. 'It's about wanting to prove something.'

THE FAMILY

At the top of Corbyn's inner circle of advisers going into the election sat the three 'executive directors'. Milne was in charge; Murphy, the gatekeeper and de facto chief of staff, ran the day-to-day operation; Andrew Fisher, the former PCS union man and parliamentary researcher to John McDonnell, oversaw policy development. What united them all was their loyalty to the project – the Corbyn project. They were true believers.

McDonnell, shadow Chancellor, Corbyn's right-hand man, political bodyguard and leadership campaign chair, sat alongside this triumvirate. He is the man prepared to roll up his sleeves to get things done and has earned a reputation at Westminster as a behind-the-scenes fixer and a schemer who arouses suspicion in the parliamentary party.

The other key figures in the Corbyn camp are his real family: his wife, Laura Alvarez, and three children, Seb, Tommy and Ben. The rule, according to one of Corbyn's close friends, is that if there is a political problem that needs fixing, they take it to Seumas. 'If it's personal, it's his wife.'

In 2016, Corbyn's aides were all conscious that his scruffy appearance – in an ill-fitting jacket and trousers that did not match – was not winning over many sceptical voters who were already unimpressed that he had not sung the national anthem at a Second World War memorial service. David Cameron even taunted him over his dress sense at Prime Minister's Questions in February 2016, telling the Labour leader: 'I know what my mother would say. I think she would look across the despatch box and she would say, "Put on a proper suit, do up your tie and sing the national anthem."' It took almost two years of persuasion to convince Corbyn to wear a suit and tie like almost every other male MP. In the end, it was only after his closest aides begged Alvarez to intervene – and she agreed – that he did.

MOMENTUM

The largest and probably most important group in the Corbyn movement is his supporter base, which solidified into an organisation of its own a few weeks after he won the leadership: Momentum. Lansman established the group 'to build on the energy and enthusiasm generated' during the 2015 Labour leadership campaign. At the time of writing, it has more than 150 local groups, 23,000 registered members and 200,000 supporters, 'united by their shared vision for a fair and equal society'.

As a political organisation, Momentum is fast, nimble and cutting edge. It is not a political party or a traditional group of any kind. It can post online videos that push the boundaries of taste, mock politicians of any party if it suits the Corbynite cause, and arrange huge events that test the limits of public order. If the Labour and Conservative parties are the giant corporations of British politics, Momentum is a sparky start-up company, free to take risks that mainstream political machines cannot afford.

By the time the Prime Minister called the 2017 snap election, Momentum had earned its spurs as a campaigning machine in the country. It was Momentum that swung to Corbyn's aid in June 2016, when Labour MPs launched their attempt to oust him, and triggered a leadership contest.

The challenge to Corbyn's leadership had long been expected. His supporters had been preparing for it from the moment he was elected. They knew Labour MPs would make their move before 2020; it was just a question of when. Defending their leader from the Blairite counter-revolutionaries was the main reason Lansman established the body in 2015. 'We knew we had to prepare for a future leadership election,' he says. 'It was the birth of Momentum.'

In the days following the Brexit referendum, distraught EU-supporting Labour MPs were desperate to get rid of Corbyn, but had not agreed on either a successor or an alternative political vision. In the end they settled for Corbynism without Corbyn in the shape of Owen Smith. He was chosen ahead of Angela Eagle because he had not been in the Commons to vote for the Iraq War. It appeared to be a choice born of desperation rather than conviction.

The contest that followed allowed Corbyn's newly organised mass of supporters to test their strength, and also gave Corbyn the chance to take his love of campaigning onto the national stage. Niall Sookoo said it was the perfect platform for him to re-engage with his supporters. Where he struggled in the Commons, he was able to get back to being himself on his stage; 'Jeremy has basically campaigned his whole life. He believes in it – to him, it's how you win the argument.'[60]

Corbyn and his defenders at Momentum rallied their supporters to see off the challenge, winning an even bigger mandate than the previous year, with more than 60 per cent of all votes cast. It was Corbyn's second national campaign in two years. He was getting good at it – and so were his large and loyal band of followers in the country. Soon, Momentum supporters would deploy the lessons they had learned in the leadership contest in the battle with Theresa May. 'We learnt our trade in leadership elections,' says Lansman. 'We had grown from an organisation which had three staff, but lots of volunteers, to an organisation which had fifty staff. We were a fast-moving, dynamic organisation which knew how to grow quickly and react.'[61]

While Labour MPs failed to remove their leader, their attempted coup helped ready the party for the general election they were dreading. Party membership swelled to over 500,000, about four times the size of the Tory Party. The leadership election itself, which charged supporters £25 to vote, raised £3.5 million for the party. This pot of petty cash would prove invaluable when Theresa May caught Westminster by surprise and called the early election.

*   *   *

The battle over Corbyn's leadership exposed the Labour Party's bitter divisions and pushed it to record lows in the polls as 2016 drew to a close. The widespread impression was of a party in terminal decline as newspapers and broadcasters focused on infighting and division. The leader's office used the media narrative of Labour's 'civil war' as an alibi to explain the party's poor polling. 'Labour's appeal had been artificially suppressed by the way Jeremy's leadership of the party had been covered,' a senior Corbyn aide says. 'The process-ification of everything, the constant reporting of internal conflict – inevitably that's going to be damaging.'[62]

The Conservatives' advantage over Labour received a further shot in the arm with the election of May as leader in July 2016. 'They got a huge boost after Theresa May was chosen,' the aide says. 'We lost five points and stayed there.' Over the next nine months, Corbyn, his fans and his enemies could only watch as the Tory lead grew.

CHAPTER 5

THE SNAP

HOUSE OF PEACE

Forty-one miles from Downing Street, set in more than 1,000 acres of Buckinghamshire countryside, lies Chequers, the official country residence of the Prime Minister. The sixteenth-century, ten-bedroom Tudor manor house was given to the nation at the end of the First World War. It was a grand and generous gesture, typical of its time. The idea was to make sure all future Prime Ministers would have access to a peaceful rural retreat, even if they did not have their own private estate but instead came from 'the ranks of the manual toilers' who could, the government conceded, one day end up running the country. A Schedule to the Chequers Estate Act of 1917 sets out the rationale:

> To none of these in the midst of their strenuous and responsible labours could the spirit and anodyne of Chequers do anything but good. In the city-bred man especially, the periodic contact with the most typical rural life would create and preserve a just sense of proportion between the claims of town and country. To the revolutionary statesman the antiquity and calm tenacity of Chequers and its annals might suggest some saving

virtues in the continuity of English history and exercise a check upon too hasty upheavals, whilst even the most reactionary could scarcely be insensible to the spirit of human freedom which permeated the countryside of Hampden, Burke and Milton.[63]

Lord and Lady Lee of Fareham, who bequeathed Chequers to the nation, commissioned a stained glass window for the long gallery of the house, complete with an inscription to ensure visitors and tenants unfamiliar with the detail of the 1917 Act remember the purpose of their gift: 'This house of peace and ancient memories was given to England as a thank-offering for her deliverance in the great war of 1914–1918 as a place of rest and recreation for her Prime Ministers for ever.'

A hundred years later, it was to this 'house of peace' that the Tory Party's top brass travelled on the cool, damp morning of Thursday 16 February. During their secretive 'away day', they were to engage in the most sensitive kind of political discussion: how to win an election. If the benefactors of the Chequers bequest were correct, the calming atmosphere of the red-brick house and the surrounding landscape should have been the ideal place to reflect. There, amid the wood-panelled halls and the tranquil rose gardens, May and her team could reconcile the competing demands of the 'revolutionary' and the 'reactionary', the city-bred men of money and power, and those who have never known life inside the political whirl of London.

The presiding theme of healing a divided nation, which runs through the Schedule to the 1917 Act, was just as relevant in the aftermath of the Brexit referendum as it had been a century before.

Instead of bringing peace, though, the Chequers meeting on that late winter day sparked a conflict at the heart of Theresa May's election team, a clash of ideas between her own visionary and reforming chief of staff and the man she had hired to design her election campaign. Four months later, this schism would prove fatal to her hopes of winning the majority and the mandate she craved. It is an enduring irony that the fracture that undermined May's electoral gamble can be traced back to this meeting at Chequers, where the spirit of the Chiltern hills and woods was supposed to exert 'a check upon too hasty upheavals'.

It was not how the day was meant to unfold. Under the Fixed Term Parliaments Act, the next general election was still a comfortable three years away, and Patrick McLoughlin, the Conservative Party chairman, merely wanted to put the subject of campaigns on the Prime Minister's radar. May hadn't attended an HQ-organised campaign meeting since becoming leader seven months earlier, and neither she nor her chiefs of staff had been involved in running a national election before.

Working with Fiona Hill, McLoughlin set up a private away day, and invited the two election experts who had been central to winning the unexpected majority for David Cameron in 2015. These were Sir Lynton Crosby, the Australian political consultant, and Lord Gilbert of Panteg, the long-serving Tory official who directed Cameron's ground operation from Conservative campaign headquarters.

Crosby brought with him Mark Fullbrook, his British business partner, and had prepared a presentation on the 2015 campaign. Among those who joined May on

the trip out of London were Nick Timothy and Fiona
Hill, the deputy chief of staff JoJo Penn, Stephen Parkinson, May's political secretary, and Chris Wilkins, No. 10
director of strategy. The event was private. Only members of May's inner circle were invited from Downing
Street and the media operation was neither briefed nor
allowed to attend, fuelling suspicions back in London
that the chiefs were secretly plotting an early vote.[64]

In truth, a snap election was not on the agenda at
this meeting. Although Timothy, Hill, Penn and Wilkins
had separately raised the idea with May during the early
months of the year, she had warned them she was not
interested.[65] McLoughlin had been trying to cool down
Tory MPs who were demanding an election to finish off
the Labour Party for the next twenty years and win May
a landslide that would rival Thatcher's record. George
Hollingbery, the Conservative MP who served as May's
parliamentary aide, approached the Tory Chief Whip
Gavin Williamson to tell him what his more excitable
colleagues were saying. He had a separate meeting with
McLoughlin, pointing out the strength of feeling on
the backbenches about the benefits of an early election.
McLoughlin gave Hollingbery short shrift: 'The Prime
Minister has said there will be no early election so
let's just stop talking about it because it's not going to
happen.'

In preparation for the Chequers away day, Timothy
asked Wilkins to draft a paper to present to the group.
As director of strategy, Wilkins should set out Downing Street's vision for governing the country, taking up
the public's desire for fundamental change that May's
team believed lay behind the Brexit vote, Timothy said.

Wilkins, a quiet, thoughtful Conservative from Wales, was wholly committed to the cause and very much a core part of May's inner team. His role included working as May's chief speechwriter and, with Timothy, he had been responsible for producing a trio of well-received interventions on foreign policy at the start of the year, including her famous Lancaster House Brexit speech.

In his presentation, Wilkins set out an agenda that was radical and, according to Tory research, popular with the public: overhauling social and industrial policy, taking a hard line on immigration, and with it a harder line on the reality of Brexit. This would mean being the party of change, and making May the leader of that political revolution, he said.

Wilkins recalls:

> The referendum, as she always said, wasn't just to leave the EU, it was a call for change in the country. She had to be the person who always fought for relentless change. That's how she had to come across. I presented the strategy and it was one of the things I said.

* * *

May invited her guests to sit down to lunch around the large table in the dining room. Crosby quipped that it was possible to tell a lot about a leader from the menus they serve. As they sipped their glasses of wine, some of the guests privately noted the somewhat eccentric fare that the Chequers chefs had produced: chicken lasagne served with boiled potatoes. But, to Crosby, Wilkins's menu for governing was even less palatable.

The logic behind the programme that Wilkins and Timothy set out was clear: their approach was working. It had catapulted May to a healthy lead over Labour in the polls and the party was on the point of gaining a seat from Labour in the Copeland by-election, a rare triumph for a government in mid-term. She was consistently ahead of Corbyn in her personal approval ratings among men and women in every age group.

But Crosby was unmoved. The plain-speaking Australian was said to have regarded Wilkins's presentation as 'classic populist woolly bullshit'. Grand political theories about the world dreamt up by thinkers in their studies did not impress him. For Crosby, political science – and, specifically, the science of polling and evidence-based research – was the key to any successful campaign. 'By the way, mate, it's not about being the change candidate, it's about doing what people want,' Crosby told the gathering.

The Australian strategist believed the Tories had been here before and made the same sort of mistakes. In 2010, Cameron's policy guru Steve Hilton set out an agenda based on the ill-defined idea of a creating a 'Big Society'. Voters just didn't get it, Crosby believed. Reflecting on the problem, he says: 'Political parties sometimes get themselves into trouble when advisers or others try to prove their particular theories of the world. You have to base your strategies on the evidence from the research.'[66]

For Wilkins, the clash with Crosby at Chequers should have been a sign of the trouble to come. 'For me, that's one of the critical things that went wrong in the election campaign,' he says. Wilkins believes that Crosby never understood the importance of the personal brand Theresa

May had built as a different kind of Conservative, one who was ready to champion change and deliver better opportunities for ordinary working people, rather than a hard-edged Tory from the nasty party of old. Wilkins says:

> In the campaign, we basically just screwed the brand completely. Both her brand and the party's, really. We suddenly became the establishment when we were supposed to be the candidate for change. Jeremy Corbyn became the candidate for change. That's what happened. Loads and loads of things went wrong in the election campaign but that is the fundamental thing that people need to understand.[67]

DOWNING STREET DELEGATION

As the daughter of a Church of England vicar, Theresa May takes her faith seriously. She is a regular on Sundays at St Andrew's Church in Sonning, the wealthy Berkshire village which she shares with the likes of George and Amal Clooney and Led Zeppelin founder Jimmy Page. Her husband serves communion to the congregation. As a diabetic, May avoids chocolates and sweets, but she is keen on crisps. It was a significant sacrifice when she decided to give up her favourite savoury snack for Lent. Announcing the Prime Minister's decision on Shrove Tuesday, 28 February, her spokesman revealed that salt and vinegar is her flavour of choice. 'I don't know how many packets of crisps the Prime Minister consumes per week, per day or per month, but she will be giving them up,' the spokesman said.

Three weeks later, as she prepared her letter to the European Union triggering Article 50, the PM's commitment to her Lenten fast would be tested to the full at a meeting with her team. May's four most senior advisers wanted to talk, and their purpose was deadly serious: for the first time, they were formally proposing that she should call a snap election. For the first time, she was ready to listen.

What helped to open the Prime Minister's mind to such a radical course of action was the battle she'd had to fight in Parliament to make progress with her Brexit plans during the previous weeks. The House of Lords defeated the government twice on her Article 50 Bill, writing in clauses to guarantee the rights of EU citizens living in Britain and to give Parliament a veto over the final Brexit deal. On 13 March, after more than seventy hours of debate, the Bill giving May legal authority to trigger the EU's exit mechanism passed its final parliamentary vote. The path was clear for May to invoke Article 50 of the Lisbon Treaty and give effect to the referendum result. Although Labour peers dropped their opposition to the Article 50 Bill, Jeremy Corbyn promised to fight the government's 'bargain basement Brexit' plan at every stage in the future.

If May thought she would have a straightforward run to the start of Brexit negotiations, Scotland's First Minister Nicola Sturgeon had other ideas. On the day the Bill cleared Parliament, the Scottish National Party leader announced she would be taking forward the option of a new referendum on independence for Scotland. Sturgeon's countrymen had not voted for Brexit and could not afford to be tied to the good ship Britannia as May sailed it out of the single market. Suddenly, it seemed the PM would have to negotiate Brexit in Brussels at the same time as fighting a referendum campaign in Scotland to stop the break-up of Britain.

SOFA SUMMIT

One evening after work in the week of 20 March, the Prime Minister's core team of Timothy, Hill, Penn and Wilkins went upstairs to the Downing Street flat which serves as the Mays' London home. The group sat on sofas and sipped glasses of red and white wine. May laid out two bowls of her beloved crisps for her guests. One by one, the PM's advisers took it in turns to tell her – and her husband – why she should call an election now.

Her response to the dramatic proposal was typically cautious. 'She was instinctively nervous,' one of those present recalls. May's concerns were threefold. She had only just made it to No. 10, and there was a risk – as always – that the election could go wrong and the Tories could lose. She was genuinely concerned that calling a snap vote would bring added insecurity to the country, something she had taken pains to avoid. But she worried most about how the public would react, after she had promised so many times that there would not be an early election. 'I've said before that I don't want this to happen and I'm really concerned about how people will respond,' the Prime Minister said.

The four aides tried to reassure May that she could make a strong case for why an election was needed: it would be easy to sit in No. 10 on David Cameron's majority but the brave and bold thing to do would be to seek to win your own mandate, to say to voters, 'If we're going to make this time purposeful and do something with it, we need your support.'[68]

May's aides knew that they did not just have to convince her; they needed to persuade Philip too. He was there, in part, because the meeting took place in the flat after work, partly also because of the gravity of the subject under discussion, but mostly because he is the one adviser whom May trusts and relies on above all. 'A decision of this magnitude did have to be a joint thing,' one of May's team explains. 'Philip is an important adviser for her. It's not normal for him to be in meetings but she relies on him a lot privately.' During the meeting in the flat, Philip May raised the same concerns as his wife, worrying how the public would react. He was the most reluctant member of the group and the last to be persuaded that an early election was a good idea. According to one of May's senior advisers, Philip asked how previous occupants of No. 10 had fared when they called snap elections in the past. 'With hindsight, this would have spoken against calling it,' the aide says.[69]

When the discussion drew to a close, May thanked her team but was still unsure. 'It was a classic Prime Minister's reaction – she listened intently and then resolved to go away and think about it,' one aide says. Despite the pressure of the decision she faced, May did not reach for the crisps.

*   *   *

Naturally cautious, and inclined to meticulous deliberation, Theresa May is famous across Whitehall for wanting to see a problem from every angle before she decides how to approach it. Those close to her say she values advice from people who are more intellectually self-confident, who will be willing to push an argument harder than she will, to throw caution to the wind, to gamble if the reward on offer will outweigh the risk. But only if she trusts them.

Few have won the Prime Minister's trust as quickly in government as her buccaneering Brexit Secretary, David Davis. A former SAS reservist, Davis is nothing if not self-assured. He is known at Westminster for always having a ready smile and a cocksure confidence. He has been described as a rare example of someone who can swagger sitting down. Davis wanted an early election. As he war-gamed the next two years of Brexit talks, he was sure a vote now rather than in 2020 would deny his European adversaries the chance to pressurise Britain into accepting a poor deal in 2019 on the brink of an election a year later. Call a snap election, thump Corbyn's Labour Party, and then thump the EU in the Brexit talks, was the broad thrust of his argument. Davis wanted an election and set about getting one.

Three weeks before Easter, Davis called Lynton Crosby, demanding to see him urgently. The pair had not spoken properly for about a year. Nevertheless, Davis knew that Crosby and his team of consultants at Crosby Textor Fullbrook (CTF) were the best in the business, and had been responsible for the Tory Party's electoral triumph in 2015. Davis made two points to the strategist: 'No one is closer to Theresa May than I, and I, Philip Hammond and Theresa May really run the country,' was his opening salvo. The second point he made startled Crosby. 'I'm urging her to have an election as early as possible. We're well ahead in the polls and we'll win.'[70] The Australian was not convinced.

'Support is broad but shallow,' Crosby replied. 'Polls in this climate are superficial. They sort of say what's going on but they are not stress-tested to the impact of a campaign.'

But Davis had made up his mind, and was determined to make up May's, and then Crosby's too. 'I'm persuading her and I just wanted you to think about it,' he said. Crosby declined to engage in a discussion. He was about to have some time away and didn't want to contemplate running a full-blown general election campaign.

REVELATION

On the evening of Thursday 6 April, Theresa and Philip May arrived amid light drizzle at the luxurious Penmaenuchaf Hall Hotel near Dolgellau, a small town nestled among the hills of Snowdonia. The Mays love hillwalking and are regular visitors to the area. Over the warm Easter weekend that followed, the spring sunshine and scenery seemed to work some magic on the Prime Minister. In a local bookshop, May bought a copy of a hiking guide, Michael Burnett's *Walks in and around Dolgellau Town*. The Mays followed Burnett's two and a half-mile route through the hills and woods above the town, with two armed bodyguards trailing a short distance behind. 'During the walk,' Burnett said later, 'there are a series of revelations. Those moments of discovery are mind-cleansing. They focus you, give you that moment of clarity you need to make those important decisions.'[71]

Little by little, May's caution turned to confidence that her advisers were right. Despite the risks, an early election was necessary to give Britain the best chance in the Brexit negotiations, and to win her own mandate for the social and economic reform programme she wanted to enact. It was time to be bold.

Although she confirmed her decision in Wales, May was close to making up her mind before she left for her holiday. She had already asked Nick Timothy and Fiona Hill to find Stephen Gilbert, the head of Tory campaigning in 2015, and gently test him on what would need to be done to fight an election in practical terms. 'Go and talk to Stephen to see how a campaign might look,' she told her chiefs of staff. 'I haven't decided but just go and have that conversation.'[72]

Timothy called Gilbert, who then travelled to the Mays' home in Sonning for an election summit, with Patrick McLoughlin, the Tory chairman, and Darren Mott, the party's director of campaigning. May raised her worries with Gilbert directly: 'I've got a reputation for just getting on with the job, for doing the right thing,' she said. 'Would calling an early election put that at risk?' Her second concern was about losing Tory-held seats in the south-west.

Gilbert said he understood the benefits of an early vote for navigating Brexit but he saw the risk that the public would think May was just trying to gain narrow political advantage, to fight Labour when Corbyn was at his weakest. Timothy asked who should be part of the campaign team. Gilbert already knew who he wanted; he told May that Crosby was the only man to run her campaign.[73]

* * *

At sixty, Lynton Crosby had been trying to take life a little easier. He was away in Fiji on holiday to celebrate his wife's birthday when his phone rang and he missed the call. It was his Australian mobile and he didn't recognise the number, but it was Theresa May. When he called back, the Prime Minister had a quick question: would he mind speaking to Stephen Gilbert? Crosby, a loyal Tory supporter who had worked closely with Gilbert in 2015, agreed.

When the two eventually spoke, Gilbert brought Crosby up to speed. Gilbert asked him to run the campaign but, for a combination of personal reasons, he refused. The Australian also raised other questions and was the least enthused of all the top campaign team about the idea. 'Hasn't she ruled this out several times?' he asked Gilbert. 'Why does she want an election now? I'm not so sure I'd be calling an election.'

Eventually, Crosby agreed to think about how CTF could help, even though he did not want to be leading the campaign. He immediately commissioned a poll and a round of focus groups because the Tories had not done any research on the public's readiness for another election campaign. The results were clear: nobody wanted one.

THE MEMO

Crosby compiled the findings into a memo to May (reproduced in Appendix 1). CTF Partners conducted two pairs of focus groups among undecided voters in marginal seats in London and north-west England, plus a national poll of 1,000 adults. Crosby's memo did not mince its words about the risks of May's election gamble, but he never explicitly advised her not to do it. For a consultant, he reasoned, the final call will always be for the party leader to make:

> The research shows there is clearly a lot of risk involved with holding an early election – and there is a real need to nail down the 'why' for doing so now. Voters are actively seeking to avoid uncertainty and maintain the status quo, and yet by calling an election the Conservatives are the ones who are creating uncertainty. Therefore, Theresa May must be able to show that by holding an election now she is minimising future uncertainty and instability.
>
> Furthermore, if an election was held today there is a risk that the Conservative vote share would end up broadly similar to that the party secured in 2015. And as earlier research has shown, there is the potential for a significant number of seats won from the Liberal Democrats in 2015 to return to Tim Farron's party – largely based on the performance of incumbent MPs compared to their predecessors.[74]

'It was very clear nobody wanted an early election,' Crosby says. 'People thought things were uncertain and they were sick of change. Some people argue that voters want change. They don't want change; they just want a few problems fixed and the world to calm down.'[75]

For Crosby and Gilbert, the first critical task was to convince voters that an election was necessary. The CTF research showed May had been right to worry that the public would not take kindly to an electoral ambush. Happily, everyone on the Tory campaign agreed that the case justifying the election would need to focus on Brexit.

In addition to the warnings about the risks, though, Crosby's memo confirmed the most persuasive finding from other polls that led May's team to recommend an early vote. The Prime Minister was far more popular and more trusted than any other party leader across a broad 'coalition' of voter groups. Chris Wilkins explains:

> People think we went into the election expecting a land-slide. We didn't, actually. When we discussed going for it, the view was that we thought we could get a majority of 50 to 60. We knew it was a gamble – it was a calculated risk – but the critical bit of polling that was convincing was the fact that over a period of time the Prime Minister was ahead of Corbyn in both male and female voters, across every age range, and across every social group. That was something we tracked and it gave us the sense that, actually, this is working. What we were trying to do was build a really broad coalition that included the 'Cameron coalition', if you like, but then also pushed out into traditional Labour voters. It's quite difficult to keep that coalition together – but the polling suggested we were doing it.[76]

*   *   *

When May returned from her Welsh walking trip, she called Timothy and Hill. Her advisers were impressed. It was a big call, they thought, but the right thing to do. For the next week, Gilbert chaired daily meetings of the small circle of aides who knew May's secret plan. Critics say little was achieved in this short window between May returning from Wales and making her announcement because Gilbert was waiting for Crosby to arrive.[77]

Over Easter weekend, the wheels of the Downing Street machine started to spin. Hill called a meeting of only the most trusted members of the No. 10 team for 17 April, Easter Monday. Some of those who got the message thought they were being summoned to work on a bank holiday to be sacked. Others thought a crisis was unfolding, or their bosses had been fired.

Staff who spoke to Timothy at this point found that he was elated. 'Nick was saying, it took David Cameron and George Osborne four years to change the face of the Conservative Party and we've done it in nine months,' according to one insider. 'They were so sure that the change was solid and real. It just shows that hubris as a condition was rife – they were going to win over all these new voters, winning over Labour territory. That was going to be Nick's legacy.'[78]

FIXING TERMS

'I have just chaired a meeting of the Cabinet, where we agreed that the government should call a general election, to be held on the 8th of June.' With the whirr of TV news helicopters hovering over Downing Street, at 11.06 a.m. on Tuesday 18 April, Theresa May dropped her bombshell. It was a testament to the iron grip she and her chiefs of staff had on the business of government that no hint of what was to come had made it into the media. The country was stunned.

With Crosby's warnings that the public did not want to be told to vote yet again still fresh, May set out to explain why another election was necessary. In short, it was all about Brexit.

'At this moment of enormous national significance there should be unity here in Westminster, but instead there is division,' May said. 'The country is coming together, but Westminster is not.' Labour have threatened to vote against the final Brexit deal Britain reaches with the EU, while the SNP have promised to try to block the law that formally repeals Britain's EU membership, she said. 'And unelected members of the House of Lords have vowed to fight us every step of the way.'

Our opponents believe because the government's majority is so small, that our resolve will weaken and that they can force us to change course. They are wrong. They underestimate our determination to get the job done and I am not prepared to let them endanger the security of millions of working people across the country.

Because what they are doing jeopardises the work we must do to prepare for Brexit at home and it weakens the government's negotiating position in Europe. If we do not hold a general election now, their political game-playing will continue, and the negotiations with the European Union will reach their most difficult stage in the run-up to the next scheduled election.

Division in Westminster will risk our ability to make a success of Brexit and it will cause damaging uncertainty and instability to the country. So we need a general election and we need one now, because we have at this moment a one-off chance to get this done while the European Union agrees its negotiating position and before the detailed talks begin.[79]

May admitted that she had previously ruled out an early election, and had only recently 'and reluctantly' concluded that a vote was needed after all. She challenged Labour and the other parties to put forward their own plans for Brexit and for running Britain 'and then let the people decide'.

Then came the campaign message that Mark Textor's research had identified for her; the slogan that would define May's bid for a mandate, and one that would eventually rebound on the Prime Minister as her campaign disintegrated over the weeks to come.

'The decision facing the country will be all about leadership,' she said. 'It will be a choice between strong and stable leadership in the national interest, with me as your Prime Minister, or weak and unstable coalition government, led by Jeremy Corbyn.'

When she stepped out of the shiny black door of No. 10 to tell the world she wanted an election, photographers zoomed in on the Prime Minister's hand to capture an unusual item of jewellery. It was a sterling silver ring she had bought a few days earlier, as she weighed up the greatest gamble of her career, on holiday in Wales.

*   *   *

Most of the Cabinet found out only during the meeting that had finished minutes earlier. Boris Johnson, the Foreign Secretary and Amber Rudd, the Home Secretary, received slightly more warning earlier in the morning, while David Davis and Philip Hammond discovered May's decision only the night before, despite being instrumental in shaping it.

For most of the Downing Street staff heading in to No. 10 after the long Easter weekend, the day was expected to unfold like any other. Communications director Katie Perrior had her first inkling that something was up when she saw Fiona Hill in the building unusually early, at 7.30 a.m., with her hair blow-dried, and wearing her best designer suit. Chris Brannigan, the No. 10 government relations chief, spotted May herself looking the part with freshly styled hair.

At 9.15 a.m., Hill called Perrior to a meeting in the 'Bollocking Room' inside No. 10 with Nick Timothy. 'We are going for an election, Lynton Crosby's on board,' Hill told Perrior. 'I don't quite know what you want to do, but there's only room for one communications director, and that's me.' For Perrior, the news was double-edged. She had always known she would not stay to fight an election campaign. Although she had given up a job she loved running her own consultancy firm in order to work for May, she did not want to end up in politics for life. More pressing was the dismal state of her relationship with Hill and Timothy. She knew she had to leave. 'I think I'm going to take this as my cue to go. You promised me things would change but they got worse,' Perrior said.

Timothy, apparently too embarrassed to speak, sat silently throughout the meeting flicking through messages on his phone. Hill was typically blunt. 'We don't want this to leak so make sure you don't say anything until the PM makes the announcement herself,' she told

Perrior. 'I've spent ten months here and I haven't leaked a thing,' a furious Perrior responded. 'I object to being told I've got to keep it quiet.' Perrior assured the chiefs she would be supporting the Tories, as she always did.

'Thank you very much for the opportunity,' she said as she stood up, placed her chair under the table and walked out of the Bollocking Room for the last time.[80]

* * *

When she got back to her desk, Perrior knew that leaving Downing Street was the right move. She drafted a post to announce her departure on Facebook and waited for May to make her statement to the cameras in the street outside.

An email popped into her inbox. It was from the previously silent Timothy. 'Are you alright?' he asked. 'Don't you worry about me. I'm a big girl and I'm out of here,' Perrior responded.

Once the Prime Minister had finished, Perrior made her own announcement. 'Always said I wouldn't stay past an election. Good decision, right choice. A vote for Theresa May and a Conservative Government is the only route forward. As for me – new opportunities ahead. Exciting times!'

In a private one-to-one meeting inside No. 10 with the PM, about half an hour after May's announcement, Perrior decided it was time to come clean.

'I have not been able to do my job here,' she said.

I am going to just pick out one of over 100 examples of that. But I find it staggering that we've been here ten

months and we've done nothing with *The Sun* newspaper. We have an open goal there, they've offered us
plenty of opportunities and we've pretty much told them
we take them for granted and we don't really care. But
we've done five hours with *Vogue*, a photoshoot with
leather trousers in the *Sunday Times*.

Those were not my call and yet when journalists ask
me about them, I defend them because I defend you –
day in, day out. But I don't make the decisions here in
terms of communications and therefore I shouldn't take
the salary. It is a joke to have that title on my business
cards.

Fiona and Nick make those decisions and I don't
think you'd be Prime Minister without them. I totally
understand the loyalty. But they made you – and they
will break you. They will be your downfall.

A startled May replied: 'Noted. Thank you, Katie. I
think you're going to go on to do a great job.'

'No, no, no. I had a great job,' Perrior said. 'I gave it
all up for you.'

May said she was 'sorry it's not worked out' and
Perrior wished her the best of luck. But with Perrior's
warning ringing in her ears, the Prime Minister must at
least have paused to wonder whether all would indeed
be well.[81]

*   *   *

The biggest immediate worry inside No. 10 was that
Labour and the SNP, who between them made up the
bulk of the opposition presence in the Commons, would

combine forces to block the election. Under the Fixed Term Parliaments Act, May needed a two-thirds majority in favour of her motion to call an election early. But her aides worried Labour would try to fight the plan. This would force a delay on the process, and mean the government would instead have to seek MPs' backing for a motion of no confidence in itself. This, clearly, would not be a good image to project to the electorate, however much it was dressed up as a parliamentary technicality.

The concern over Labour's reaction contributed to a fateful decision – to hold the election back until 8 June.[82] No. 10 had to build in extra time to the schedule in case Labour tried to block the election and they needed to resort to plan B to dissolve Parliament. Looking back, May's aides believe that such a long campaign, effectively lasting seven weeks, was a critical mistake. Some Labour strategists think that with another two weeks, they would have won.

'I think we all accept that – at seven weeks – the final campaign was too long and didn't really meet the requirements of a "snap" election,' says Chris Wilkins, May's director of strategy who left No. 10 in July. A short, four-week campaign was impossible partly because the House of Lords was in recess for an extra week, meaning the final pieces of legislation would take longer to pass before Parliament was dissolved. The second consideration was to avoid polling day falling during school half-term, which caused another week to be lost.

'I should have tried to stop things when that became clear, but the reality was the decision had been made and the train was rolling,' Wilkins says. 'I think that fundamentally changed things though from the "snap" four-week campaign we were advocating in late March, and in which it's fine to do things like not take part in TV debates, to the heavy slog that it became.'

For others, even a shorter, four-week campaign would have been too long. 'You're joking,' a woman called Brenda from Bristol told the BBC in a video clip that went viral online. 'Not another one. Oh, for God's sake. Honestly, I can't stand this. There's too much politics going on at the moment. Why does she need to do it?' It was Lynton Crosby's point precisely.

TEAM 2015

One by one, Stephen Gilbert and Patrick McLoughlin began putting their campaign team together. Just two years after the party won an unexpected majority – in a ruthlessly effective, precision-targeted campaign de-signed and executed by Lynton Crosby – the Tories set about assembling the same winning team. Crosby was confirmed, along with his business partner, the brilliant pollster Mark Textor, and about thirty staff from their London-based firm CTF. Although Crosby apparently insisted he would serve as a consultant to the campaign, rather than as campaign director, his expertise would be vital to fashioning the party's strategy and messaging during the seven-week contest.

Next on the list of consultants who had helped Cam-eron win was Jim Messina, regarded by many as the best centre-left political campaign strategist in the world. He had been responsible for Barack Obama's 2012 presidential re-election bid and served as deputy chief of staff in the White House. Messina and Crosby became friends during the 2015 campaign and held each other in high regard. The American also knew and liked Stephen Gilbert, with whom he had worked on the Remain campaign alongside Cameron before the 2016 EU referendum. Importantly for Gilbert, he could be confident that Messina and his team knew their way around the data that was available for profiling voter types in the UK.

Gilbert and Darren Mott, head of campaigns, would run the Tory ground operation, liaising with the grassroots and overseeing the key seats. When he landed in London on 28 April, Crosby and his team would road-test key election messages and design the overall strategy for how the Conservatives would pitch their offer. The final key element was the Tory digital campaign. Tom Edmonds and Craig Elder had worked on the past two Conservative elections, in 2010 and 2015. They were credited with helping the party break through to a majority by targeting voters on Facebook, especially in Liberal Democrat-held seats across the south-west. The pair, who now run their own consultancy, were persuaded to rejoin the band.

* * *

Seven minutes' walk along the edge of St James's Park from Downing Street lies the Conservative campaign headquarters. Known as 'CCHQ' to all in Westminster, though still sometimes referred to by old hands as 'Central Office', 4 Matthew Parker Street was the nerve centre from which the Tory election campaign was run. May's political team vacated No. 10 as soon as Parliament was dissolved and moved in to the building. Timothy spent most of his time on the fourth floor, along with almost the entire Downing Street Policy Unit, where, along with Ben Gummer, they set about fashioning the manifesto. Hill took charge of the media operation in the war room on the ground floor. Here, at a central table in the middle of the open-plan office, was what had become known as the 'power pod' in the 2015 campaign. Some of the same faces were there, including Crosby, Gilbert and Textor, but also Timothy and Hill.

Pretty soon, a daily routine took shape. Staff would arrive early, at 5.30 a.m. or 5.45 a.m., in preparation for the first meeting of the campaign chiefs at 6 a.m. Meals were provided, often involving traditional British dishes such as shepherd's pie. And days were long. Although the final meeting of the power pod took place at 6 p.m., most people stayed later. It was not unusual for Tory staffers to be putting in fifteen- or sixteen-hour days. With this in mind, the campaign's most senior figures booked rooms and stayed in the St Ermin's Hotel, five minutes' walk away, for the duration of the election.

*　　*　　*

For May, Hill and Timothy, the choice of commanders to run their campaign was really no choice at all. They knew little about how to organise a campaign themselves. Stephen Gilbert had recommended putting the team behind the 2015 majority back together

– and there was no time to come up with an alternative plan.

One of May's advisers says she was not convinced about Crosby. She remembered how the 2005 Tory campaign, which Crosby ran for Michael Howard, had been criticised as nasty and full of 'dog-whistle' messages about immigration and crime, designed to stoke fear and division, the aide says. Crosby has also been controversial in Australia, where he earned his reputation by winning successive elections for John Howard's Liberal Party using messages critics attacked on similar terms. His many successes, however, had earned him the nickname the Wizard of Oz.

May disapproved of Zac Goldsmith's failed run for the London mayoralty, another Crosby campaign which again deployed hard-hitting negative attack lines and attempted to toxify the eventual winner, Labour's Sadiq Khan, with allegations that he fraternised with Islamist extremists. 'She was quite sceptical,' the aide says. 'But the view was, well, we haven't got much time, we need to do this quickly, we just need to bring in the people who know what they are doing.'[83]

A senior Tory who knows both Crosby and May well says the Australian was also reluctant. He did not feel close enough to May to want to take directorship of her campaign himself, the Tory says.[84]

This proved to be a major problem, especially as Stephen Gilbert – who was initially the figurehead – never wanted to run the campaign himself either. Soon after Crosby arrived on 28 April, he took over chairing the twice-daily strategy meetings in CCHQ from Gilbert. Both men were happy with the switch. Those who know

Crosby well say he finds it difficult to step back and watch when he knows he can help provide leadership, yet he was not formally made the boss.

The distinction is important. When Crosby agreed to direct Cameron's 2015 election campaign, he demanded total control over every aspect of the strategy. Cameron agreed and submitted to Crosby's rule.

For Timothy, there was every reason to think that Crosby and company would deliver the numbers they needed, and that the magic they worked in 2015 would work on the electorate again. 'A lot of the criticism of Theresa and Fiona and me is we kept things too tight – and maybe in government we might have done sometimes,' Timothy says. 'But nobody can say we did that in the campaign because we brought in Lynton, Tex, Stephen and Messina and said, "You guys know how to run national campaigns, you do it."'

Timothy accepts that the leadership structure of the campaign itself was 'a little bit messy'.

At first Lynton said, 'I don't want to be campaign director, Stephen should be campaign director.' CTF insisted on a form of words to Stephen about their role: they were to be advisers to the campaign and Stephen was the campaign director. What actually happened was that within two weeks of him getting there, Lynton effectively became the campaign director. Because it's kind of impossible for him to not want to take charge in that situation, so it was kind of messy but it didn't feel very messy at the time because Stephen and Lynton worked quite well together. Stephen was the figurehead. Lynton effectively became the figurehead and that's how it worked.[85]

Here, Timothy omits to mention his own role. Key decisions still went to the two chiefs of staff for signing off during the campaign. Timothy and Hill would veto plans on the basis that the Prime Minister had already made up her mind and disagreed with what was being proposed. As for May herself, she was out touring the country, delivering the slogans and messages designed for her by her campaign team in London.

There is a plausible case for saying that each of Gilbert, Crosby, Textor, McLoughlin, Timothy and Hill were running May's operation, at different times. Compared to the campaign that delivered Cameron's miraculous majority in 2015, it was messy indeed.

PART TWO

THE
STRATEGIES

CHAPTER 6

LABOUR REACTS

Seumas Milne had been expecting an early general election for months.

Like his Tory opponent, Nick Timothy, Milne could see the logic of an early vote long before Theresa May herself accepted it. 'Why wouldn't they?' he asked colleagues. The Conservatives had an apparently unassailable lead over Labour in the polls. May's own approval ratings were approaching the levels usually reserved for dictators.

Then came the Budget. On 8 March, Philip Hammond stood at the despatch box in the Commons offering voters nothing but tax rises and fiscal belt-tightening. He even broke a 2015 manifesto pledge and had to perform a humiliating U-turn. Suddenly the Tories didn't seem quite so invincible, and were clearly not even trying to sweeten the electorate with give-aways from the Chancellor's red box. Everyone could relax.

'It looks like there won't be an election after all,' said Andrew Fisher, Corbyn's influential policy chief, turning to Milne that afternoon. 'Which is good, because if there was an election we'd both die,' added Fisher, to laughter.[86]

Corbyn's key lieutenants were exhausted after what had been a punishing two years. First came his shock victory in the leadership contest, then the backlash from MPs, then the EU referendum, followed by the failed coup and another leadership election. 'It was very gruelling,' says a key ally. 'We had one election after another, constantly under a barrage.'[87]

SHOCK AND AWE

Labour were in a slump. The morning the election was announced was a classic example of their dismal situation. Corbyn went on ITV's *Good Morning Britain* breakfast show, where he received a rough ride from Piers Morgan, the show's presenter, who compared his position to that of Arsenal football manager Arsène Wenger, saying they were 'both in deep denial about the institutions they're destroying'. Corbyn, seemingly unruffled, said the comparison was 'nonsense'.[88] Afterwards, he returned to his office in Parliament to meet two women who ran small businesses. They were being shown around the Palace of Westminster by producers for the BBC's *Victoria Derbyshire* show for a programme about voter apathy. It was just the sort of encounter Corbyn loves.

'It was meant to be a short, "Hello, I'm Jeremy Corbyn, I'm the Leader of the Opposition, this is what the Leader of the Opposition does," and that would be that,' says an aide. 'But, of course, Jeremy was very interested in them, and they were very interested in Jeremy and they ended up sitting down and talking for half an hour. In the end, the producers had to say, "We need to move on."'[89]

Suddenly, a blizzard of text messages and phone alerts hit Corbyn's team. Twitter, Sky News and BBC News were in turmoil at the announcement that the Prime Minister would be making a statement outside No. 10 at 11.15 a.m. Political correspondents, bookmakers and City analysts frantically tried to guess what it could be. Was it her health? Was she stepping down? Had there been a royal death? She had already ruled out an early election many times – but could that be it? Some journalists seemed to think so.

The Labour leader's office sprang to life. James Schneider, Corbyn's media adviser, drew up a list of six potential possibilities, ranging from military action against North Korea to a snap election, and prepared responses for all eventualities so that party spokesmen knew what to say in the television and radio interviews that would follow.

The election Milne had long expected – but had only recently felt ready to rule out – was dramatically back on the table. His mind returned to the conversations he'd had with Corbyn and others about how May would legally set about calling a snap poll under the Fixed Term Parliaments Act. She would need to propose a motion in the Commons for an early general election – and then win a two-thirds majority in favour of it among MPs. The question was: would Labour support it? Milne and Corbyn were always clear that they would. 'If you're the opposition and you want a change of government, why wouldn't you vote for one?' a senior figure close to Corbyn explains.[90]

The first concrete sign that May's announcement was of an early election came when a No. 10 aide set up her lectern in Downing Street. The official crest of her office was missing, indicating that whatever she was to announce, it was party political in nature, rather than business conducted on behalf of Her Majesty's Government.

In Parliament, officials in Labour's Whips' Office took this as their cue and began frantically warning MPs and the leader's office that an early election was likely. Corbyn was in a 'positive' mood as the political order was torn up, say those who were with him that day. There was never any suggestion from him or his senior advisers that they should consider trying to stop the election. That would come later from the parliamentary party – those MPs who feared that voting for an election amounted to volunteering for unemployment. 'Obviously it's daunting,' one figure in Corbyn's office says, recalling the magnitude of the task they faced. While they were confident they could cope, 'It's a level of work which doesn't exist in normal life. We were also coming from a long way behind.'[91]

*   *   *

At Labour headquarters that morning, party officials were equally oblivious to May's intentions. But a strange coincidence meant they were more ready for what came next than almost everyone on the rival Tory side.

Corbyn's election campaign coordinator, the Denton and Reddish MP Andrew Gwynne, was cloistered in a meeting with Patrick Heneghan, Labour's executive director of elections. Heneghan was the party's campaigns supremo and the closest thing Labour had to a Lynton Crosby figure.[92] Gwynne would not normally have been there at all, but it had been his turn to chair the local election campaign meeting that morning. The pair had already concluded there was little chance of an early election being called – and even if May did have a surprise in store, she would not make an announcement until after the local elections on 4 May, at the earliest. Purely as a precaution, though, Heneghan talked Gwynne through an outline plan he had been preparing for the steps the party would need to take in the event of a campaign.

Heneghan's phone buzzed, interrupting his flow. It was a WhatsApp message from Labour's shadow Health Secretary, Jonathan Ashworth. There are rumours about an election, it said: 'What's going on?' Almost immediately, there was a knock on the door and an aide burst in: Theresa May is about to make a statement in Downing Street. 'It will be that snap election, good job we've prepared this,' they joked.[93]

Heneghan quickly drafted an email to an old adversary who had become something of a friend: Stephen Gilbert, the Tory stalwart who had been director of campaigning for David Cameron in 2015. Despite being party rivals, Gilbert and Heneghan came to know and like each other in 2016 when they had worked together on the Stronger In campaign during the EU referendum.

'You're not calling an election, are you?' Heneghan asked in his email to Gilbert. He did not know it, but Gilbert was at that point in charge of the Tory operation, and had been the first person outside May's tight circle of aides to be brought in on her plan. Gilbert did not respond, heightening Heneghan's suspicions. That draft plan on the table suddenly took on a new significance.

When the announcement came, pandemonium

followed. 'We were watching the TV, they brought the podium out and it was running live on Sky,' Gwynne says. 'There's no crest, this is it, a political announcement, it's got to be an early election. And then half an hour later she came out and announced it. It was like a scene from *Dad's Army* and I was Corporal Jones, saying, "Don't panic."'[94]

*   *   *

Corbyn, meanwhile, was in his parliamentary office with his most senior staff when the Prime Minister spoke. Before he could respond, Labour MPs began to panic – in public. Tom Blenkinsop, the MP for Middlesbrough South and East Cleveland, announced he was standing down, rather than contesting the election. Blenkinsop had been a fierce Corbyn critic. He would be joined later by others, including Michael Dugher, a former shadow Cabinet minister who had previously worked in Downing Street for Gordon Brown.

It took more than half an hour for Corbyn to comment publicly on May's announcement, but when he did, he was unequivocal. Labour wanted to go to the country and all the party's MPs would be ordered to back the motion proposing an early general election. 'I welcome the prime minister's decision to give the British people the chance to vote for a government that will put the interests of the majority first,' said Corbyn's statement, which was emailed to the media at 11.40 a.m.

Labour will be offering the country an effective alternative to a government that has failed to rebuild the economy, delivered falling living standards and damaging cuts to our schools and NHS. In the last couple of weeks, Labour has set out policies that offer a clear and credible choice for the country. We look forward to showing how Labour will stand up for the people of Britain.

Corbyn then recorded a short video clip with the BBC, shot in his parliamentary office, which laid out a message that would not change over the next seven weeks. He had survived MPs' attempts to stop him before he could lead them into an election, and now he had the chance to put his case to the British people. Two years previously, he did not even want to be Labour leader. Did he really intend to become Prime Minister? 'We are campaigning to win this election,' he told the BBC reporter Iain Watson. Asked if this meant he would be the next Prime Minister, Corbyn responded: 'If we win this election, yes.'

THE FEAR

All was not well in the Labour family. Some MPs were so distraught at the prospect of fighting an election that they begged Corbyn's office not to back May's motion for an early vote. A poll published later that afternoon showed why. ICM asked the public whether they thought the party leaders were doing a good or bad job. May's approval rating was a startling +33 points. Corbyn's was -48. On which team was best able to manage the economy, 51 per cent said May and the Chancellor, Philip Hammond. In contrast, 12 per cent said Corbyn

and John McDonnell, his shadow Chancellor. Andrew
Gwynne recalls the panic that day. 'She's called this
because she was guaranteed a landslide victory, bigger
than Thatcher, bigger than Blair. The Tories knew it.
Their tails were up. The PLP [Parliamentary Labour
Party] was in absolute disarray.'[95]

As Corbyn's election coordinator, it fell to Gwynne
to brave the media and talk up the party's prospects in
the hope that his appearances would calm colleagues'
nerves. He did his best, valiantly claiming that Labour
were 'in it to win it', however little he may have believed
the statement himself. After the interviews, Gwynne
went back to Labour HQ for a crisis meeting with the
party's general secretary, Iain McNicol, campaign chief,
Heneghan, and other election officials. He already felt
the pressure and it was about to get worse.

The party's private polling was no better than the
public results. Labour were lagging 20–25 per cent
behind the Conservatives. While the team sat at the table
discussing their options, an email arrived from a pollster
giving them advance notice of some new research. A poll
that night was giving the Conservatives a startling 26-
point lead.

As part of Labour's preparations for a snap vote,
Heneghan's team had calculated which seats were most
at risk. The five-strong internal modelling unit analysed
the demographics of each constituency, using data from
the credit reference agency Experian that the party had
brought in. They then overlaid this constituency information with national polling data that showed the
voting intentions of sections of the population from
different social classes and age groups. The results of

these calculations allowed Labour to project how each seat was likely to vote, based on the make-up of its population. 'It was pretty grim reading,' one of those in the room recalls. In the worst case, Labour would be left with just 125 MPs. The most optimistic scenario was for 175, still a catastrophic outcome that would see the party lose fifty-seven seats from its 2015 tally.

The analysis covered all the seats the party held and projected the likely outcome of the election for each one. Gwynne himself took the report and began leafing through it, starting at the back, with the safest seats. 'You can see the blood drain from my face,' Gwynne recalls.

> I'm sitting on a 10,500 majority in a seat that has not had a Conservative MP since it was formed in 1983. Most of the area hasn't had a Tory MP since 1945. I was the last seat predicted to fall on the demographic shifts with a 0.2 per cent predicted Tory majority. That shows the scale of where we were on 18 April. Every decision we took was based on that position we were in. Just how bad it was. Initially, it was all about making sure the losses were limited.[96]

Even those closest to Corbyn in the shadow Cabinet feared the worst.

THE RESPONSE

Against a backdrop of impending electoral Armageddon, Labour's top brass gathered at Southside on 19 April to thrash out their battle strategy – which seats had to be defended, targeted and ignored. The three most senior figures at party headquarters assembled to confront the grim reality of their situation: election supremo Patrick Heneghan, general secretary Iain McNicol and party executive Emilie Oldknow. Corbyn sent his chief of staff Karie Murphy, loyalist MP Jon Trickett and election co-ordinators Andrew Gwynne and Ian Lavery.

Their task was to decide which seats would get the money. Normally before an election, the key seats are chosen well in advance – based on an assessment of which constituencies need reinforcements and which can look after themselves, says one of those in the room that day. 'In this election it was massively different. There were no defined key seats on 18 April when the election was called. It was just like, "What are we going to do?"' Nor were there any staff in the target seats to run campaigns on the ground, or any time to recruit them.

But thanks to Heneghan and McNicol, the party had done some preparation. They had written a sixty-page guide for MPs on what to do in the event of an early general election. The moment May called the vote, Labour HQ updated the timetable in the document for 8 June and then emailed the guide out to MPs so they had the guidance they needed within hours. A draft leaflet was ready to print, and the party also had the cash to print it: £3.5 million from the leadership election the previous year. 'We don't usually have that,' the party insider said. 'We usually have to start fundraising. This was put to one side and kept for a general election. All the costs of a general election, new computers, new cars – all this sort of stuff – we could afford it on day one.'

Two crucial decisions were made that day, and both were unanimous. First, the senior officials in that meeting realised they needed to use the money quickly before the Electoral Commission spending limits came into force ten days later. Second, because there were no candidates selected in seats Labour did not already hold, they could not spend the war chest on leafleting constituencies held by other parties where they might – albeit optimistically – hope to make progress. The party arrived at these decisions quickly because there was little else it could feasibly do. 'You had a period of ten days where you could send candidate-facing material in unlimited quantities and not have it count against the election limits,' says one Labour figure in the meeting that day. 'The decision was we should do that now, get the money out today. We can only do that in seats where we have candidates.'

Yet, there was a discussion about whether to write off some seats – even from within this narrow list of Labour-held constituencies – because they were 'hopeless cases'. One person at the table that day recalls: 'We are twenty-five points behind in the polls. That means we are going to lose seats – so why are we going to plough money into Chester and other super-marginals like Ilford North?' Ultimately, this approach was rejected. 'We said, "We are not at that stage – at the start of the campaign, everybody is going to get some funding."'[97]

Had the decision gone a different way, Labour would have ceded ground to the Conservative Party at the outset of an election during which its fortunes improved beyond recognition. The only areas that did not get money in that first tranche of funding were the seventy-five safest Labour seats in the country. Critically, the party machine moved fast, buying a mail-shot of a million leaflets which went out that weekend, before the official spending limits came into force. 'We got the money out of the building within twenty-four hours,' one official says with pride. 'Two million pounds, out of the building and into seats.'

One thing is clear from individuals in the room for that critical meeting: nobody was planning an aggressive, attacking strategy designed to win new ground at the start of the campaign. Why would they? Labour was facing disaster and it needed to shore up its base. 'We did the right thing,' insists one senior figure involved in the discussions. 'It provided stability to the Parliamentary Labour Party that there was a plan. Everyone was in panic mode and it did look like we had a grip.'[98]

THE GOAL

While the Labour Party's most senior figures were locked in a room in Victoria Street working out how to avoid disaster, Jeremy Corbyn was in the House of Commons. As he stood to speak, Tory MPs opposite mocked him in delight, while his own colleagues sat glumly and silently behind him.

The Labour leader, in a suit and tie, with John McDonnell to one side and Tom Watson to the other, appeared relaxed and confident, welcoming the election but accusing Theresa May of breaking her word. He also went on the attack, dismissing the Tory record on the economy and blaming the government for overseeing a slump in living standards for ordinary workers. He had heard

May's charge that he was a weak leader, ignored it and moved on to his preferred area of combat – austerity.

At the end of Prime Minister's Questions, the political reporters based in Parliament – known collectively to all at Westminster as 'the Lobby' – gathered in a crumbling ante-room just outside the door to the Commons press gallery for the routine briefings with spin doctors that take place after the clash of leaders every week. First it was the turn of the Downing Street team to answer questions about May's comments in the Commons. Then Corbyn's chief spokesman and thinker, Seumas Milne, gave his forecast for the contest ahead.

Tall and languid, Milne remained calm under some typically hostile questioning, explaining to a largely disbelieving pack of reporters why Corbyn was about to prove them all wrong. 'We said there were two reasons why the polls would narrow sharply,' one Labour executive explains. The first was that election broadcasting rules would help Labour get their message across without it being filtered through 'the white noise of character assassination'. The second was that Labour's policies will prove popular. 'For the first time in eighteen months we will be able to speak in a less mediated way and people will hear Labour's voice in its own terms – and they'll hear Jeremy on his own terms,' the executive says. 'We know that the policies that we're standing on are very popular. People will respond.'[99] The executive explains:

> The mythology around Jeremy was that he could only
> appeal to activists. Anyone who'd seen him in the wider
> campaigning knew that potential was clearly there and
> that he does have an appeal that goes far beyond his

immediate base. We discovered this two years ago – we
did not know it before then. No other left candidate in
the Labour Party was able to have the appeal and cut-
through that Jeremy had.

Over the coming days, Labour began working out a
strategy to capture the groups of people who were
not going to vote Tory. It amounted to a plan that, if
everything went their way, could deliver them 40 per
cent of the vote, according to party officials. But in order
to do this, Labour would need to hope that the enthusiasm of young Corbyn fans outweighed their generation's
typical apathy towards voting on polling day. It was the
same dilemma that faced Ed Miliband's team in 2015.
The youth vote loves Labour, it just doesn't love voting.

INSURANCE POLICIES

If Jeremy Corbyn and Seumas Milne were outwardly
confident and privately ambitious, many of their closest
allies were less sure and had already begun preparations
for defeat – the ultimate defensive strategy. It started
with setting the minimum result that Corbyn would
need to cling on to his job.

'There were two benchmarks,' explains one close
Corbyn friend candidly. Firstly, to achieve a higher vote
share than Ed Miliband managed in 2015. Secondly, to
restrict May's majority to no more than twenty.

These were the benchmarks which meant Jeremy could
not be ousted. Some of the early predictions would have

left Jeremy in an untenable position. There was a view [in the leader's office] that there had to be a position which was politically and practically defensible in terms of share of the vote and majority. Ed's strategy was 35 per cent so if Jeremy got 35–36 he was safe – he would've beaten Ed's target. In terms of [the Tory] majority, once you get above 20, [Labour MPs] start losing their seats so that's tough.

The attempt to frame the election result as success or failure for the Labour leader received a public airing on 16 May when Len McCluskey, the general secretary of Unite the union, Labour's biggest donor, put it on the record. 'I believe that if Labour can hold on to 200 seats or so it will be a successful campaign,' McCluskey said – almost a month after May triggered the snap election which would eventually cost her party its majority. 'It will mean that Theresa May will have had an election, will have increased her majority but not dramatically.'[100]

Senior Labour officials even claim that members of Corbyn's innermost circle were calling colleagues in the days immediately after May's election announcement, asking whether people wanted to 'work on the Jeremy campaign' – by which they meant Corbyn's part in the seemingly inevitable leadership contest that would follow a clear defeat on polling day. A WhatsApp group was set up for loyalists: JC Team 2017. 'It was never said but there was a view at HQ that they [Corbyn's aides] were as much running a post-election leadership election as a general election campaign,' said one official sympathetic to Corbyn.

CORBYN UNCHAINED

On the day that Theresa May shocked the country with her election announcement, the orthodox thing for Corbyn and his team to do would have been to cancel their engagements and lock themselves away to plan their strategy. They were twenty points behind in the polls and heading for catastrophe. No party had ever made up such a deficit over an election campaign.

Corbyn had other ideas. The Prime Minister might have called an election but he had a prior engagement. A meeting with carers in Birmingham was in his diary for 18 April, and he was determined to keep it. One aide involved in the discussion says:

> She calls the election and obviously the traditional instincts are to cancel that, to get into crisis meetings, what are we going to do? Jeremy said, 'No, we're going – on two principles. One, we have a room full of carers whose time is extremely precious, who've come to talk, so I want to do that. And secondly, what better way to start the election?
>
> 'If the media are desperate to have a pool clip of me responding to it, I'll give a very short one now and they can pick something up later coming to see me talking to carers.' If the leader of the party says that's what he wants to do, it's quite difficult to stop him.[101]

It was a decision Corbyn took on instinct. This was to be a pattern that he repeated throughout the campaign, and one which marked him out from Theresa May, whose method was one of cautious, careful planning, weighing up risks before reaching considered decisions, or putting them off until more persuasive evidence could be found. Not so for Corbyn – he was going campaigning.

'In fifty days, the country will go to the polls,' Corbyn told the carers in Birmingham. 'We founded the NHS, we created the social security safety net, we created the Open University, we developed the minimum wage, we've done so much on human rights and equality. A Labour government, elected on June 8, will build on that legacy.' There was no attempt to 'triangulate', to tack to the centre in order to poach Tory voters. It was Corbyn in his socialist comfort zone, talking about the issues that he always talked about.

*   *   *

Corbyn showed few signs of self-doubt, even at the start of the 2017 contest. He made his first campaign stop the Tory marginal seat of Croydon Central in south London. The constituency was Labour-held from 1997 to 2005 and had been represented by Conservative Gavin Barwell, the housing minister, since 2010. He held it with a majority of just 165 in 2015.

In a glimpse of the Corbynmania which was to come – often orchestrated by Momentum – the Labour leader arrived at the key target seat to be greeted by hundreds of activists. 'This election is about the future of all of us,' he said.

The future of our children, the future of social justice, the future of our jobs. Are we going to be a country that gives riches and makes riches for all of us, or are we going to be a country that works only to make the richest even richer?

It was undiluted Corbynism in a London commuter town that voted Tory. It's not what the numbers suggested was sensible.

Whatever was happening behind the scenes, Corbyn carried on. He had done his own thing his entire career; he was not about to stop now just because there was an election on. And with Milne at his side, he had the intellectual support to continue making his authentic pitch to Britain. Here was the real Corbyn offering a vision he believed in completely. It was a relief for him to be out of Westminster and the internal party politics that he hated. Corbyn was on the road again.

CLASS WAR

The following day, Thursday 20 April, the Labour leader set out his vision for the campaign, which he would stick to for the following seven weeks. In his first speech of the contest, hastily arranged at Church House in central London, Corbyn laid out his plan. 'The dividing lines in this election could not be clearer from the outset,' he said.

It is the Conservatives, the party of privilege and the richest, versus the Labour Party, the party that is standing up for working people to improve the lives of all. It is the establishment versus the people and it is our historic duty to make sure that the people prevail.

Much of the media and establishment are saying that this election is a foregone conclusion. They think there are rules in politics, which if you don't follow by doffing your cap to powerful people, accepting that things can't really change, then you can't win.

But of course, they do not want us to win. Because when we win, it is the people, not the powerful, who win ... It is the establishment that complains I don't play by the rules: by which they mean their rules. We can't win, they say, because we don't play their game. We don't fit in their cosy club. We're not obsessed with the tittle-tattle of Westminster or Brussels. We don't accept that it is natural for Britain to be governed by a ruling elite, the City and the tax-dodgers, and we don't accept that the British people just have to take what they're given, that they don't deserve better.

And in a sense, the establishment and their followers in the media are quite right. I don't play by their rules. And if a Labour government is elected on 8 June, then we won't play by their rules either. They are yesterday's rules, set by failed political and corporate elites we should be consigning to the past.

Corbyn accused the Conservatives of being 'drunk on a failed ideology' of austerity, 'hell bent on cutting every public service they get their hands on'. Corbyn declared that if he was 'the CEO of a tax-avoiding multinational corporation, I'd want to see a Tory victory ... Why? Because those are the people who are monopolising the wealth that should be shared by each and every one of us in this country.'

The speech was antagonistic, populist and direct.

It was authentic Corbyn but with an intellectual edge brought by Milne. It was the language of revolution. Corbyn's speech was a rejection of 'conventional wisdom' and it defined Labour's entire campaign, one aide recalls. 'It was about the people versus the powerful, which becomes the many versus the few, and it incorporates a much more antagonistic approach. It says, if I was a tax-dodging press baron, I'd want the Tories to win. It says we're going to break all the rules.'[102]

CHAPTER 7

GROUND WAR

THE ARMIES

Reality hit home for the Tories terrifyingly late.

On Thursday 8 June – polling day itself – Lynton Crosby was ensconced in the war room in Matthew Parker Street, monitoring feedback from field teams across the country. His phone buzzed with a text message from a campaign official fighting a marginal seat in Southampton. 'Fuck me – there's ten buses of Labour activists here,' it said. 'There are 200 activists on the street. They're running out of things to do.'[103]

At 5.54 a.m. the following morning, the city's results were declared. Labour held the seat of Southampton Test with a hugely increased majority of 11,000 votes. It was a crowning blow to the credibility of the Conservative operation. The seat was high on the Tory target list and Theresa May had visited it twice in the campaign.

In the neighbouring constituency of Southampton Itchen, the Conservative incumbent, Royston Smith, only just clung on, after three recounts, with his 2,300-vote majority slashed to thirty-one. The Southampton results, announced together, were the point on the morning of Friday 9 June when the Tories officially lost their majority and a hung parliament was confirmed.

The Tory activist who sent that panicked text message to Crosby wasn't quite right. The army of campaigners who swamped Southampton on polling day were not just from the Labour Party. Many came from a separate, highly organised, mass movement of Corbyn supporters who had transformed themselves into the most powerful electoral ground force of 2017. Its name was Momentum.

For all the preparation, arguments about policies, finely honed campaign slogans and lovingly drafted manifestos, elections are won and lost – and also drawn – in the 41,000 polling stations across the UK. The battle for supporters, and then the battle to turn those supporters into election-day voters, is fought in town squares and on residential streets by party activists, faithfully handing out leaflets and knocking on doors. This is the election 'ground war'. To win it, you need three essential items: a message to sell on the doorstep, an army of volunteers to sell it and a really good map.

The story of the 2017 ground campaign is a dramatic mismatch between a Conservative Party comprehensively outnumbered by a Labour Party that could draw on tens of thousands of enthusiastic supporters of their leader's personal movement. The big problem that faced both camps was that the cartographers mapping the battlegrounds from their respective London headquarters were hopelessly confused.

MOMENTUM

Momentum is not the same thing as the Labour Party. It is a political organisation that grew out of Jeremy

Corbyn's first campaign for the Labour leadership in 2015 and it remains primarily loyal to him and his socialist project. Corbyn's friend Jon Lansman knew the Labour leader would need to keep hold of the thousands of supporters who backed him and campaigned for him when the inevitable coup attempt from Labour MPs came. Momentum was born. By the 2017 general election, it had amassed 23,000 members and 200,000 registered supporters.

Lansman and Corbyn remain close. After the election, the Labour leader sent his friend a birthday message, scrawled in marker pen onto a large red campaign placard carrying the slogan 'For the Many Not the Few'. 'Jon!' it said. 'A very happy birthday and thanks for all you do. Jezza.'

According to Lansman, the tens of thousands of new activists who have flooded into Momentum are not interested in ordinary political parties. They want their politics to be as easy as the rest of their lives are, especially online. 'They don't want to be told what to do,' he says. 'They just want a space to organise.'[104]

Yet there is nothing laidback about Momentum's campaigning. It is revolutionary and disruptive. Momentum does not develop policies or field candidates, but instead works, often aggressively, to win support for Corbyn's socialist agenda. It was vital in helping Corbyn keep his job when 80 per cent of Labour MPs wanted him to quit and forced a new leadership election in 2016. 'We had to mobilise lots of people, organising mass rallies to give the feeling of additional momentum,' recalls Lansman. Momentum specialises in training its volunteers in techniques for how to talk to voters they meet on the doorstep. A team from Bernie Sanders's campaign for the 2016 Democratic presidential nomination in the US worked closely with the organisation, developing the training programme during the general election. The key insight into this work is that activists faced with a hostile voter who hates Jeremy Corbyn should move the conversation immediately onto issues, such as the NHS, often starting with a personal story of their own. Activists were told to turn the conversation to individual voters' concerns and focus on policy rather than personality or leadership in areas where Corbyn's personal standing was low.

During the course of the 2017 election, Momentum trained 3,000 people in using these techniques.[105] Their next task was to send them out onto the streets.

HACKATHON

Momentum's potency came from its ability to adapt and grow rapidly online. This would prove crucial in both the digital campaign and the ground war. It developed a piece of software that allowed its thousands of volunteers to club together with people living nearby and share cars to drive to a swing seat for a day's campaigning. The story of how the software was created is typically grassroots-led.

'We have teams of people voluntarily doing coding,' says Lansman. 'We have a "hackathon", which is a whole bunch of coders coming together to solve problems for us. Teams of people do this all the time. In the digital world this is totally normal.' In British politics, it was revolutionary.

The result was called 'My Nearest Marginal' and it was essentially a dating agency to allow volunteers to find a lift to a constituency where they were needed. 'My Nearest Marginal was the software we used to enable people to catch lifts to by-elections and ultimately to our target marginals,' Lansman says. 'You said who you were, where you lived and what your phone number was. Drivers would put in where they were going. It was a lift-sharing system and got large numbers of people to marginals.'

During the 2017 campaign, more than 100,000 individuals used My Nearest Marginal to campaign in more than 100 seats across the country, according to figures provided by Momentum. These seats included Battersea, which Labour won from the Tories; Leeds North West, which they took from the Liberal Democrats; Brighton Kemptown, which they snatched from the Conservatives; and Hampstead and Kilburn, a marginal in 2015 which the Tories were targeting but which instead turned into a safe Labour seat with a huge 15,560 majority.

After the election, Momentum tallied up the scale of its involvement in a report that it released to the media. It found almost 10,000 people had pledged to take the day off work to get the Labour vote out on polling day, knocking on more than 1.2 million doors. Labour won twenty-five out of the thirty constituencies that Momentum activists targeted.

Even Lynton Crosby, the mastermind of the Tories' 2015 election victory who was back in the Tory war room, was impressed. He says:

Corbyn had the advantage of two leadership campaigns and Momentum campaigning for him, as well as numerous other third-party groups which were campaigning all the time. Labour had an infrastructure in place. These third parties had a big role and influenced the campaign. You can have the best techniques in the world and all the money you want but it doesn't matter if you can't get people out to vote on the day. You need people out knocking on doors on polling day.[106] [107]

DAD'S ARMY

Using vast digital resources from a support base of 200,000 potential contributors, Momentum had solved a problem that the Conservatives have grappled with for years: how to move activists from safe seats, where they are numerous, to campaign in the swing seats where they are needed but are scarce. The My Nearest Marginal software solution for Momentum was simple: share cars.

In 2015, the Conservatives ferried activists around the country in buses. While it was successful in helping deliver a majority, by the time Theresa May was preparing to call the snap election two years later, the Tory battle bus tactics had exploded into a full-blown scandal.

The party's use of buses was investigated by the Electoral Commission for breaching the strict legal limits on constituency spending during elections. The Tories were fined a record £70,000 by the commission for the 'significant failures' in how the party had declared its 2015 electoral spending. There was no way the buses were going to be used again.

As the party went into the 2017 election, there were fears that the Crown Prosecution Service would announce formal charges against more than twenty Conservative MPs – a cloud which never fully lifted throughout the campaign. On 10 May, the CPS announced there would be no charges against any Conservatives over the battle bus investigation, but inquiries would continue into the contest in South Thanet, where the Tories had narrowly seen off Nigel Farage in 2015. On 2 June, less than a week before polling day, the CPS announced it would charge the Tory candidate, Craig Mackinlay, as well as his election agent and party organiser, for breaking expenses rules.

The case loomed large in the minds of those running the Tory campaign from the start, not least because Nick Timothy had played a major role in Mackinlay's fight against Farage in South Thanet. Concerns were raised among the Prime Minister's most senior aides about launching the Tory battle bus should the CPS announce a decision on charges the same day. 'We couldn't afford to have the PM pictured in front of a bus on the day that battle buses became part of some kind of criminal investigation,' an aide to May recalls.[108] Another senior adviser says the Tory campaign machine was 'soft pedalling' on the question of moving activists around the country to fight in marginal seats after the controversy over their battle bus campaign in 2015.

Yet, if there was ever an election where the buses were needed, it was 2017. For the first time, the Tories were facing a genuine mass movement marshalled and despatched by a new force in British politics. And the Conservative election machine was not ready for the snap contest when the Prime Minister called it.

Under Corbyn, Labour's membership had grown

to 500,000; he could also count on an army of online activists, the trade unions and Momentum. Officially the Conservatives had more than 120,000 members, although even CCHQ did not know the true figure because no central register was kept. Each local Conservative association was charged with keeping its own record of membership, making any national estimate fraught with problems. In 1952, the Tory Party had 2.75 million members.

Strategists who worked on the 2017 campaign believe the official number of active members could be as low as 50,000 – one tenth of Labour's. This was an impossible situation when it came to targeting seats the party had not held for decades – or ever – at the general election. Nobody was available to knock on doors. 'You can do some through social media but ultimately the closer you get to an election, the more you need people on the ground to help turnout – and they just weren't there,' a senior Conservative strategist says.

The timing was also critical. In the run-up to the 2015 election, the party had two years in which to develop methods for filling the holes in its ground operation. In 2017, there was no time to make any plans at all. The Conservatives were less battle-ready than Labour and no amount of last-minute funding or expensive professional expertise could hide the fact.

In 2015, the Conservatives had embedded campaign directors in every one of the party's 100 target seats and they had been active in their constituencies for months or more. By 2017, almost all of these local election managers had left. Those who could be deployed had their work cut out. They had to cover up to ten seats each, which meant they could not run effective campaigns. The most they could do, when spread so thinly, was get a 'top-line' picture of how the campaign was going. 'The party's on-the-ground stuff was shit,' one senior figure recalls. 'The place was run-down. The party was ill-equipped for an election. It was nothing like the operation in 2015.'

It's a point even the most senior figures in the party now admit privately. Asked how ready the Tory machine was to fight an election on 18 April, one Cabinet minister says simply: 'It wasn't.' Even ministers who are long-standing supporters of May believe this opening mistake – failing to prepare – cost them a significant advantage. 'This point is massively underrated,' says Damian Green, the First Secretary of State, who is a friend of May's. 'We called a snap election and our troops weren't ready. None of us were expecting a snap election, but Labour were. When you get a lot of very close results, that matters.'[109]

The failure to prepare for a snap election was also a necessary corollary of the desire to keep the plan secret. May's team were conscious of wanting to avoid leaks. As one of her closest advisers in No. 10 explains, 'You are either calling one or not; you don't have room to deliberate in public.'

TARGET PRACTICE

None of it should have mattered.

The Tories began the seven-week campaign more than twenty points ahead in the polls, a margin no rival party could hope to overcome merely by putting extra pairs of boots on the ground.

May's closest advisers called the election expecting a majority of at least sixty, although expectations were much higher in CCHQ as soon as the announcement came.[110] Ten days into the campaign, Jim Messina, the American data consultant working with the Tories, told Stephen Gilbert, Lynton Crosby, Mark Textor and other senior figures that his modelling suggested the Conservatives would win 470 seats – enough for a staggering majority of 290, more than double Margaret Thatcher's 1983 landslide – and an exponential improvement on David Cameron's winning margin of twelve. It was an extraordinary moment and one that caused serious concern among those at the top of the campaign who already feared expectations were spiralling out of control. Messina's forecast was the high-water mark for the tide of Tory optimism, but right up to election day the most senior campaign officials thought they would make strong advances into Labour territory.[111]

Gilbert and his team drew up an initial list of constituencies to target. As in previous elections, it was a mix of seats to defend – those marginals deemed potentially at risk from a surge of support for other parties – and constituencies the Tories hoped to take from their rivals. At the start of the campaign, this target list comprised forty-nine defensive seats, and sixty-one seats to attack, most of which were Labour-held. Of the attack seats, fifty-one were considered to be the key 'battleground' that would decide the outcome of the election. The Tories prioritised these fifty-one seats when it came to selecting candidates. The battleground seats also received more visits from May and senior ministers, more direct mail and more targeted Facebook advertising than other constituencies.

Unusually, the 2017 campaign included a massive live polling exercise involving millions of people casting real votes: the local elections. These contests took place in thirty-five English councils and all local government districts in Scotland and Wales, alongside elections for mayors in six areas, including Greater Manchester, Liverpool and the West Midlands. It was a rare opportunity for the political parties to gauge their progress in a real – but less important – set of elections before the main event on 8 June. If the Tories did well in the locals, they planned to expand their campaign to include another thirty-three offensive seats. This showed the scale of ambition among senior CCHQ strategists in the opening few weeks of the campaign. When the party carried out a review ten days into the campaign, seats 'well beyond' this extra target group of thirty-three seats were projected to turn blue.

Following the local elections, which pointed to a comfortable general election victory but not the landslide many expected,[112] the Tories pulled funding out of most of the seats threatened by the Liberal Democrats, including Bath, Oxford West and Abingdon, Eastbourne and Portsmouth South, in order to concentrate their fire on Labour-held constituencies.

The target list in a campaign is constantly evolving as data comes in from polling and activists in the field. As the Labour surge began to be picked up in the final three weeks, CCHQ scaled back its ambitions, but continued fighting to win 35–40 attack seats in what the party still assumed was the battleground.

Labour, in contrast, did not have a single attack seat on its list of constituencies due to receive central party funds for a whole month after May called the election. It was only after the manifestos were published, and the real backlash against the Tories began, that the party started to think about offensive targets. But even then, on 18 May, when it produced its second target list, the party's priorities were overwhelmingly designed to limit the losses, with 100 defensive and thirty-nine attack seats.[113]

Throughout the campaign, Cabinet ministers, MPs and ordinary activists were sent to constituencies the Tories expected to gain but where they ended up losing significant ground to Labour. In return, the Labour Party sent activists to seats it already held in a bid to fend off a Tory advance that never came.

WASTED EFFORTS

The battleground as far as both parties were concerned was in northern England, the Midlands and Scotland. The south-east and south-west were safe Tory territory. Here, the Conservative Party expected huge majorities as UKIP voters turned blue thanks to May's Brexit policies.

When drawing up their target seats list, the Conservatives gave all 650 constituencies in the Commons a code number from 0 to 7. Tory-held seats that needed to be defended were marked '0' or '1' and regarded as probably safe, although Gilbert and his team became increasingly concerned as the campaign wore on about the threat from Labour in metropolitan seats, particularly in Remain-voting London. The top tier of target attack seats were marked with a '2' – these were the constituencies the Conservatives had come close to winning in 2015. More ambitious targets came further down the number scale. For much of the campaign, seats marked with a '2' were considered to be in the bag, according to losing candidates who discovered the party's mistake too late.[114] Category '3' seats were considered the main battleground, while those marked '4' were considered realistic possibilities until the publication of the manifesto, which halted the party's progress and forced CCHQ to reassess. On polling day, the Tories lost thirty-three category '0' and '1' seats – constituencies they held before the election – and won only twenty new seats, including twelve in Scotland.

The final election map bore almost no resemblance to the one both the Tories and Labour had been using to navigate their strategies. This abject failure to understand what was happening on the ground as it moved beneath them is one of the most striking aspects of the 2017 election.

When the results came in, Labour seats given up as lost to the Tories not only stayed loyal, but returned their MPs with increased majorities.

Tory marginals went red and even safe heartland seats for Theresa May, with barely a Labour presence on the ground, voted for Jeremy Corbyn. 'Clearly there was a significant data failure,' says one senior Tory aide close to the Prime Minister when asked what went wrong. 'We were targeting places we were never going to win.'

Nowhere was this clearer than in the north-east of England. Here, in the working-class areas that had been passionate about Brexit, the Tories pushed their messages hard all the way to polling day. In the final week and a half, Boris Johnson, the charismatic Foreign Secretary and former figurehead of Vote Leave, hit the streets of Bishop Auckland, while then Work and Pensions Secretary Damian Green – now First Secretary – travelled to Hartlepool and Michael Fallon, the Defence Secretary, to Darlington. Such was the Conservative Party's confidence in the north-east that category 2 targets like Darlington and Middlesbrough South and East Cleveland were considered safe. Resources were redirected to nearby Stockton North, where Labour had an 8,000 majority. On election day, just one seat in south Durham and the Tees Valley area voted Conservative. James Wharton, the MP for Stockton South, saw his 5,000 majority overturned. He became one of eight ministers to lose their places in Parliament that night.

In the Midlands, it was a similar story. The Conservatives were targeting Walsall and North East Derbyshire, which did turn blue, but continued – wrongly – to believe they had a chance in seats like Bolsover right up until and on election day.[115] The seat has been represented by the veteran left-winger Dennis Skinner since 1970 without his vote ever dropping below 50 per cent.

Less far-fetched, but ultimately just as unsuccessful, was the Tory pursuit of seats in and around Birmingham. Capturing this working-class territory from Labour was a deeply held ambition, especially for Nick Timothy, a proud Brummie. May launched her 2016 leadership campaign in the city and it was people who were 'just about managing', in areas like this, to whom her government had pledged to dedicate itself.

The Midlands constituencies on the Tory shopping list included Birmingham Northfield, Edgbaston and Wolverhampton South West. Despite intense campaigning efforts by CCHQ, Labour's majority went up in each of these seats. The Tories also believed they had a chance in Wolverhampton North East but only managed to knock 1,000 votes off MP Emma Reynolds's 5,500 majority. For much of the campaign, Labour's deputy leader Tom Watson was concerned about his chances of holding on in West Bromwich East, but in CCHQ this was never seen as a realistic target, according to senior party insiders.

Timothy had his eye on taking Birmingham Erdington, where he grew up, but it was not to be. 'We'd have needed a 100-plus majority to win Erdington,' one senior Tory says. During much of the campaign, however, a Tory landslide of this scale seemed likely.[116]

*　*　*

It was a picture of confusion. The map that candidates and campaign generals were working from seemed to bear little relation to the reality of the contest, even in the Conservative heartlands of the south-east. 'We didn't appear to know we were a mile away from winning places like Ealing and Brentford, where we were campaigning hard,' says one concerned Cabinet minister. In Ealing Central, Labour's majority went from 274 to almost 14,000 and in Brentford from 465 to 12,000. One defeated candidate reveals the frustration felt by many of his colleagues: 'There were examples around the country where afterwards you thought, "Why did we put so much effort there?" We lost it by 10,000. Why that happened, I don't know.'[117]

The extent to which the Tories took their eye off the ball was exemplified by the deployment of Conservative MPs from safe seats to campaign in nearby targets only to turn up at their own count on the night to find they had lost. Canterbury MP Julian Brazier was asked to go to Eltham in south London, only to see his own 10,000 majority overturned. To rub salt into the wound, Labour more than doubled its majority in Eltham to more than 6,000. In Reading East, Rob Wilson, another minister, was asked to go to help in Slough because his seat was deemed 'safe'. He lost by 4,000 votes.

FIGHTING BLIND

No matter how bad it was for the Tories, it could have been much worse.

In the final weeks of the campaign, the Labour Party had the perfect combination of an army of enthusiastic activists and a rising tide of support in the country. By the day of the election, Labour was within striking distance of more than forty Conservative-held seats. The party won twenty-eight and came within 1,000 votes of taking fourteen more, but at the time, nobody knew.[118]

In Labour HQ on polling day, strategists still expected a Conservative majority of 80–90. Momentum, which has accurately boasted of pursuing a more offensive campaign than Southside, campaigning in Tory-held seats throughout the campaign, spent their final days embedded in many defensive marginals. 'We were going into polling day completely blind to what was going on,' says Sam Tarry, the trade union organiser and Momentum activist.[119]

If Momentum had known what was happening on the ground, they would not have wasted huge effort and resources on seats which turned out to be rock-solid Labour and turned their considerable fire to nearby constituencies which to everyone's surprise turned out to be up for grabs. Tarry explains that, with a better early warning system, Labour could have taken up to fifteen extra seats, a result that would have left the Conservatives unable to form a majority government even with the Democratic Unionist Party. 'I don't think the Tories realise just how close they were to losing the general election,' he says.

On 8 June, thousands of Momentum activists descended on defensive seats which they assumed were in danger of falling to the Conservatives. In east London, 350 activists spent the morning and much of the afternoon in Dagenham, where the Labour MP Jon Cruddas was sitting on a majority of 5,000. At 4.30 p.m. they were joined by people from Ilford North, where Labour's Wes Streeting was defending a slender 600-vote majority. In both seats there was a sizeable UKIP presence. The question was where would these UKIP voters choose to put their faith in 2017? Many assumed they would all switch to the Tories, who had become the party for hard Brexit, thanks to May's promise to quit the EU single market. But it wasn't that simple.

Momentum did not think of sending their activists on the thirty-minute drive to Thurrock, a three-way marginal, fought over by the Tories, Labour and UKIP. The Conservative candidate Jackie Doyle-Price had a wafer-thin majority of 500 votes but it was assumed she would be returned easily because the 15,000 UKIP voters in her constituency seemed unlikely to switch to support Jeremy Corbyn.

On election night, Momentum looked on in horror as Labour came within 350 votes of taking Thurrock despite a collapse in UKIP's vote, while Jon Cruddas was comfortably returned in Dagenham and Wes Streeting turned a majority of 600 into one of 10,000. They had the army, but they were stationed on a Maginot Line of their own imagination while the battle was quietly raging nearby.

*   *   *

The same story unfolded all over the country. In Norfolk, buses full of Momentum activists engaged in a battle to save the Corbynite MP for Norwich South, Clive Lewis, even though he was sitting on a majority of more than 7,500. In neighbouring Norwich North, the Conservative incumbent Chloe Smith, who had a 4,000 majority, was largely ignored. When the results came in, Clive Lewis more than doubled his majority to 15,000 while the Labour challenger in Norwich North came within 500 votes of toppling Smith.

On the south coast, huge efforts were made to take Brighton Kemptown from the Tories. Simon Kirby, the Treasury minister, was returned in 2015 with a slender 700 majority but Momentum were determined to capture it from him. In the end, Labour won the seat by 10,000 votes. Momentum had done more than enough there. Nearby, in Hastings, Home Secretary Amber Rudd clung on with a majority of just 350, down from almost 5,000 two years earlier. Somehow, she had avoided heavy Momentum assaults in the closing stages of the campaign.

Momentum's supporters rightly point out that they played a crucial role campaigning in offensive target seats like Battersea, Sheffield Hallam, Leeds North West and Croydon Central, which all fell to Labour. But, in many respects, 2017 is a story of an opportunity missed: had Momentum known just how many more seats were up for grabs, they could have achieved even greater success.

MIRAGE?

Such was the shock of the final result, MPs have taken to asking whether the polling and modelling data – which decided where the ground forces should focus their energies – were ever right.

The number crunchers of both parties still believe their initial target lists were right at the time. The commanders poring over campaign maps in their respective war rooms are confident that in April, the Tories really were heading for a landslide and Labour really was going to be buried under it.

'It was real,' insists one senior Labour insider.

Fast forward to the first week in May and the local elections. It's easy to forget this now but that was the worst performance of any opposition party for forty years. It was like, 'Wow, you can't be in opposition and do that bad. It's not possible.' And it was. It was real at that point.[120]

Labour's private pollsters, BMG, spelt out the scale of the oncoming disaster in its weekly seat predictions to the party leadership. At the beginning of the campaign, the Tories forecast a majority of about 150, according to party officials. This did not change significantly until the week of 15 May, when the manifestos were launched. Even after that, BMG never suggested anything other than a comfortable win for Theresa May.[121]

Senior figures on the Tory side agree that they were genuinely streets ahead at the start. 'Something changed,' says one of the most senior figures at CCHQ, who watched in horror as the Tory poll lead collapsed over the final three weeks. 'At the beginning of the campaign, the seats we were looking at were looking very, very good for us, there's no doubt about that.'[122]

By convention, election campaigns are not expected to change anything. This one did. There was a significant and dramatic surge in support for Corbyn's Labour which became clearer over the final three weeks of the campaign, without an equally dramatic fall in support for the Conservatives. What is more puzzling is why the parties themselves, who had thousands of people tuned in to the election on the ground, appeared so unaware of the scale of the movement.

The Corbyn surge did show up in polling, but the extent of it simply was not understood – by either Labour or the Conservatives. Election strategists on both sides point to the shortcomings in their internal polling, as well as the public polls; this research simply could not keep up with what was happening on the ground, they say.[123] Corbyn's increase in support came in part from energising young people and other voters who by habit are less likely to vote.

Pollsters take their raw research findings and then 'weight' them against the likelihood of different respondents to turn out on polling day and vote the way they say they will. It was these calculations that led to variations between the pollsters during the campaign. One of the key questions was how likely they believed young people who said they would vote Labour were to make it to a polling station and cast a ballot on 8 June.

Then there was the speed of the changes in support for Corbyn. It was a fast-moving phenomenon which took off at a time when campaigning had to be stopped twice because of terrorism. The sharp tightening in the polls came largely after the launch of the Tory manifesto, which proved to be one of the most influential policy documents in recent election history. The effect of that manifesto, and the U-turn that followed, on the Conservative lead was like a gust of wind on a house of cards.

THE WRONG CONVERSATIONS

In campaigns, political parties need troops and a good map but they also need to know what to do when they arrive in those swing towns and suburbs where elections are decided. They need to know exactly who to speak to – and what to say when they do.

This is where the mysterious wizardry known as

'modelling' comes in. There is a wealth of information available to political parties – some free, much paid for – which they can use to identify the swing voters they are most likely to win over. These are the voters who decide elections. They may have voted a different way at the last election but 'modelling' helps parties understand which arguments will be most likely to persuade them. The exercise is highly complex, meaning it can go wrong. All mainstream parties model their potential voter types; it is simply sensible market research. They use a combination of data from Facebook, the electoral roll and the credit checking agency Experian. This information reveals what specific voters in specific target seats are like. Reliable polling evidence, broken down by age, social class, gender, education level and other factors, can then suggest how people with particular characteristics might vote.

Targeting specific voter types is fundamentally a question of time and resources. 'There are 40,000 doors to knock in each constituency. You simply can't knock on 40,000 doors,' says one senior strategist in the Conservative campaign. (Momentum would later challenge this theory. If you have the resources, you can knock on 40,000 doors, but for the Tories this was not an option.)

*   *   *

In the wake of the result, there have been many complaints about the information given to Conservative activists on the ground. One of May's advisers spent the last day of the campaign in Dagenham and Rainham, 'which actually felt very upbeat', he says. But he noticed a troubling trend: he seemed to be knocking on doors with committed Labour voters inside. 'I was putting leaflets through doors and there were just lots of Labour posters in the windows of the houses we were knocking. When there are lots of people living in the same house you get that, but it felt a bit wrong.'

Yet, other Tory candidates insist the canvass data was good. Why was the picture patchy, at best? MPs and activists on both sides now argue the micro-targeting of voters and old-fashioned canvassing methods were simply overwhelmed. The tide of support surging back towards the two main parties after the EU referendum – and the number of new voters switched on to politics by Brexit – meant the old techniques did not work, or were not viable, especially in a snap election with little time to prepare.

To start with, Labour MPs understandably concentrated on the core of voters who had backed them in 2015 because the party was so far behind in the polls. Yet neither main party saw that vast swathes of the electorate, 25–45-year old new voters in particular, were moving en masse behind Jeremy Corbyn. This swing group were up for grabs but nobody was talking to them. 'The Labour Party did not see this coming whatsoever,' says Momentum's Sam Tarry. 'We weren't talking to anyone who shifted in the last three weeks of the campaign.'

The one organisation which did not use micro-targeting was Momentum. They simply bombarded their target seats with activists in the hope of persuading people to vote for Corbyn. In doing so, they knocked on doors none of the main parties were bothering with.

Even internal Tory modelling experts now question the value of what they were doing. 'Maybe Corbyn's plan to build a big groundswell of support, ignoring the seat-by-seat numbers etc., is the right way to go,' says one. 'How do you ever factor in for that? This is what happened with Trump, this is what happened with Brexit. People voted who you never expected to vote. How do you work out a way to tackle that?'

TALE OF TWO CAMPAIGNS

Another group of people who did not see what was happening was Labour MPs. While Corbyn went campaigning, his MPs hunkered down in their constituencies, many of them doing all they could to distance themselves from their leader.

'You've got to remember, a major part of about half of Labour MPs' campaigns was that Corbyn could not win but the country needed a strong opposition,' says one senior Labour Party executive. On WhatsApp, Labour MPs began sharing examples of how to subtly – or not so subtly – disavow their leader to boost their support locally.

In Stoke-on-Trent, Ruth Smeeth produced leaflets with the message: 'Your REAL Labour voice for the Potteries.' The Labour brand was still strong, MPs felt, but the leader was killing their chances. An image of the leaflet was shared between MPs.

Others went much further. The evening after May announced her intention to call an election, the fierce Corbyn critic John Woodcock uploaded a video on his Facebook account declaring that while he would be seeking to stand again for the Labour Party, he would 'not countenance ever voting to make Jeremy Corbyn Britain's Prime Minister'. He said: 'I cannot countenance endorsing him for a role which I think even he, although he may say different in front of the cameras, does not think he is fit to carry out.' He then added, for good measure: 'There is still of course time for Jeremy to stand down rather than lead Labour to defeat.'

Other Labour MPs chose different forms of words, but the message was the same: don't worry about Corbyn becoming Prime Minister, a vote for Labour is a vote to keep Theresa May honest.

In Tony Blair's old seat of Sedgefield, Phil Wilson wrote a letter to his constituents: 'Your vote in Sedgefield on June 8 won't affect who is in Number 10 on June 9,' he said, 'but it will affect who is your local MP. I am no supporter of Theresa May and I am no supporter of Jeremy Corbyn – the only people I support are you, the people of Sedgefield constituency.'

In Enfield North, Joan Ryan had a strikingly similar idea, writing to her voters to say that Corbyn could not win the election.

I know from speaking to people around here that many who have previously voted Labour are thinking hard this time because, they tell me, they have more confidence in Theresa May as Prime Minister than they would have in Jeremy Corbyn. The polls are all saying that the Conservative Party will win a large majority, possibly with more MPs than they have ever had before. Realistically, no one thinks Theresa May will not be Prime Minister, or that she will not have the majority she needs to negotiate Brexit.[124]

Ryan warned that with a big majority the Tories could make further cuts and 'may be tempted', even, to privatise more of the NHS.

Theresa May's most senior election advisers believe the message was potent. The looming prospect of a landslide Tory government was not something the country had had to contemplate for thirty years. It meant every policy or hint of an idea from the Conservatives was a potential vote loser. For much of the campaign, Labour MPs were focused solely on stopping a Tory landslide, not a Tory majority.

'The way Labour had to do it was to distance their local MPs from Corbyn, which they did,' says Lynton Crosby.[125]

> Some of their MPs literally said, 'I don't support Jeremy Corbyn but I'll be a good MP for you.' Expectations were so high that the Tories were going to win anyway that voters were thinking, 'Well, I can keep my local Labour MP, he'll fight for the local hospital, and I'll still get Theresa May as PM.'

The message from Labour MPs was given extra credence by the Lib Dems, whose MPs were pushing the same line. Crosby says:

> Vince Cable said, 'The Tories have got this election in the bag. Theresa May is going to be Prime Minister. But you can have me as your local MP.' The expectations made it very hard for us to do what we did in 2015, which was to say, 'If you want David Cameron as Prime Minister, you've got to vote Tory.' The expectations that

the Conservatives would win a majority were much higher.[126]

This is the kind of electoral analysis that claims people only voted Labour because they wanted to protest, and did not think Corbyn would get anywhere near No. 10. This interpretation, while persuasive to campaign insiders in both parties, is rejected by academics from the British Election Study (BES). They found that, in fact, the more likely someone thought Labour were to win a majority, the more likely they were to vote for the party.[127]

The truth is, certainly in the intensity of the campaign itself, nobody really knew what was happening. According to the BES, voters who switched to Labour in their droves did so because they believed in Corbyn and liked his politics. This phenomenon was largely missed by the party machines grappling with data, target lists and voter models in their campaign war rooms in Westminster.

Labour was a movement that split into competing camps amid ideological disputes, each faction pulling in separate directions. By accident rather than design, their efforts combined to drag the party's tanks out of the mud and enabled Corbyn to roll on towards the Tory trenches.

CHAPTER 8

DIGITAL CAMPAIGN

THE CALL

On 17 April – Easter Monday – Craig Elder was enjoying a holiday in Aberdeenshire with his wife. They were looking forward to eating at the Bay fish and chip shop in Stonehaven, an award-winning restaurant famous for its battered haddock. Then the phone rang.

Elder was in the queue at the time and didn't answer but there was a voicemail from his friend and business partner Tom Edmonds, with whom he had set up a consultancy after their success running the Tories' digital campaign together for the 2015 election.

'You'll want to ring me back,' the message said.

After an argument with his wife at a crowded fish bar, and a day of negotiations with Conservative HQ, Elder was persuaded. The pair signed up to May's campaign and, with just a day's notice, began devising a digital media strategy for the election seven weeks later.

For Stephen Gilbert and Lynton Crosby, bringing in Edmonds and Elder was essential. Digital campaigning is now an indispensable part of political communications, in part because of the impact that Edmonds and Elder had on the contest against Ed Miliband's Labour Party in 2015. During that election, their work also helped

the Tories win a swathe of Lib Dem territory across
south-west England. Their success transformed Labour's
attitude to digital, too. This time, the task for Elder and
Edmonds was to defend the seats they had helped the
Tories gain two years previously, and make inroads into
Labour heartlands in the Midlands and the north.

*   *   *

When they arrived at Matthew Parker Street, Edmonds
and Elder were shocked by what they found. Rather
than building on their success, the Conservatives' digital
operation had gone backwards. In part, the EU referendum of 2016 (at a time when the next election was not
due until 2020) had sucked resources away and meant
the party leadership had not focused on building its own
links with voters. However, with the arrival of a new
leader and Prime Minister in Theresa May, there had
been an opportunity to win more followers, rebuild the
Conservative website and expand the party's email list.
Nothing had been done.

To a degree, this reflected a firm desire from May and
her two gatekeepers, Fiona Hill and Nick Timothy, to
do things differently. David Cameron once famously re-
marked that 'too many tweets might make a twat' – but
then became a prolific user of Twitter to get his party's
messages out directly to voters. May was not Cameron,
in style or in policy choices, and the trio that ran her
government were determined it should stay that way.

Before the 2015 election, Elder and Edmonds spent
two years preparing. They tested their methods, won
the internal argument for more funding, and were ready

when the time came. The consequence of May's sudden decision to call an election out of the blue meant there was no time to plan a strategy. Nor was there a clear narrative to sell online about Theresa May and what she stood for. David Cameron had been readying the country for his battle with Ed Miliband over economic competence for months before the short campaign in 2015. He promised the Tories would stick to their 'long-term economic plan' until even his own MPs laughed when the slogan appeared in the Commons.

Just like Crosby and Textor (who deployed almost identical messages in some cases to those they had used in 2015), the Tory digital team needed to choose their weapons quickly. Their golden rule was to go where the audience is, not to follow the latest shiny new trend. That meant one thing: Facebook.

PAYING FOR IT

In 2015, Elder and Edmonds made their names with a stealth campaign that used highly sophisticated targeting techniques to contact specific types of swing voters in marginal seats. First, they had to find those voters. Facebook sells advertising to many types of company: supermarkets, insurance firms, car rental businesses. It also sells to political parties.

It works because Facebook users provide a wealth of information about their lives to the social network – how old they are, whether they have children, what they are interested in and where they live. Companies use this information to target their products at particular types of consumer who are most likely to be persuaded to buy them – and political parties can do the same. In 2015, this meant Edmonds and Elder could target tailored advertisements to tiny batches of voters – as few as 1,000 at a time – in key marginal seats.

In 2015, Elder and Edmonds realised they had to spend the bulk of their budget on Facebook because that's where 55 per cent of the whole population was to be found. Two years later, this proportion had gone up to 60 per cent – a higher share than even the United States. The social network leads all other platforms for audience figures and has grown across all age ranges, for both men and women, since the 2015 election, according to figures drawn from the Ipsos Connect tracker. YouTube videos and Google were also significant in terms of their ability to reach into voters' lives.

The Tory digital unit did not want simply to repeat their 2015 campaign. In the short time available, they tried out two other channels that had grown significantly. Instagram had overtaken Twitter in popularity among women of all social classes and every age group up to forty-five, making it vital in any campaign to reach female voters. Elder and Edmonds set May up with her own Instagram account. Snapchat had also burst onto the social media scene, dominating younger age groups. The Tories allocated £10,000 for a trial of Snapchat but halted it before the project had finished when it became clear that the experiment would not work for them.

In 2015, the Conservatives spent £1.2 million on Facebook advertising, and this goes a long way online. Labour, however, was said to have spent as little as £16,000 during that campaign, though this figure has been disputed since it first emerged. By 2015, Labour had learned its lesson and set aside £1.2 million for its digital budget, and spent the vast majority of it on Facebook ads.

Elder warned his campaign masters that there was no prospect of Labour repeating its mistakes of two years previously and he would need more money. The Tories allocated £2 million for their digital campaign, spending 70 per cent on Facebook, with just 1 per cent going to Twitter. 'As far as we were concerned, Facebook was still the go-to platform to reach the majority of voters. Throw on top far better targeting options, and it was the obvious choice for the majority of the budget,' Elder says.[128] May also took it seriously, appearing on a Facebook Live video interview, for which 45,000 questions were submitted by viewers.[129]

In 2015, the Tory Facebook operation was so sophisticated that it required them to send out 350 different advertisements, matched to different types of voters, in different seats. This degree of segmentation of the British electorate was unprecedented at the time. There were 350 different ways of telling voters that David Cameron's long-term economic plan would help them and their families while Ed Miliband, propped up by the SNP, would cause economic chaos – it all depended on where voters lived, how old they were, what their social and marital status was, and what their personal and political interests were.

By 2017, the picture was dramatically more complex. On 8 June, when people were heading to the polls, the Tories sent close to 4,000 different Facebook ads, more than ten times as many messages tailored to specific types of voter as in 2015. They were variations of the core messages: vote Conservative for a good Brexit deal, a strong economy and, in Scotland, where the party made remarkable inroads, to stop a second independence referendum. The operation to get the vote out involved promoting adverts with pictures of ballot boxes, and repeatedly using the word 'vote', during the week of the election.

Elder and Edmonds worked intensively in the southwest, where Crosby had identified a risk to the Tories from a Liberal Democrat revival. Some of the Tory MPs in the seats the party took from Nick Clegg in 2015 had failed to perform well enough in their constituencies, according to Crosby's research, and so were judged to be vulnerable. As well as defending these seats, the Tory digital operation reinforced the main battleground as the party saw it – in the Midlands and Scotland, where it was most successful in taking new territory.

Even with the most sophisticated targeting on Facebook, however, it's hard to convert Labour voters into Tories in a short campaign, irrespective of their disdain for Corbyn. 'There's a huge swathe of people who are nailed-on Labour voters who wouldn't vote for him [Corbyn] in a million years,' says one Conservative campaign official.

> They are the voters you're looking to talk to. It's more challenging for voters to come to the conclusion 'I'm going to vote for Theresa May and the Conservatives'. There needs to be more done further out in the build-up period before people will turn away from him and towards the Tories. That's the challenge.[130]

ORGANIC PRODUCE

In 2015, targeted Facebook ads represented the sprint finish to the marathon digital effort that had begun in earnest two years previously. The foundation for the Tories' online success was traditional routes, such as building a big email list of 1.5 million voters and sprucing up the party website so it reflected the manifesto pledges and the arguments in the air war. It also relied on building a network of supporters who would spread David Cameron's messages on Facebook in an 'organic' way, rather than through advertisements.

Yet, again, the time to lay these foundations was not available to the party in the snap election campaign of 2017. 'The organic stuff is incredibly important,' says Elder.

> You've got to build the website, you've got to be great at the Google search stuff. You've got to build an organic Twitter reach for the Prime Minister. If you don't have that foundation underneath you, Facebook ads just end up being something that keeps your head above water in seats where you're not doing as well as you'd like.[131]

Cameron built a huge personal following on social media, with 500,000 Facebook followers when the 2015 full-time campaign began, compared to Ed Miliband's 80,000. Craig Oliver, his communications chief, was especially keen on Twitter and worked hard to build Cameron's network and craft his 'voice'. The loss of Cameron's personal following was keenly felt. May almost never tweeted and her Facebook page had just

350,000 likes by the time she announced the snap election in April 2017. Jeremy Corbyn had more than twice as many, with 843,000.

Corbyn himself won the Labour leadership after a mass social media campaign that galvanised party members. 'In 2015, our organic social media was very effective,' a senior Tory figure says. 'It was built up over a long period of time and we had more Facebook followers and more on Twitter. I'm pretty confident that we still outgunned Labour on paid social media but Labour killed us on organic this time.'[132]

Why had May's Conservatives allowed Labour to catch up in the race for digital disciples who could spread the word?

In part, it was about a structural blockage: it was hard to get lines signed off when all decisions had to go through the two chiefs of staff, who were already overworked in their respective jobs running the media operation and drafting the manifesto. 'Stephen would take advice to Nick and Fiona and they would make a decision after a couple of days,' one Tory campaign official said.

> Even if they were the best decision makers in the world, even if they were right 100 per cent of the time, which no one is, you can't fucking do it like that, especially in the age of social media. You've done too much damage by the time you've played around and made a decision.[133]

Some Tory insiders claim May's aides were too interested in their feud with the Cameroons at a time when they should have been focused on winning an election.

'There were things they said they wouldn't do because that's what David Cameron did. One was social media engagement,' a senior Tory says. 'But if that's how you're thinking, you're not really serious about the campaign. It's amateurish and unprofessional.'[134]

The impact of this policy of social media restraint was never more dramatic than in the immediate aftermath of the Manchester terror attack on 22 May. The digital team in Tory HQ were desperate for May to make a short, strong statement on Twitter, but her aides refused.

GOING VIRAL

Labour campaign chiefs believed the terrorist atrocities in Manchester and two weeks later at London Bridge would damage them and help May, who looked un-deniably prime ministerial, standing outside No. 10, commanding the country's security infrastructure in the hours after the attacks. Security was one of the Tories' strongest arguments against Labour, and they promoted their case relentlessly online. Diane Abbott, the shadow Home Secretary, had fallen to pieces in an LBC radio in-terview when she could not answer even basic questions on Labour's plans for recruiting more police. But it was the leader, Jeremy Corbyn, whom the Tories regarded as the weakest link in Labour's defence offer to voters.

At every opportunity, Lynton Crosby pushed May and the Tory campaign team to highlight Corbyn's al-leged record of opposing anti-terror laws, campaigning against Trident nuclear weapons, and choosing a selec-tion of 'friends' and associates who included Hamas and the IRA. The Tories' biggest social media hit of the election came as a result of this policy: an attack video highlighting Corbyn's previous comments on national security and his apparent reluctance to condemn the IRA's record of bombings.

'This man is only six seats away from being Prime Minister...' the opening caption says in one version of the video. The lettering is stark white capitals on a black background. Then, a clip of Corbyn: 'I've been involved in opposing anti-terror legislation ever since I first went into Parliament in 1983,' he says. The most controversial section of the one-minute, 22-second production was an edited extract of an interview Corbyn gave to Sky News's Sophy Ridge. In it, he was asked to condemn IRA bombings. When he condemned 'all bombing', he was asked again if he would condemn IRA bombing, without caveats; the clip shows him saying 'no' before cutting away.

The video was being watched 300 times a minute in the days after the Manchester attack, but the editing of this section sparked a huge row. Labour said the Tories had misrepresented Corbyn's views by failing to show what he said next. They accused the Conservative campaign of promoting 'fake news'. In his interview with Ridge, Corbyn went on to say:

No, I think what you have to say is all bombing has to be condemned and you have to bring about a peace process. Listen, in the 1980s, Britain was looking for a military solution in Ireland, it clearly was never going to work. Ask anyone in the British Army at the time. And therefore you have to seek a peace process. You condemn the violence of those that laid bombs that killed large numbers of innocent people. And I do.

Pressed further, Corbyn eventually said: 'I condemn all the bombing by both the loyalists and the IRA.' Corbyn's office issued a statement which accused the Tories of 'running a hateful campaign based on smears, innuendo and fake news' because 'they have nothing to offer the British people'.[135] The row made the front-page lead story for *The Guardian* and was covered elsewhere. It was, in the words of one Conservative, 'a piece of contrast campaigning' designed to make Labour voters think twice about their man. The video was the most watched social media election video ever produced by a British political party, according to *The Times*, notching up some 9 million views.[136]

'That Corbyn video just went crazy. The nature of the shares and people pushing it on tell us it was successful,' a CCHQ strategist says. 'It's not a positive piece of content, you're trying to focus people's attention on what Jeremy Corbyn has said and what his actual views are. You want floating voters to say, "We didn't know that and actually he has serious questions to answer." They are very legitimate questions.' The controversy over the claims probably helped the Tories too, by forcing questions about Corbyn and security into the media agenda. It was a move straight out of the Corbyn playbook.

Hardly anyone in the Tory campaign thinks attacking Corbyn over his alleged links to the IRA did them much good. To most people under the age of forty, the Troubles simply seem like ancient history. One senior Labour figure close to Corbyn says the failure of the Tory strategy showed how impotent the traditional right-wing alliance of the Conservatives and the press barons has become: 'For half the population the IRA means nothing and people could see it was a campaign of vilification and it didn't work. It's obviously quite symbolic of the rise of social media versus normal media. It was a demonstration of a lack of power.'[137]

CATCHING UP

By 2017, Labour's more professional approach to digital campaigning meant their online communications were versatile, flexible and creative. As a whole, the central party spent about £1 million on Facebook ads. Before the election even started, Labour campaign teams launched a drive to get MPs and candidates to spend more time on their Facebook accounts, for the same reasons that Craig Elder and Tom Edmonds chose the social network as their primary channel for reaching floating voters over the more politically engaged audience on Twitter.

Labour also used social media effectively to promote its manifesto, with the document's page on the party's website receiving an estimated 5 million hits before polling day. Was there a big difference between what the Tories were doing and what Labour was doing? No, but that in itself represents major progress for Corbyn's party since the previous election.

'Fundamentally, we do the same things,' one senior Labour campaign official says. 'I would say our digital operation is better because our people are ingrained in British politics, they're Labour Party staff working full-time, rather than Americans who turn up for seven weeks.'[138]

One element of the campaign the Labour Party is particularly proud of is a new piece of software which was completed only just in time for the election. Called 'Promote', it is an election database containing all the modelling of voter types that would be used traditionally to tell canvassing teams on the street which doors to knock on, and who not to bother with, as they seek to persuade swing voters face-to-face. The new system was built with the credit reference agency Experian, during a year-long project. The feature of the database of which Labour figures are proudest is its ability to automatically match voters with their Facebook accounts, enabling Labour to target individuals with social media ads. 'The tool was literally used for the first time in the general election. It was just about ready,' a Labour strategist says.[139]

Although Labour officials are pleased they spent money working with Experian on the Promote project, they wrongly believe the Tories didn't have access to the same data from the credit checking agency. Jim Messina's team was modelling voter types using data bought from Experian, taken from the electoral roll and elsewhere. Three members of the American consultant's staff also worked closely with Edmonds and Elder producing thousands of Facebook ads. In truth, these data models for both parties proved fallible.

SNAPCHAT

In the final week of the campaign, both Labour and the Tories splashed their resources on social media. By this stage, it was too late to write new leaflets for mail shots,

so only online advertising, which is far quicker to gener-
ate and distribute, could respond to the latest campaign
developments.

Labour spent a late windfall of donations in the final
few days on getting their voters out, many of whom had
not bothered or been eligible before. On polling day
itself, the party paid £90,000 to buy the top 'trending'
spot on Twitter for their campaign hashtag, VoteLabour.

Another channel, Snapchat, also came into its own. The
app is wildly popular among crucial young voters, who
like it for sending temporary text messages, videos and
pictures, all of which disappear after a short time. More
than half of under-25s were Snapchat regulars, across
almost every social class bracket. Snapchat was largely
unable to reach older voters, who are the most likely to be
Conservative supporters, in the kind of numbers to make
it worthwhile. This led the Tories to abandon their experiment with the app – the party knew it was unlikely to
win among the younger age group. For Corbyn, however,
these young people represented some of his wildest fans.

Labour built a simple but clever digital tool, which
matched voters' addresses in key seats to their nearest
polling station. All you needed to do was enter your
postcode into the polling station finder and it would tell
you where to go to vote, and plot you a route to get
there. After Labour saturated Snapchat with adverts,
one million young people used the map to plan their
trip to the polling booth.

A senior Labour figure recalls:

We spent £100,000 on Snapchat in the last three days.
We targeted every single young person in the country

irrespective of seat. We got 7.8 million young people to see our advert. A million people clicked the link to see where to vote in the final forty-eight hours. Nobody has ever spent £100,000 on Snapchat before in British politics.[140]

THIRD PARTIES

Clean-cut, smartly dressed and handsome, Dr James Crane gazes intensely, straight into the camera. A stethoscope hung around his neck, Dr Crane delivers his health warning in the tone of medical authority that's halfway between friendly and stern: 'If you care about the NHS, vote for anyone but the Conservatives.'

This is the final scene of an extraordinary campaign video that was one of the most viewed and shared of the entire election and among the most alarming for the Tory digital specialists battling for supremacy online. One after another, GPs, hospital doctors and nurses talk directly to camera to warn viewers that voting Conservative will damage the health service.

'I live with it, day in, day out. I work within it,' Dr Fionna Martin, another registrar with a stethoscope, says. Dr Jackie Appleby, a GP, also sporting a stethoscope, says: 'I feel terrified. I feel terrified for what's going to happen.'

The 'Vote NHS' video was viewed 10 million times before polling day. But it was not produced by the Labour Party, or the Liberal Democrats, or even the SNP or the Greens. The Tories were impressed – and worried.

'It was so well shot that you think you're actually

talking to your GP – and they're saying, whatever you do, don't vote Tory,' one CCHQ strategist says. 'I must have seen that from about twelve different groups, shared by about twenty or thirty of my friends on Facebook, and I saw that and went, "Oh. There's a big third party swell."'

In fact, it featured no politicians and it was not obviously a political party product at all. The credits at the end name two groups: the People's Assembly Against Austerity, and Health Campaigns Together. Although no Labour branding appears anywhere on the video, both groups have links to the party, and specifically to Jeremy Corbyn's socialist movement now leading it.

The People's Assembly Against Austerity says on its website that it is not aligned to any party's agenda. The claim seems potentially open to debate. It was founded in 2013 with a joint letter to *The Guardian*, with signatories including film-maker Ken Loach (who produced a party election broadcast for Labour in May 2017), journalist John Pilger and a rebellious backbench MP called Jeremy Corbyn. In 2016, it demanded the resignation of David Cameron over the Panama Papers scandal and since the 2017 election it has been campaigning for Theresa May to step down. Three weeks after the 8 June election, Corbyn spoke at a huge rally in London that the People's Assembly organised as part of a national day of demonstrations to get the 'Tories out'.

Corbyn told the crowds in Westminster: 'We are the people, we are united and we are determined, we are not going to be divided or let austerity divide us. We are increasing in support and we are determined to force another election as soon as we can.'[141]

What about the other group behind the video? Health Campaigns Together (HCT) does not trumpet claims to political independence. Its board has included members of Momentum. Constituency Labour Party branches are also affiliated with HCT and the organisation has worked on motions to submit to the Labour Party conference. Published board minutes from meetings in 2016 show HCT sent a delegation to form an advisory group for Corbyn, John McDonnell and Diane Abbott, who was shadow Health Secretary, in a concerted attempt to influence Labour policy on the NHS. The alliance is supported by the health workers' unions, including Unite and the GMB, which also bankrolled Labour's election campaign.

In its election 2017 resources for supporters, Health Campaigns Together urged volunteers to turn out to 'roadshow' events in marginal seats to put pressure on Tory MPs. 'All of us as healthcare professionals and NHS campaigners have a public duty to hold the government to account for its unacceptable record in the NHS. By taking the facts to the public, we can make this general election a vote on the National Health Service,' the group said. HCT organised more than forty events around the country during the campaign, starting with a rally on Saturday 13 May in Croydon Central, where the sitting Tory MP, housing minister Gavin Barwell, would soon be defeated, giving Labour one of its biggest scalps on election night.

Speaking afterwards, Barwell said the anti-austerity sentiment played a significant part in his downfall:

There is a conversation I particularly remember with a teacher who had voted for me in 2010 and 2015 and said, 'I understood the need for a pay freeze for a few years to deal with the deficit but you're now asking that to go on potentially for ten or eleven years and that's too much.' That is something Jeremy Corbyn was able to tap into.[142]

The Vote NHS video is one example of how third-party groups played a major role in boosting Labour's campaign on social media. Inside CCHQ, they certainly noticed. Tory staff estimated that fifty or more different organisations engaged in opposing the Conservatives – or some of the party's policies – online, with trade unions promoting Labour plans to their members, activists in the League Against Cruel Sports opposing fox hunting, campaigning organisations like 38 Degrees pushing for money for the NHS, and Momentum's pro-Corbyn movement all committed in the digital battle. A Tory insider says: 'The groups that deserve an enormous amount of credit are these third-party campaigning groups who share a very obvious objective with the Labour Party: to "get rid of this Tory government".'

Brutal humour is a feature of many of the most successful social media productions. One video from Momentum, 'Daddy, Do You Hate Me?' was viewed more than 7 million times on the group's Facebook page. The video shows a father talking to his young daughter about life in Tory Britain in 2047. The girl asks why class sizes are so big, whether she can go to university, and why her school meals aren't free any more. He replies with a smile: 'Because I voted for Theresa May.'

The girl then asks: 'Dad, do you hate me?'

'Obviously,' he chuckles.

The video then displays a message in what looks like official Tory white-on-blue campaign lettering: 'VOTE THERESA MAY', it says. 'Because your children deserve worse.'

*   *   *

According to Momentum's records, nearly a third of UK Facebook users viewed at least one of its videos over the course of the campaign. In the crucial final week, nearly one in four Facebook users in Britain had viewed a Momentum video. The group's influence extended to getting the vote out on polling day. Momentum says it contacted more than 400,000 mostly young people on election day through WhatsApp messages.

One senior Tory ruefully concludes: 'Momentum were OK at generating content but the third-party groups, I take my hat off. If their mission was to come together online and batter the Tories like we'd never been battered before, they did a great job.'

*   *   *

In a pattern that seemed emblematic of the entire election, it turned out that the Tories' costly, precision-targeted social media machine was no match for a mass movement of disparate groups and enthused supporters, all spreading the Labour word for free.

One long-standing Tory pollster who worked on the party's successful campaign in Scotland, Andrew Cooper, says Labour's new-found mastery of digital campaigning is bad news in the long term for the Conservatives.

Labour's use of digital campaigning and social media seems to have been much cleverer, subtler and more sophisticated than what the Tories did. Certainly, Labour's social media campaigning seems to have played a big part not just in the big increase in turnout among younger voters, but also the even more significant achievement of a landslide-scale Labour lead among this age group. In 2015, David Cameron's Conservatives trailed Ed Miliband's Labour by 4 per cent among under-30s. In 2017, Theresa May's Conservatives trailed Jeremy Corbyn's Labour by 40 per cent. This is an existential threat to the Conservatives who have, for much, much too long, been dependent electorally overwhelmingly on the elderly.[143]

A senior Conservative campaign strategist puts it more bluntly: 'This truism has been established that Labour were much more effective with young people on social media. Well, actually, young people's vote share didn't go up much; their turnout did. Sixty per cent of young people vote Labour anyway. It was just more of the fuckers turned out to vote.'

CHAPTER 9

PRESIDENT MAY

POKER FACE

It is something of a political tradition for Prime Ministers to use the first Sunday back after New Year to outline their vision for the next twelve months in a major, set-piece TV interview. The BBC's *Andrew Marr Show*, broadcast at 9 a.m. every Sunday, was David Cameron's vehicle of choice. More recently, rivals have appeared, including ITV's *Peston on Sunday*.

On 8 January 2017, a new show was launching. This one was different: the presenter was a woman. Sky's Sophy Ridge had bagged the big interview for her first outing in the role of Sunday political host, in part because Theresa May likes to encourage female journalists in an industry which, like politics, is dominated by men. May's communications director Katie Perrior thought it would be a good opportunity to signal that May wanted to do things differently, as well as to send a message to the BBC that they wouldn't always get their way. There was just one problem: Donald Trump.

On Sunday 8 January, May went to church at St Andrew's, Sonning, as was her weekend routine. Rather than head home to cook a roast lunch, May climbed into her prime ministerial limousine and sped through

Berkshire to the studios of Sky News in Osterley, west London.

During her preparations for the interview, Perrior became concerned that Ridge could try to pull a stunt in her first show, in an attempt to grab headlines. The US President-elect had just supplied the obvious and perfect question: what did May feel, as a woman, about the newly unearthed (but twelve-year-old) video of Trump saying his celebrity status gave him the ability to grope women whenever he liked, adding, 'You can grab 'em by the pussy'? As she waited for May in the official car outside the church, Perrior knew she would have to find a way to prepare her boss for such a question. She decided she would just have to say it.

'Prime Minister, it's possible she will ask what you think of Donald Trump saying he can grab women by the pussy.'

In the front seat of the Jaguar, the PM's police protection officer snorted on his bottle of water.

May said: 'Right. How would you like me to respond?' Perrior told her the camera was likely to zoom in on her face in a close-up, because they would be expecting her to grimace in the way she sometimes does.

'I don't do that,' the Prime Minister said.

'You do,' Perrior replied.

'I don't.'

'Actually, you do,' Perrior persisted. 'Don't do it. Keep completely and utterly still – poker face. It's all about the face. They want to be able to say, "This is the face Theresa May makes when she talks about Donald Trump."'[144]

In the end, May remained perfectly composed, waiting, expressionless, for Ridge to finish her shock question about the President-elect groping women. 'I think that's unacceptable,' May told Ridge in response, 'and in fact Donald Trump himself has said that and has apologised for it.'

*　　*　　*

According to numerous aides and campaign officials, May 'hates' doing media appearances. She particularly dislikes broadcasters posing long-winded questions during press conferences. These TV stars are never interested in the answers, or in finding out new information, she has complained to her aides. They only want the opportunity for 'grandstanding', so the evening news bulletins will show footage of the BBC's X or ITV's Y taking a tough line with a politician on TV.

Every election campaign is fought and won on the ground, by getting people to turn up at polling stations and cast their ballots for particular parties, but the essential context for those individual decisions is framed in the national media, usually for months, if not years, before polling day. The task for the rival parties is simple: to cast the choice that voters will have to make so it works to their own best advantage.

In the 'short' campaign, between the dissolution of Parliament and the day of the election, this 'air war' is a genuine battle for media attention, a contest over which party or leader can command the most airtime and the biggest audiences on television and radio and in the pages of the newspapers. The prize is huge: the chance to move the election debate onto your most favourable subjects. Elections are rarely won by the party that fails to get its core messages across, or cannot convince voters that its story about the choice they face is more compelling than the versions offered by its rivals. The burden of this work almost always falls on the shoulders of the party leaders. However much she hated it, May had to perform.

PRESIDENT MAY

The PM is private, shy and has never particularly sought the limelight for herself, a fact that astonished Tory campaign insiders given her position at the very top of British politics. In part, it is nerves. She doesn't want to make a mistake. But she also fundamentally doesn't understand why the media want to know about her personal life outside her role as PM.

With this in mind, May's closest aides initially planned a traditionally structured election campaign in which a rotating cast list of Cabinet ministers would present a policy for each day, often with their own press conferences. It might be Jeremy Hunt, the Health Secretary, outlining the Tories' proposals for the future of the NHS, or Philip Hammond, the Chancellor, analysing Labour's spending plans. Nick Timothy wanted what he saw as a grown-up campaign that levelled with voters about the difficulties ahead and put policy at the centre of the party's offer to the electorate.

Before moving from No. 10 to CCHQ, Timothy asked Will Tanner, the deputy head of the Policy Unit, to coordinate the manifesto and the translation of policies into news stories for the media. 'The thing you need to realise is we're probably going to need a policy a day for the next fifty days,' he told Tanner. 'I need you to operationalise every one of those policies so they can be given to the press team and we can campaign on them every day.'

Even after moving into the campaign nerve centre in Matthew Parker Street, Timothy kept asking Tanner for lists of policies that were sufficiently well-developed to be briefed to newspapers as stories ahead of the manifesto's official launch. Tanner, a policy specialist, drafted press releases for the communications team to polish, but they very rarely went any further.

The campaign strategists, led by Lynton Crosby and Mark Textor, found in their focus groups that May's personal popularity far outstripped the support base for the Tories and recommended playing to the party's strengths. In his strategic memo to the PM in April, Crosby set out what the Conservatives 'must' do. His final point was: 'Use Theresa May as the campaign's main communication vehicle – and take every opportunity to contrast her with Jeremy Corbyn.'

The Prime Minister herself was deeply wary of the prospect. She privately confided to Stephen Gilbert that she did not want to be the centre of the election contest. But Timothy, Hill, and ultimately May herself deferred to the experts. A presidential campaign was born.

Posters and placards were printed for events emblazoned with the words 'Theresa May's Team'. Almost every trace of Conservative branding was removed, apart from the colour scheme of blue and white. When the party launched its election bus, the slogans on the side read: 'THERESA MAY: FOR BRITAIN' and 'Strong and stable leadership in the national interest'. The coach (the same vehicle previously used by the Remain campaign in the EU referendum) featured May's own signature.

The word 'Conservatives' was relegated to tiny lettering on the door.

One Tory official explains the decision to focus on May: 'Voters liked what they saw when she became leader. They thought she was the right person to be leader; they thought she was considered and steady, reliable, a proven performer as Home Secretary, and she was the logical appointment.' In the early part of the campaign, the strategy seemed to be working. During field research, previous Labour voters would mention May's leadership as the sole reason they were planning to vote Conservative for the first time.

Yet these voters had a nagging doubt, according to internal Tory research conducted during the campaign. They worried whether May could be trusted with a huge majority. Was she really different from other Conservatives, someone who could be relied upon to do what she promised and deliver for them, or was she just another 'nasty party' Tory who would somehow betray their votes? 'She was a blank canvas – they didn't really know her,' the campaign official says.[145]

The longer the campaign went on, the more voters seemed to warm to Jeremy Corbyn. May, by contrast, was refusing to take part in televised debates with her rivals, and when she did appear on television, such as in interviews with the BBC's Andrew Neil, the Prime Minister came across as mechanical, unable to be spontaneous. Her robotic answers repeating the campaign slogan of 'strong and stable leadership' earned her the nickname 'the Maybot'.

She was mocked for a joint appearance on *The One Show*, the BBC's primetime evening programme, with her husband. Asked what it was like negotiating with the Prime Minister at home, Philip May replied that he got to choose 'when' he took the bins out, 'not if' he did. The Prime Minister jumped in to explain: 'There's boy jobs and girl jobs, you see.' According to one campaign source, focus groups held to gauge the reaction of the watching public showed the appearance had not been a success.

Nick Timothy explains how the Tory sales pitch ended up being all about May:

> We certainly didn't expect to make the campaign entire-
> ly about Theresa. But the advice on the basis of the CTF
> research was, 'The party brand is as screwed as ever,
> she's really popular, it's got to be all about her. Nobody
> in the Cabinet is popular – keep them away, even Boris.
> And people don't want change, they just want stability
> and continuity.' That's where I kick myself.[146]

MESSAGES

Timothy's argument with Crosby and Textor is essentially that they picked the wrong narrative to tell, and the wrong messages to sell it to the electorate. But what exactly is a political election message and how did the Tories choose theirs? On the most basic level, a message is the narrative you want voters to hear, and to believe, about the election. The critical task is to distil this into a few memorable phrases, slogans and ideas that will persuade them you are trustworthy, competent and deserving of their votes.

As outlined earlier, the snap nature of the election meant the Tories did not have time to recruit a fresh team of election specialists, so they decided to rehire the same clutch of consultants who delivered victory in 2015. When it came to choosing the campaign messages, Crosby and Textor had little time to research and design a fresh strategy. To many observers, including May's own staff, the 2017 campaign resembled a cover version of the same song the party played in 2015: strong leadership with the Conservatives, or a 'coalition of chaos' with Labour, the SNP, the Liberal Democrats and the Green Party. Three days before polling day in 2015, Cameron sent a tweet informing voters that their choice was between 'stability and strong government with me, or chaos with Ed Miliband'. For the first three weeks of the 2017 campaign, Theresa May endlessly rehearsed the contrast between her 'strong and stable' leadership and the 'chaos' that Jeremy Corbyn would unleash.

The reason May repeated lines such as 'strong and stable' so much was again drawn directly from Crosby's campaign manual: message discipline. His mantra during the Tory 2015 campaign was that without discipline – sticking to the message and never deviating, so that it lodges in voters' minds – you don't have a message at all, and without a message, you don't have a campaign. Discipline was key, and May was good at it. But that did not mean she liked it. On one occasion, the Prime Minister is said to have turned to her advisers and asked, 'How many times are you going to make me say "strong and stable"? It is making me look ridiculous.'[147]

Framing the election as a choice between the two leaders seemed sensible in April. CTF focus groups and polling showed 'Theresa May is the most favourably viewed individual tested, while Jeremy Corbyn is the least favourably viewed'. However, after the Prime Minister's infamous U-turn on the social care policy in May, which became known as the 'dementia tax', it was impossible to sustain the idea that the Prime Minister was not for turning. 'Strong and stable' morphed from a Tory asset into an easy laugh line and a potent attack for Labour.

In another strategy drawn from Crosby's 2015 playbook, the Tory campaign tried to paint Corbyn as a weak leader who would never be able to win power on his own and would depend on the support of other smaller parties to have any hope of entering No. 10. This was exactly the same scenario the Conservatives had set out so effectively two years previously, telling voters that Miliband would require the support of Nicola Sturgeon's Scottish National Party in Parliament. A weak Labour leader would inevitably be pushed around by the stronger First Minister of Scotland, the Tories said in both 2015 and 2017.

There was one critical difference. In 2015, a hung parliament seemed inevitable. The Tories and Labour were neck and neck in the polls and the media's campaign debate focused on potential coalitions and alliances. In 2017, it was hard (though possible) to find a political pundit who believed the Tories were not on course for a bigger majority, and potentially a landslide. At the start of the seven-week campaign, the Conservatives held a 25-point lead over Labour. This made May's warnings that a hung parliament would see Corbyn forced to do a deal with the SNP, the Lib Dems and the Greens seem like fantasy politics. Voters didn't buy it.

BREXIT

Brexit was another battleground where the Tories sought to contrast their strong leader with Corbyn, whom May repeatedly called 'weak and nonsensical'. The election was a choice about who would be the strongest leader to negotiate the best Brexit deal for the UK. One Tory poster said: 'Jeremy Corbyn can't negotiate a Brexit deal. The Lib Dems won't negotiate a Brexit deal. Only Theresa May can get the best deal for Britain.' To their credit, Crosby and Textor did identify Brexit as a key concern for voters in their early strategic note to May. Strengthening the PM's position to secure a better Brexit deal was the main reason for calling an early election in the first place – and this happened to be true, as well as a good tactical message to win over poll-weary voters.

May received notable help from the European Union itself. Four days after hosting European Commission President Jean-Claude Juncker for dinner in Downing Street, she was the subject of a hostile briefing in Germany's *Frankfurter Allgemeine Sonntagszeitung* newspaper. The report said Juncker left the dinner shocked at May's unwillingness to compromise and 'ten times more sceptical' of reaching a good Brexit deal. The raised eyebrow of suspicion over who was responsible for the briefing tilted in the direction of Juncker's chief of staff, Martin Selmayr. May's election strategists saw it as an opportunity.[148]

With fears that voters would not turn out because a Tory triumph seemed inevitable, May used all the trappings of prime ministerial authority to launch a stinging attack on the EU, accusing officials of issuing threats against Britain, trying to meddle in the election and wanting the UK to fail. 'The European Commission's negotiating stance has hardened. Threats against Britain have been issued by European politicians and officials,' said May, as she returned from Buckingham Palace for the formal election announcement on 3 May. 'All of these acts have been deliberately timed to affect the result of the general election that will take place on the 8th of June.'

May's bellicose language ignited the campaign and delighted Eurosceptics in her party, as well as ministerial colleagues who were ambitious for a crushing landslide victory. The PM picked a 'genius moment' to accuse the EU of meddling with the election, Europe Minister Alan Duncan said at the time. 'She never fails to surprise.'

'This was a quite deliberate attempt by Juncker and his people to try to weaken the Prime Minister during the election,' Iain Duncan Smith, the Brexit-campaigning former Cabinet minister said, reaching for a Shakespearean parallel. 'He is like Iago, whispering poison into the ears of others around him.'[149]

The dangers of Brexit and the threat from Europe was a theme that May returned to at key moments in the campaign. The Tories turned her speech into a party election broadcast that aired two weeks later. With a steady-paced orchestral soundtrack, the three-minute video consists largely of May's Brussels-bashing speech, warning about the risks of a bad Brexit deal, interspersed with clips of members of the public who say they believe she has 'our country's best interest at heart' and won't 'take any nonsense' from European negotiators or anybody else. The broadcast ends with the question that Crosby, Textor and Gilbert intended voters to ask themselves on 8 June: 'Who do you want

negotiating for Britain and your family's future: Jeremy
Corbyn or Theresa May?' Then came the presidential
slogan: 'THERESA MAY: STRONG, STABLE LEADER-
SHIP IN THE NATIONAL INTEREST.' The word
'Conservatives' appeared in small lettering underneath.

*   *   *

The CTF research found voters were worried about instability. Ironically, given the result, there was one overriding
concern, 'namely a hung parliament creating chaos over
the delivery of Brexit'. But such an outcome still seemed
remote. Given the early poll leads for May, convincing
the electorate to take seriously the prospect of a hung
parliament – or any outcome other than a thumping Tory
majority – was impossible, even for campaign specialists
as skilled as Crosby, Textor and Messina.

Research from the British Election Study showed the
Tories had picked the right subject to focus on for the
election. The Conservatives had also successfully transformed themselves into the party for Brexit, the BES
said, hoovering up 60 per cent of people who voted
Leave in the 2016 EU referendum, and more than half
of those who voted for UKIP in 2015. Yet, even though
May argued the election was necessary because of Brexit
– and the electorate believed leaving the EU was the
single most important issue facing the country during
the campaign – the Conservatives barely raised their
Brexit plans in the run-up to polling day.

Why not? Perhaps because the Tories knew the details of what Brexit would actually look like were divisive. While the country was increasingly looking for

politicians to get on with enacting the referendum result, there was no national unity on exactly how the UK should leave. The clear point the public could broadly agree on – at least at the beginning – was that May would be a better negotiator than Corbyn.

Here is the other key rule from Crosby's election playbook for running the national air war: you focus on your strengths and fight the campaign on the issues on which you can win. This means silencing discussion of subjects that are your party's biggest weaknesses. For the Tories, their traditional strengths have been the economy and security. Investment in the NHS, schools and other public services, by contrast, has for decades been Labour's home territory.

Yet in 2017 the Tories tried something different. After the manifesto, they found themselves mired in a debate about plans to reform the funding of care for elderly and disabled people, which, even though it is not part of the NHS, is a health policy that proved for the Tories to be dangerously close to it. Most people assume care costs are all funded by the state anyway.[150]

The manifesto also opened up a debate about school funding – specifically ending free school lunches for all primary-age children. When Thatcher cut the free milk allowance for older school children, the National Union of Teachers successfully labelled her 'Maggie Thatcher, milk snatcher'. Nick Timothy and Ben Gummer, the authors of May's manifesto, knew these issues would be controversial but believed it was right to include them anyway. Whether or not the Crosby-inspired campaign was ideal, the manifesto destroyed any coherence in the core messages that the Tories had deployed to fight the air war until that point.

Two terrorist attacks could have made security an easy win for May. Labour expected that to be the result of the Manchester Arena and London Bridge atrocities in late May and early June. It was a surprise to Corbyn's strategists that their attack on the Tories for cutting police numbers worked so well. That was in part because the Conservatives could not – or would not – talk about the economy and the need for spending restraint with any conviction.

The Tory reticence was partly because Labour did an effective job of raising the issue of public sector cuts and austerity. But according to a very senior figure inside the campaign, the dire state of relations between Philip Hammond and May's co-chiefs of staff was a bigger problem.[151] The Chancellor and Nick Timothy had been on frosty terms ever since the row over the abortive National Insurance reforms in the 2017 Budget.

Rumours began to swirl that Hammond would be fired in the first reshuffle after polling day. When May was challenged about the gossip during a press conference with the Chancellor, she failed to give the man standing next to her any reason to think he would keep his job. Asked if she would endorse her Chancellor, she said she was 'very happy to do so' but then added that the pair had worked together for 'longer than we would care to identify'.

Hammond's allies were angry and frustrated that he was sidelined during the campaign. They believe his poor treatment by May and her team meant the Tories never properly challenged Labour on the economy, allowing Corbyn and shadow Chancellor John McDonnell to make wild spending promises without being seriously scrutinised. As Steve Parker, from the Tories' favoured advertising firm M&C Saatchi, has said: 'The

Conservatives unable to talk about the economy is a very weakened version of the Conservatives. That's pretty much all they've got, historically, that and security.'[152]

One area on which the Tories were happy to take the fight to Corbyn was his record on national security and alleged links to the IRA. The Conservative Research Department inside CCHQ, aided by consultants who joined from Crosby's team and elsewhere, dug out as much 'dirt' as they could on Corbyn's friendship with Gerry Adams, president of Sinn Féin, and the late Martin McGuinness, former senior IRA commander, and on views he expressed before becoming Labour leader on dismantling NATO. The aim was to show voters how much of a security risk Corbyn would be as Prime Minister. But – as we have seen already – the plan crashed into two major hurdles: first, few believed he would become Prime Minister, and second, Tory campaign officials now admit that most voters under the age of forty-five regarded the IRA issue as essentially solved. The Good Friday Agreement, which heralded a new age of peace in Northern Ireland, was almost twenty years old.

Corbyn's election coordinator Andrew Gwynne says:

The world has moved on. However fragile the peace process in Northern Ireland is and remains, we're used to a sense of normality. People know the political sacrifices that were made to get us to the Good Friday Agreement – both Tory governments and the start of the Blair government. People look back and think, 'Well, past Tory governments negotiated with the IRA, what's wrong with Jeremy talking to Sinn Féin? Those are the steps you need to bring peace.'[153]

HUNTING WITH HOUNDS

Theresa May was by nature well-suited to delivering the message discipline Lynton Crosby demanded. He was impressed with her ability to make serious, persuasive set-piece speeches, and believed 'very few' would be better. Crosby, like May, disliked press conferences and media interviews. One reason he did not want the traditional, policy-rich campaign with daily press conferences that Nick Timothy originally envisaged was because it would undermine the headline message discipline. Political reporters hunt as a pack – and could hijack the day's question-and-answer session to pursue their own 'hobby-horse' issues, he warned.

May's usual tactic was to swerve around difficult questions and 'pivot' back to her key messages, that only a Conservative government with her 'strong and stable leadership' could be trusted to negotiate the best Brexit deal for Britain. This was the kind of answer that reinforced her 'Maybot' caricature. But for some reason, on one occasion, May and her aides suffered a serious and costly lapse in discipline. All now agree that the party paid for the error at the polls.

On Tuesday 9 May, the Prime Minister was visiting Yorkshire when a journalist informed the Tory press officer on duty that he wanted to ask her about hunting foxes, and whether she would reverse the ban introduced under Tony Blair. The question followed a story in the *Mirror*, which splashed its front page that day with the headline 'Secret Tory Plot to Bring Back Fox Hunting'. The press officer went backstage to brief the PM and two of her senior aides so she could prepare her response. May said she had always personally been in favour of hunting, and thought the party's policy of a free vote for MPs on whether to repeal Labour's 2004 ban on hunting with hounds was the right one. No one tried to stop her, or even raised a question over whether her proposed answer on such a highly emotive subject was wise.[154] So May went out to face the questions and confirmed her support for hunting. 'She thought she was giving an honest answer to an honest question,' one adviser says. 'It was obviously a mistake. It cut through massively in the campaign.'[155]

A Cabinet minister adds: 'The wording of our manifesto commitment to a free vote for MPs was exactly the same as in 2015 but it became a big thing in this election. Was it because people thought we were going to get a big majority so we might actually do something?'[156] A third senior May aide believes the fox-hunting row, allied to the other manifesto difficulties, meant people doubted the Conservatives' good faith on everything else: 'We just looked like mean, nasty Tories.'[157]

* * *

There were unfortunate moments for other ministers at campaign events too. When Philip Hammond and David Davis joined forces to launch a Tory election poster about Labour's 'Tax bombshell for your family', a cheeky press photographer framed the image so Davis appeared in front of the phrase 'hell for your family' and a picture of a bomb, emblazoned with the words 'debt' and 'taxes'. A poster like that should never have made it out of the door. Or at least, not at the same time as a pair of Cabinet ministers.

COALITION OF CHAOS

It's not enough to decide what a leader will say in an
election campaign. They have to have somewhere interesting to say it. But the process of planning and coordinating key news stories and the Prime Minister's press
and broadcast activities was chaotic for the Conservatives in 2017. Most decisions about the areas and venues
the PM would visit were made at the last minute. 'A lot
went right down to the wire,' one campaign insider says.
There was no venue for the manifesto launch until the
day before it happened. 'That was totally normal for the
first month. Journalists were waiting for press releases
at 6 p.m. because the policy had not been signed off. We
would be trying to organise tours on the day.'

For months, the party had been expecting a strong set
of local election results on 5 May, although there was
apparently no plan for a visit from the party leader to
give a speech or statement on the outcome. In the end,
May turned up at the Octink signage company in west
London in another hastily arranged media call. Reporters were given about an hour's notice to get to the venue.
One campaign staffer says:

> On the day of the local election results, we had done so
> much winning all over the place, but we hadn't got a
> venue sorted out and we ended up in a factory in Brent-
> ford. We'd just taken Tees Valley. We'd just taken West
> Midlands. And we're celebrating it in an area that didn't
> have any elections. We had planned to go to Wales but it
> got ditched on the day. I think some of the advance team
> had already gone.[158]

*   *   *

To May's detractors within the Tory Party, some of her economic policies – such as a cap on energy prices, or a pledge to crack down on soaring executive pay – appear closer to those of Ed Miliband than of David Cameron. Yet few Conservatives would have imagined their party leader would attempt to emulate some of Miliband's worst image blunders. When the then Labour leader was photographed eating a bacon sandwich, the resulting images went viral on social media and, according to his own aides, did a lot to undermine his credibility with voters. One Labour figure who worked with Miliband at the time insisted the Labour leader just wanted some breakfast after an early start on a visit to New Covent Garden flower market in south London. 'It was not a set-up. We didn't say, "You've got to eat a bacon sandwich on TV now."' Sadly for the credibility of the Tory media operation, the same cannot be said of the curious incident of the Prime Minister and the cone of Cornish chips.

The Tories were frustrated that they were not getting better broadcast coverage, but knew they were themselves failing to give television producers the kind of interesting images they would like. On a visit to St Austell on 2 May, the Prime Minister's team on the ground received a message from CCHQ, 270 miles away: May should be seen eating something.[159] Precisely what should be on the menu was not specified. But as she was at the seaside, a traditional cone of fresh, hot chips seemed like a good idea. Everybody loves chips, after all.

The resulting images did not meet the requirement

either to smile or to adopt a poker face. Most of all, the plan broke the first rule of political spin doctoring: never allow your politician to be photographed eating – because, as an image frozen in time, the act of human mastication generally looks monstrous.

When a Tory supporter placed a cup of tea in May's one free hand, trying to be helpful, the Prime Minister was suddenly stuck: she had a beverage that was too hot to drink in one hand and a cone of chips she now couldn't eat in the other. The image of a grimacing Prime Minister, immobilised by two of Britain's most iconic foodstuffs, went around the world. Fiona Hill, who was responsible for the Tories' day-to-day media operation back in London, was furious. *The Guardian* wondered aloud whether May's chips could be the 2017 election's 'bacon sandwich moment'.[160]

By polling day, through a combination of policy blunders, shambolic organisation and her own personal aversion to performing for the media, Theresa May's image had switched from that of the all-powerful president-elect to a malfunctioning robot mocked on Twitter for her attempts to eat 'human food'. It's hard to recall such a dramatic transformation in a leader's standing over the course of an election campaign.

CHAPTER 10

LET CORBYN BE CORBYN

For the Labour leader, the start of the campaign was a frustrating experience.

The polls were dire, he was being ridiculed in the media and even his own candidates were asking him to stay away because they believed he was an electoral liability. Then came the local elections on 4 May, the worst performance by an opposition in forty years.

On 6 May, Corbyn had finally had enough.

'We're in the fight of our lives,' he told his most senior advisers and campaign chiefs in a conference call the day after the local election results became clear. 'Let's not write ourselves off,' he said. 'Just let me be me.' It was a rallying cry, but also a plea to be let off the leash.

For those on the conference call that day, there was a simple calculation: 'At that stage, I felt, well, what have we got to lose,' says one senior Labour MP on the call. 'We are where we are in the polls and we'd just taken a battering in the local elections. Let Jeremy run this campaign the way he wants to – play to his strengths.'

With a month left in the campaign, Corbyn and his team put all their chips on their leader. It was a gamble taken out of desperation, but one that would prove inspired.

*   *   *

Over seven weeks, the transformation in May's personal standing with the public was as dramatic as it
was unparalleled in modern political campaigns. But
there is another example of a reputation spectacularly
transformed in the space of a general election: Corbyn
himself.

Shortly after May called the election, the Labour
leader's net favourability rating was -42. The PM's was
+10. Such a stark contrast in public perceptions was one
of the key reasons May's aides had pushed for an early
election. Over the course of the campaign the public's
view of the Labour leader changed dramatically, rising
to a far less toxic -14 before polling day. But that only
tells half the story. The increase in support for Labour
between the start of the election and polling day depended on Corbyn somehow keeping the voters the
party had in 2015 and taking more from other parties.
At the start of the campaign, only 40 per cent of people
who voted Labour in 2015 had a positive impression
of the party leader. By the end, this had risen to 75 per
cent. Corbyn enjoyed an even bigger boost in support
among people who voted Liberal Democrat two years
previously. Just 15 per cent had a positive view of the
Labour leader in April but by June the figure had reached
69 per cent.

How did a man ridiculed by Foreign Secretary Boris
Johnson as a 'mutton-headed old mugwump' and widely
seen as electorally toxic by the media achieve such a
turnaround?

MONSIEUR ZEN

Corbyn had an unusual media strategy to win over a sceptical public: he didn't care. Like May, he dislikes the media and what he sees as its obsession with personality. 'I don't like dragging personal things into my political life and I think it's very sad when that happens,' he told *The Guardian* shortly after making it onto the Labour leadership ballot in 2015.

While his detractors would mock the cult of personality that would soon develop, Corbyn would stay true to his word. Faced with a sceptical public, the conventional response would be to open up to journalists, invite them into your home, introduce the country to your family and show the world your personal side. Corbyn could have done it easily, had he chosen to. He could have talked about his jam-making, his three sons or his allotment. But, for the most part, he refused. Corbyn's family are strictly off limits to the media, as is his beloved garden plot. Despite repeated requests, Corbyn never allowed anyone from the media near his place of sanctuary. It is not hard to imagine Tony Blair or David Cameron on a *Gardeners' World* special. Even his jam-making is private, or at least he won't discuss it except strictly on his own terms. Corbyn gave the Queen a jar for her 90th birthday, but has banned aides from telling the story.[161]

His wife Laura does not play the game either. She is occasionally seen at campaign events but never on stage. She does not join her husband in front of the audience at Labour conference for a kiss. Nothing could be less Jeremy Corbyn. 'She does not wish to be a political wife,' Corbyn has said. This rule was even enforced for his appearance on *The One Show*, despite the Prime Minister's appearance with her husband three weeks before. Corbyn and his wife simply refused. 'We absolutely refused to do *The One Show* together,' he says. 'I said absolutely no.'[162]

Corbyn was not trying to win the country's affection, but the country was warming to him anyway. In part, this was because his dislike and mistrust of the media had softened into a recognition that there was no escaping the scrutiny. It helped that he had relaxed into the job by the time the election was called. In 2015, after winning the Labour leadership, he had been short-tempered during broadcast interviews and hostile with the press, snapping at reporters or ignoring them altogether if they approached him outside work. During a campaign visit in Oxford in May, he joked about the pressures of the job. 'I'm Monsieur Zen,' he said.

On *The One Show*, which would in earlier times have been something of a trial for Corbyn, he was the picture of relaxation, joking about his separate passions for jam-making and manhole covers. If this was a dangerous left-wing fanatic, he did not portray it to the show's audience, which regularly numbers 5 million. The practice had paid off. 'He's had two years of every interview he's done being hostile,' says one of his closest aides. 'Maybe if he'd done this two years ago it would not have gone so well.'

A prime example of his inner calm came in the interview with Jeremy Paxman on 29 May for the Sky News/Channel 4 programme *The Battle for No. 10*.

The Labour leader had a plan. 'I'll make a joke at the start and disarm him so if he keeps attacking it looks a bit much and I'll have the room on my side.' This was his logic, according to one of his most senior aides. In Corbyn's private rehearsals for the duel, it was left to James Schneider to play Paxman.[163]

As the veteran attack dog of television interviews, Paxman began his opening sequence in typically aggressive style. But Corbyn dissipated the tension with a joke: 'Oh come on, give us a chance,' he said. The audience laughed.

The more the public saw of Corbyn, the more they seemed to warm to him. It was the exact opposite of what most pundits and Labour MPs, who knew his political views inside out, expected. Here was a man with little personal charisma or hinterland somehow becoming a mainstream political icon; a 68-year-old whose politics had remained static since the 1970s leading a charge of the millennials; a man who even his closest friends and political allies admit is no great orator attracting thousands of enthusiastic supporters to open-air rallies. He was leading a campaign of contradictions, but it was working.

The contrast with May is revealing. When it came to the media performances in the air war, the Prime Minister was old-fashioned and private but trying to do what she thought was necessary in a modern campaign. Corbyn was old-fashioned and private and doing exactly what he wanted. One of his closest advisers puts it more bluntly: 'Our good campaign and their crap campaign are interrelated.'[164]

THE CONTROVERSIALIST

The air war is not just a battle for time on television and radio news, but also for attention. A very good way to gain attention is to say something outrageous. In the US presidential election of 2016, this method was a favoured technique of Donald Trump's campaign. In British politics, Nigel Farage has deployed it during his time as UKIP leader, while Lynton Crosby found a typically arresting metaphor to explain the tactic: throwing a dead cat on the table.

The theory is that when the public debate in the media is going against you, change the subject. At a dinner party, throwing a dead cat on the table would stop the conversation and suddenly everyone would be discussing the feline fatality, according to Crosby's advice. It would be repulsive, but at least people would be talking about something you wanted them to talk about, rather than whatever the troublesome topic had been before.

Corbyn's media operation adopted similar tactics. The aim was to secure primetime coverage on the 6 p.m. and 10 p.m. television news. As one of his aides explains:

> As a way to get your message across, cause some controversy, through the opprobrium you will receive from those who are utterly discredited in the eyes of the overwhelming majority of people. The more they attack you, the more likely people are to hear your message. And it doesn't matter if they think it's crazy.[165]

It is a media playbook lifted straight from Trump. It

is also reminiscent of the Vote Leave campaign, which revelled in the controversy around its claim that Britain was giving £350 million a week to the EU and could spend the money on the NHS after Brexit. The more the Remain opposition complained that the claim was false, the more they were fighting a battle on Eurosceptic territory.

For Labour, the ultimate dead cat was soon to land on the table: their entire manifesto leaked to the newspapers in such a way that it would dominate the campaign for days. Before the leak, however, came the planned roll-out of policies specifically designed to rile certain sections of the population – to create 'animosity', in the words of one of Corbyn's inner circle. One example was proposing to charge VAT on private school fees, as a way to pay for free school meals for all primary-aged children. Another was the policy of tax rises on those earning over £80,000. 'They were small but symbolically very important because they were very popular,' says an aide. It was also a clear form of class warfare: stripping cash from the rich to help everyone else.

Milne and Corbyn's other close aides believed the policies would cut through with the public because the broadcasters would be forced to publicise them under the strict election rules. Under these rules, television channels – which must be impartial – are required to balance their coverage of the political parties, with Labour and the Tories expected to receive roughly equal prominence. Outside of election time, Milne has argued, the broadcasters tend to focus more on news originating from the government.

THE MANY, NOT THE FEW

Towards the end of the campaign, Corbyn took to reciting poetry at his rallies. His aides were astonished to see the crowds of thousands roaring to the sound of English Romantic verse. The phenomenon dates back to an early decision, taken under the intense pressure of a print deadline only minutes away.

Seumas Milne and Andrew Gwynne were locked in a room desperately trying to think of a campaign slogan with twenty minutes until all the party's election literature went to the presses. Several ideas were in the mix – with the most promising being 'A Richer Britain'. But Milne was not happy. He wanted to try again, to see if they could think of something better. Labour officials at the party's Southside headquarters were 'hysterical' over the hold-up, fearful of what the newspaper headlines would be if the party failed to agree a slogan for its leaflets.

Gwynne ran through the list of options again and reached the words 'For the many, not the few'. Then Milne stopped him. It was a Blair slogan. Was this really the look Corbyn wanted? But for Milne, it worked. The phrase was written into the famous Clause IV of Labour's constitution by Tony Blair, so it was hard to object to.

'The fact that it was in the New Labour Clause IV was an appeal,' says one senior Labour figure. 'Nobody in the Labour Party is going to object to it. But also because what they were encapsulating has a resonance in this era which it didn't actually have then. It's saying the country is increasingly being run for the 1 per cent.'[166]

Ironically, Milne had been in the forefront of the campaign against Blair's Clause IV rewrite, which removed the commitment to 'the common ownership of the means of production, distribution and exchange'.

Milne was pleased with the decision, but even he did not expect it to have such resonance as the campaign wore on. 'It was one of those moments when somebody mentions something and you're desperate and you go, yeah,' a senior figure recalls. 'It didn't seem brilliant but it seemed good enough. It worked. The more you use it the more it encapsulated what you're trying to do.'

As Corbyn's campaign grew in confidence, he began to play around with the phrase, quoting the Shelley poem 'Masque of Anarchy', a standard text in left-wing circles, which finishes with a rousing cry to 'the many':

> Rise, like lions after slumber
> In unvanquishable number!
> Shake your chains to earth like dew
> Which in sleep had fallen on you:
> Ye are many—they are few!

Corbyn, a poetry lover, would repeat the lines from memory during his rallies.

'He started to use it in the latter half of the campaign,' explains one Corbyn adviser. 'People were going wild for it because of the resonance with the slogan. He was using 'the many, not the few' again and again and again. People on the left know that poem. It's a theme of radicalism.'

Part of the appeal, like much of the rest of the Corbyn package, is surely that it is so different from how any other politician speaks to voters. 'How often in British history does the repetition of a 200-year-old poem make crowds go absolutely wild?' says a Labour strategist. 'There's something quite funny about it.'

'OH, JEREMY CORBYN'

On Sunday 21 May, Jeremy Corbyn went to a gig.

The Labour leader travelled to Merseyside to join thousands of music fans packed into Tranmere Rovers' Prenton Park stadium. It was the Wirral Live music festival, and Corbyn was due to appear on stage. To his aides, it felt like a risk. What if the crowd booed? But playing safe would only guarantee that the Labour underdogs would be consigned to a heavy defeat.

In the end, they need not have worried. Corbyn received a rapturous welcome. He told the crowd he had a plan for taxing the richest clubs in football and sent a message to the giants of the Premier League: 'Give your 5 per cent so we've got grassroots football for everybody.' It was pure populism and the music fans cheered. Corbyn then returned to his core themes with even more success. 'Do you want housing? Do you want care?' he asked. 'Do you want a society coming together? Or do you want selective education and fox hunting?' At the mention of Tory blood sports, the crowd booed.

As Corbyn was speaking, his excitable, mostly young audience composed their own football chant: 'Ohhhhh, Jer-em-y Corrrrbyn. Ohhhhh, Jer-em-y Corrrrbyn', they sang to the tune of the White Stripes's 2003 hit 'Seven Nation Army'. It became his anthem and was chanted everywhere he went by crowds large and larger. Corbyn's fans posted clips of the Tranmere rally on social media, with video footage quickly going viral, shared hundreds of thousands of times between supporters. The craze astonished Corbyn's aides as much as it surprised him. 'It was a moment that makes you think, is there something going on under the radar?' says one Labour official who was with him that day. 'Thousands of people spontaneously start chanting "Oh Jeremy Corbyn".'

The images of Corbyn's rallies began to unsettle CCHQ, multiple sources working at Matthew Parker Street admit. The scenes from the Wirral rattled even May's closest aides, who asked colleagues to begin planning a similar rally for the Prime Minister. The difficulty was twofold: firstly, May would be unlikely to draw the same numbers of people who would express their passion for her leadership with the same enthusiasm, meaning the Conservative event would look pathetic by comparison. The second obstacle, according to Tory sources, was the need to control the PM's events to protect her security.

The contrast between May's allegedly stage-managed campaign appearances and Corbyn in front of 'real people' became a theme of the election. One party, representing the establishment, was out of touch. The other was a living revolution. Though a caricature, the portrait contained some truth.

*   *   *

For Lynton Crosby, the plan at the outset in April was obvious: make the election a straight choice between

Theresa May and Jeremy Corbyn, and the Tories will win big. If Crosby had been right, Labour's decision to make its campaign all about Corbyn should have been a stunning and decisive own goal. It was not, for one critical reason: the character of the leaders themselves.

Crosby and Textor did not know May well, but they knew the public liked her and believed she was a far better Prime Minister than Corbyn when the campaign began. Their decision to hang their entire campaign on May's personal leadership ratings was based on polling, not personal understanding. Corbyn's team saw the same dire polling figures but simply ignored them. They had faith that the numbers would change as the public got to know their man. It was a strategic gamble, based on intuition rather than evidence. It was also born of necessity.

By 2017, Jeremy Corbyn was the Labour movement. He had fought and won two leadership elections and simply could not be separated from the party's brand.

Apart from the leader, Labour also had few options for key spokespeople who could carry its message on television. The cast list was short: shadow Chancellor John McDonnell, shadow Education Secretary Angela Rayner and shadow Health Secretary Jonathan Ashworth helped with media interviews. For a time, Diane Abbott took a prominent role but disappeared from view after a series of disastrous interviews in which she failed to explain how much Labour's policy of recruiting 10,000 extra police would cost. Labour said Abbott was unwell and she took a temporary break from her frontbench duties on health grounds.

Abbott's performances were so bad that they became

a key part of the Conservative campaign. Tory focus groups found that the idea of Abbott taking control of national security was horrifying for voters. On Wednesday 7 June, the day before the election, the *Daily Mail* had photos of Corbyn, McDonnell and Abbott above a front-page editorial. The splash headline said: 'Apologists for Terror: The Mail accuses this troika of befriending Britain's enemies and scorning the institutions that keep us safe'. The paper also carried an interview with May. Voters could choose security with the Tories, 'or they can vote to put Jeremy Corbyn in charge of the Brexit negotiations, John McDonnell and his Marxist policies in charge of the economy and Diane Abbott in charge of our police, our borders and our national security,' she said. The *Mail* report explained that 'Tory strategists have dubbed Corbyn, Abbott and McDonnell the "toxic trio", believing that their hard-Left views will repel Middle England.'

Corbyn's aides argue that the fact that the party could win 40 per cent of the vote despite predictable hostility from papers such as the *Daily Mail*, *Sun* and *Daily Telegraph* was a clear sign of how the mainstream press is losing its influence. They see this as another argument for investing in social media communication strategies and building a following on Facebook, YouTube and Twitter to communicate directly with voters.

Labour realised, however, that their perceived weakness on national security was a problem, especially given Tory attacks on Corbyn's record. They chose to tackle the issue in a party election broadcast on 15 May. Directed by film-maker Ken Loach, the profile of Corbyn was the most watched of Labour's election broadcasts,

with 7.2 million viewers, amounting to 23 per cent of the
available audience. In it, Corbyn gives an interview at a
wooden table in a coffee bar in his Islington constituency. He discusses his values and views, while members of
the public say why they support him. Over video footage
of Corbyn being greeted like a hero as he walks among
cheering crowds, the voice of a man says: 'As a former
British soldier who served in Afghanistan and lost friends
there and in Iraq, I support Jeremy Corbyn's opposition
to the wars. I trust Jeremy to keep us safe.'

CONSTRUCTIVE AMBIGUITY

For Theresa May, Brexit was the single justification for
breaking her promise not to call an early election that
made sense to voters. She needed a clear mandate for
the negotiations, and she needed to avoid being held
to ransom at the end of the process in 2019, with an
election looming in 2020. For Labour, however, devising
a policy on Brexit to keep all parts of the party happy
and at the same time appeal to voters was perhaps the
biggest strategic headache of all.

Many Labour MPs are passionately pro-European
and were distraught when they lost the referendum.
May herself set out her Brexit vision in January 2017,
promising to take Britain out of the single market and
customs union. Labour's stance was far less clear.

In February, Corbyn and his aides faced a painful dilemma over how to handle the Commons vote on the
government Bill authorising the Prime Minister to trigger
Article 50, the formal legal mechanism for withdrawing

from the EU. If he tried to block the Bill, Corbyn would be accused of betraying those working-class voters in Labour heartlands in the north, especially those who supported Brexit. If he whipped MPs to vote for the measure, he would have a rebellion on his hands. Clive Lewis, the shadow business minister and a leading supporter of Corbyn and his left-wing politics, had made it clear that he could not support a vote to trigger Brexit. Corbyn's team felt they had no choice – opposing the will of the people on the biggest policy decision in a generation would be impossible to recover from.

'These decisions aren't easy at the time,' explains one figure in the Labour leader's office. 'You know you are going to come in for heavy criticism.' Corbyn issued a three-line whip, ordering all Labour MPs to support the government in the division lobbies of the Commons. Lewis resigned, one of fifty-two Labour MPs who defied Corbyn's orders because of their passionate belief in EU membership. 'We knew when we put a three-line whip on Article 50 that we would lose Clive. That's not good. We like Clive. But it was the right thing to do,' the Corbyn aide adds.[167]

The Article 50 Bill gave the green light to the government to start the Brexit process. It did not detail what type of Brexit would then follow. May proposed a clean break. Labour was again divided, this time over whether the UK should leave the single market, a trading bloc of 500 million consumers which most Remain supporters regarded as vital to the health of the British economy. Reconciling these pro-European Labour supporters, who were most numerous in London, with the Leave voters who traditionally back the party in the north and the Midlands seemed an impossible task. It was more painful because the Tories had let it be known that they planned to use Brexit to seize swathes of territory in these Leave-supporting regions from Labour.

Keir Starmer, the party's shadow Brexit Secretary, and Corbyn's aides carved out a position of 'constructive ambiguity' – commonly known as a fudge. Labour made clear it would take Britain out of the single market but would seek a 'jobs-first Brexit'. In its manifesto, the party said:

> We will scrap the Conservatives' Brexit White Paper and replace it with fresh negotiating priorities that have a strong emphasis on retaining the benefits of the Single Market and the Customs Union – which are essential for maintaining industries, jobs and businesses in Britain. Labour will always put jobs and the economy first.

Starmer hoped the position would mean Leave supporters trusted that Labour would not try to undo the EU referendum result, while Remain supporters would believe the party wanted to soften May's 'extreme' plan for Brexit. To everyone's surprise – not least those who constructed the carefully woven compromise – it worked. 'I really don't think anyone expected it would work as well as it did,' says one senior figure who was closely involved.[168]

By making the early decision not to campaign for a second Brexit referendum, Corbyn was able to move the debate on to austerity, public services and other subjects on which the Labour message was more popular. It was a piece of political positioning and compromise that Corbyn is not known for – and that many of his supporters frequently decry – but it was vital to neutralising a serious weakness. It showed that when he needed to, Jeremy Corbyn could play political games of the old school, too.

SHOWING UP

It was late on Tuesday 30 May when Andrew Gwynne's phone buzzed. It was a text message from Corbyn, agonising over whether to take part in the final leaders' TV debate in Cambridge the following day. He wanted advice.

The Prime Minister was sticking to her decision not to attend – Home Secretary Amber Rudd was due to go in her place. Corbyn's aides were worried that he could become the chief target for the other party leaders in May's absence.

'I'd like your honest opinion,' he told Gwynne.

'My honest opinion is I think you should do it,' Gwynne replied.

The Labour campaign coordinator thought it would be a win–win for Corbyn. By showing up, he would force May to review her decision not to go. Whatever she decided, he would look stronger. Gwynne also believed Corbyn had to take a risk if the party was to stand any chance of closing the gap in the polls with just over a week to go.

Corbyn's advisers were split. Chief of staff Karie Murphy and the Unite union organiser Andrew Murray pushed him to do it, but Milne and Ian Lavery, Corbyn's other campaign coordinator, worried about the risk that it would backfire. Corbyn decided to sleep on it.

The next morning, he decided he would take part.

RUNNING AWAY

Corbyn's bold decision undermined one of the key pillars of May's pitch to the country: strong leadership. Her refusal to take part in head-to-head debates with Corbyn or any other party leader was seen as high-handed, or potentially a sign that she was afraid, according to focus groups. Labour grabbed its chance to reinforce the point.

Momentum produced a video mocking the Prime Minister's decision to stay away from the BBC debate in Cambridge. It attracted 4.5 million views on Facebook. 'If you're so strong and Jeremy Corbyn is so weak,' asks Sky News' political editor Faisal Islam in the clip, 'why have you sent Amber Rudd to take on his arguments at the debate tonight?'

For Corbyn's closest aides, the day of the debate was the moment in the campaign that something radical shifted.

After Corbyn had made his decision, Milne ordered the party's officials to book the most boring hotel they could find near Cambridge so they could prepare for the debate in peace, away from excitable members of the public, BBC executives and the press. It was a tactic he had used three days earlier before the Sky/Channel 4 programme in Osterley, west London, where the Labour team had booked some bland accommodation for the day.

After the rehearsal, Corbyn then got into the waiting Special Branch jeep with one of his aides for the two-mile journey to Senate House in the city centre, where the debate was taking place. 'It was at that point that I realised Jeremy's popularity had transcended the level it was in the past,' explains a Labour official with Corbyn that day. 'When people saw there were police outriders, they knew it was somebody interesting and when they saw it was Jeremy, they started cheering spontaneously. I'm not just talking students, I'm talking ordinary shoppers. All along the route they were cheering.'

Even the Special Branch drivers taking Corbyn into town were taken aback by the reception. 'That was quite some welcome,' one said. The officer had spent sixteen years working in close protection and said he had 'never seen anyone in Britain as popular as Jeremy', according to one Labour aide's account.

If May hoped to avoid an attack from the party leaders by staying away, she failed dismally. To cheers from the audience, the Green Party leader Caroline Lucas launched the opening assault. 'I think the first rule of leadership is to show up,' she said. Lib Dem leader Tim Farron was next: 'Good leaders don't run away from a debate. How dare you call a general election and then run away from the debate?'

Corbyn's mockery was gentler: 'Where is Theresa May, what happened to her?' he asked.

May's campaign advisers knew the decision to stay away was cutting through with voters at the time. Their logic for it was that she started the campaign far ahead of Corbyn in popularity – a debate would only hurt her and boost her opponents, they believed. But the longer the campaign went on, the more difficult it was to shake off the criticism.

With hindsight, Chris Wilkins, May's director of strategy, believes it was a mistake to boycott the debates, a strategy he now thinks could only have been tenable in the type of four-week snap campaign that the PM's aides originally envisaged.

AMBUSH

Less than a week before polling day, the leaders and their teams reconvened for their final televised encounter in York. In the spin room outside the BBC studio, senior Cabinet ministers and their Labour shadows toured the TV cameras and talked to huddles of reporters to tell them why their boss had won the *Question Time Leader's Special* on 2 June. This has been a tradition ever since the first televised leaders' election debates in 2010. But it's not without its risks, especially when two combative politicians end up face to face on TV.

On duty in York were Boris Johnson, the Eton-educated Foreign Secretary, and Andrew Gwynne, the chirpy and energetic Manchester state-school boy who was running Corbyn's election campaign. Before *Question Time* began, Johnson and Gwynne had been due to appear together in a live interview on Sky News. The pair had history. They clashed during the pre-match warm-up before May and Corbyn took turns to answer questions from the audience and endure a Jeremy Paxman interview in the Sky/Channel 4 *Battle for No. 10* show. During that fiery exchange, Gwynne had his hand on

Johnson's shoulder and could sense the Foreign Secretary's fury. 'It really wound him up,' one source recalls.

Johnson's team declined to repeat the double act in York, even though Gwynne was willing. When the Foreign Secretary was being interviewed live on Sky on his own, Gwynne's adviser David Prescott suggested an ambush. It fitted perfectly with Labour's guerrilla-style, unpredictable, attention-grabbing campaign methods. 'You don't have to do this, but...' Prescott began. But Gwynne did not need encouragement. He smiled to his colleague, marched over to the camera and put his hand on Johnson's shoulder.

'Long time no see,' he said. 'Why wouldn't you go head to head with me today, Boris?' he asked, before walking off.

'I'm being heckled,' Johnson protested, before inviting Gwynne to return to join in. 'Come on then, you big girl's blouse,' the Foreign Secretary shouted, on air.

Gwynne returned – again resting his hand on Johnson's shoulder. This seemed to be too much for the blond Brexiteer. Johnson put his own arm around Gwynne, and applied force. The Labour MP stumbled forward and almost crashed into the camera. Johnson pulled him back again just in time, smiling, and said: 'I'm so sorry. Sorry.'

Gwynne recovered his balance, if not his manners. 'Don't be a pillock,' he said.[169]

*   *   *

For most voters, the air war *is* the general election campaign. It is where they experience the day's comings and goings, policies and gaffes: played out on radio and television in the morning as they are getting ready for work and taking their children to school. It is on in the background when they get home and watch the evening news. In the final few days of the campaign, it is almost impossible to escape politics in the media, which now includes news delivered to smartphones and tablets.

For those who pick up a newspaper or check a website, the noise of national media election messages is deafening. In 2017, May's ratings slumped while Corbyn's soared. His achievement was a personal vindication – for the simple reason that he had only his own belief, and the enthusiasm of thousands of supporters, to work with. Corbyn and his small group of trusted aides followed their instincts, rode their luck and rolled with the punches when they came. Their strategy was to do what they wanted, and what would work, and to hell with the mainstream media and its conventions.

One of the Labour leader's advisers sums it up like this: 'The politico, media, punditry, expert, commentary class – the people who get everything wrong – do the opposite of whatever they say.'

PART THREE

THE
CAMPAIGN

CHAPTER 11

SABOTAGE

On the evening of Wednesday 10 May, Lynton Crosby left his seat inside the busy and often noisy campaign war room on the ground floor at Matthew Parker Street and went upstairs.

The fourth floor was, by comparison, monastic; a place of refuge where the party's brightest intellects could have the space and quiet they needed to think.

Here, Nick Timothy and Ben Gummer were crafting the manifesto with John Godfrey, Will Tanner and the Policy Unit team from No. 10. They spent their days refining the party's vision for how Theresa May would use her likely landslide victory to refashion British society and mould the Tory Party anew. They had a little time to spare; the battle of the manifestos was not due to begin until the following week, with Labour publishing its blueprint for government first, before the Tories took their turn.

Crosby had a present for Timothy, and handed it to him with a smile. It was Labour's entire manifesto – Corbyn's plan had leaked.

'Thanks,' said Timothy, and the room burst into uproarious laughter.

As political security breaches go, this was the equivalent of the Russians stealing the blueprint for America's atomic bomb. It gave the Tories the chance to trawl through the 43-page document, line by line, preparing their attack.

Corbyn's inner circle were locked in a crisis meeting trying to work out how to respond to the news of the leak. They did not know that their manifesto was in the hands of their political enemies.

At 9.04 p.m., the dam finally broke, with a tweet from the *Mirror*'s political editor Jack Blanchard. 'SCOOP – Labour's entire draft manifesto leaked to the Mirror.' One minute later, at 9.05 p.m., the *Telegraph*'s Kate McCann published her version. 'Read Jeremy Corbyn's leaked left-wing manifesto in full, Telegraph has seen draft copy,' she tweeted.

Earlier in the day, the two journalists had separately received the full draft of the manifesto which was due to be launched on Tuesday 16 May. Extracts of the manifesto had already started to drip out earlier that day. The trade magazine *Schools Week* was first out of the blocks, publishing a story at 5.45 p.m. that revealed some of Labour's planned education policies. Half an hour later, at 6.17 p.m., more policies appeared on the *New Statesman* magazine's website, detailing a proposal to ban arms sales to Saudi Arabia.

By the time the *Mirror* unveiled its scoop, at least three other publications and the Conservative Party had seen part or all of the document. At 10.33 p.m. the BBC political correspondent Chris Mason tweeted that he had managed to obtain a copy, too. Then *The Guardian* trumpeted its own scoop just after 11 p.m., before the Guido Fawkes website published a full version online shortly after midnight.

It appeared to be yet another incomparable shambles for the Labour Party. Not only was Corbyn trailing hopelessly in the polls, but he could not even keep control of his own manifesto.

FIND THE MOLE

Furious Labour officials demanded to know who had betrayed them. Two broad theories emerged: it was either the Labour right, under the Machiavellian guidance of deputy leader Tom Watson, or the Labour left, with the tacit approval of Corbyn himself or someone close to him.

When the *Mirror* approached Corbyn's office with the news at around seven o'clock that evening, the Labour leadership team was scattered around the country. Corbyn was in South Yorkshire with James Schneider when Schneider took the call from the *Mirror*.

'Hello, mate. There's something I need to tell you,' said Blanchard. 'We've got the entire manifesto, do you want to comment?'

The other end of the line fell silent. 'Of course you have,' replied Schneider, somewhat taken aback. 'OK. We don't comment on leaks.'[170]

Corbyn was giving a speech at the time, unaware of the pandemonium taking place all around him.

Schneider immediately tried to get hold of his boss Seumas Milne. Nothing is agreed without Milne's approval, but he was in a meeting at Unite's headquarters and could not be reached by phone. Labour officials began frantically calling their friends in Unite to get through to him.

If Schneider was in on the leak, acting on Milne's behalf, he must be a fine actor, according to those who witnessed his reaction on the Labour battle bus. After finishing a phone call he slumped next to the *Sunday Mirror* political reporter Keir Mudie. 'The thing is – the really disappointing thing – is that it's a really fucking good manifesto,' he said. 'We would have liked more control over it but it's out there now.'[171]

It was an intriguing choice of words – a recognition within minutes that Corbyn's team would need to rip up their media strategy and start again. If, that is, it was not part of their cunning plan all along.

When Milne was finally tracked down and told the news, he exploded, cursing loudly and gesticulating in front of his colleagues in the meeting room at Unite's offices. Milne has since confided that he found it a 'discombobulating experience'.[172] Alongside him at the meeting were Labour's campaign directors Ian Lavery and Andrew Gwynne, shadow Chancellor John McDonnell, head of policy Andrew Fisher – the man who had drawn up the manifesto – and Andrew Murray, the Unite official who had been drafted over to the leader's office to help during the campaign.

'Everybody was angry,' a witness in the room that night recalls. 'We were planning a really big launch of the manifesto and we just felt as though the rug had been whipped from under us. We stayed up until two o'clock in the morning working out how we would deal with it.'

DEPUTY HEADS WILL ROLL

Inside the crisis meeting, the inquest began immediately. Milne ordered a full investigation, to report to him, as soon as possible. Meanwhile, suspicion turned towards Watson, the man the leader's office appeared to blame for every plot, real or imagined, against Corbyn.

The leader's aides initially believed that different versions of the manifesto had been leaked to the two papers and that the draft given to the *Mirror* was the latest.

This was the proof the team thought they were looking for. There were only three people who had seen the copy of the manifesto leaked to the *Mirror* – Corbyn himself; the author of the manifesto, Andrew Fisher, who was in room; and Watson. Therefore it had to be Watson, they felt.[173]

But the pressure of the crisis in the middle of the night was pushing people to the wrong conclusions. Officials involved later admitted the information they had that night was 'partial'. One of those who has seen the conclusions of the leak inquiry says it absolves Watson of blame.

The version that was given to the *Mirror* was, in fact, the same as that given to the *Telegraph*. Both papers were leaked a draft version given to the Trade Union and Labour Party Liaison Organisation, or TULO as it is known, at a meeting at 10 a.m. at Southside on Tuesday 9 May, the day before it was leaked. Every copy of the manifesto handed out at the TULO meeting had been numbered and collected before people were allowed to leave, so the leak was unlikely to have been from the union officials who attended. Nevertheless, the number of people who had been given access to the leaked manifesto was significantly larger than the three individuals initially identified.

Furthermore, although the findings of the leak inquiry remain closely guarded, it concluded that Watson could not have leaked the manifesto because he did not have the draft that made its way into the hands of the two journalists.

DOUBLE INTRIGUE

To confuse matters, according to the party's internal inquiry there were in fact two separate leaks: first, the full TULO draft manifesto to the *Mirror* and the *Telegraph* and then, later on, sections of a different version 'fed in' to at least one of the newspapers' coverage.

It was this second part of the leak which had only been seen by a small number of people, according to senior Labour sources who have read the internal inquiry's findings. The second leak threw Milne and the other amateur investigators off the scent, incorrectly pinning the blame on Watson, who was not involved.

Corbyn himself gave a hint of his suspicions when he was asked about the leak by *The Guardian* shortly after the incident. He told the paper he was 'very disappointed' and claimed it had been sent to 'a very small number of people', other than himself. 'It is very difficult to countenance it as anything other than people trying to undermine the party.'[174]

The initial assumption that the leak was somehow orchestrated by Watson has left a lasting fissure in his relationship with Corbyn. Watson's team remain furious at the suggestion that they were involved in the treachery and have threatened to take legal action against anyone who suggests so.

The deputy leader's director of communications, James

Robinson, was so angry he confronted Milne and Schneider about the 'utter bollocks' the day after the leak.

Whoever it was, the ill feeling and mutual suspicion remain.

A CUNNING PLAN?

Once the manifesto was out, Corbyn's aides knew it would be impossible to keep it secret any longer. According to one official close to the leader, his advisers decided the best course of action would be to make sure broadcasters who were covering the story of the leak had their own copies. Although convinced the leak had been a hostile attempt to damage them, the leader's team felt they had no option but 'to roll with it', one senior Corbyn ally says. 'A strong case was made and agreed that the broadcasters got it too – the logic of it being once it was out then give it to all,' one official says.[175]

But was it really a hostile leak at all? Or could it have been an elaborate double bluff? On the day of the leak, Labour was staring at the prospect of a landslide election defeat. The party was seventeen points behind the Tories, who were on 47 per cent, based on a Survation poll. Labour needed a game-changing moment to grab the public's attention and shift the debate in their favour. Perhaps the leak was a deliberate move by people who wanted Corbyn to succeed but knew something dramatic had to be done. If so, it certainly worked.

There were other reasons why the leak potentially helped the Corbynite left of the party. At the time, Corbyn's aides were not thinking about triumph on 8 June, but about how they could keep their man in his job after the expected drubbing on polling day. If the leak did not succeed in delivering better media coverage for Corbyn's radical policies, and Labour failed to avoid a bad defeat, the left would at least have a ready-made alibi for the disaster – sabotage. As for Corbyn's enemies in the party, they had little need to leak the manifesto because he was already staring at a defeat of historic proportions. So goes the theory of the 'inside job'.

Corbyn's old friend Jon Lansman was watching the drama unfold with a smile. He knew James Schneider well from their early days together at Momentum and he suspected that the 'clever boy' he once shared an office with might have pulled off a stunning political ambush. Lansman asked Schneider directly if he was the genius behind the leak – but his friend denied it.

If it was not the leader's office, could Corbyn's old friend and committed socialist John McDonnell have been responsible? One possibility is that McDonnell, or his aides, believed such a dramatic step was necessary to force their internal opponents within Labour's ruling National Executive Committee (NEC), the shadow Cabinet and elsewhere in the party to accept Corbyn's radical left-wing programme for government. The NEC, MPs and other top officials were due to meet the very next day to sign off the document.

Moderates who opposed Corbyn's socialist policies would have found it far harder to argue against popular giveaways in the manifesto, such as abolishing tuition fees and providing more free school meals, if those policies had already been made public.

According to one senior union organiser with close

links to Corbyn, bouncing Labour right-wingers into accepting the manifesto would be a 'classic John Mac' tactic. However, the party's internal inquiry found that neither McDonnell nor anyone in his office had a copy of the draft of the manifesto that made its way into the *Mirror* and the *Telegraph*, according to a senior source who has read the findings.

HOSTILE INTENTIONS

Corbyn reacted angrily to the leak when Schneider told him the news before they boarded the train back to London. 'He doesn't get angry often but he was really pissed off,' says one Labour aide who witnessed Corbyn's reaction. 'It was a hostile act, no question, but it backfired.'

One senior Labour figure involved in the writing of the manifesto said the leader's office was 'in genuine panic'. Trusted members of Corbyn's team who were on their way home when the leak became known were called into the office at some point not long after 7 p.m. Once Milne was aware, he went into immediate 'firefighting' mode – he called the editor of the *Mirror*, Lloyd Embley, direct, in a bid to limit the damage.[176]

'I would like to say we'd planned it but we actually hadn't,' says one of the figures handling the crisis that night. 'Seumas's reaction and the reaction of others in that room led me to believe that it certainly wasn't planned.'

*   *   *

The internal party inquiry suggested the leak was not a deliberate plot from the leader's office to win publicity but rather an act of sabotage or internal political calculation. The investigation was led by Labour's internal compliance unit and reported directly to Milne.

'It is unable to pin it on an individual,' says a senior party figure familiar with the secret report. 'It has found that it was distributed on email wider than initially thought, including emails to non-Labour Party networks, so it's untraceable. Too many people had it, basically.'

The official adds:

> I don't believe there was a conspiracy in the end. I think it just got shared with too many people. There was a copy lying on somebody's desk in the office. The notion that it was tightly controlled just isn't true. There were lots of people who could've seen it and some of them are on non-Labour Party networks and email addresses. We cannot get to a definitive conclusion.

Analysis of party officials' email chains from that day identifies a group of up to half a dozen potential culprits who were forwarded the document by email and may have subsequently leaked it, according to senior party sources. This group of people represent a faction within the Labour Party that is hostile to Corbyn, the leader's office believes.

Labour's general secretary Iain McNicol told a meeting of the party's NEC on 19 September that the leak came from 'a stakeholder' from Scotland or Wales, but did not name an individual.

What is undeniable is that somebody leaked the entire manifesto at a moment when they could not be traced. By mid-afternoon the *Mirror* and the *Telegraph* had copies. By the evening, Lynton Crosby and Nick Timothy were looking over its contents. If this was a ploy by the Labour leader's office, it carried huge risks, potentially undermining the credibility of the party at a crucial moment in the campaign.

*   *   *

Two miles away from the Unite union HQ in Holborn, Crosby and his Conservative colleagues were fine-tuning their attack lines. At 10.18 p.m., they put out their response: 'This is a total shambles,' said a Conservative spokesman in the comment emailed to journalists. The statement continued:

> Jeremy Corbyn's plans to unleash chaos on Britain have been revealed. The commitments in this dossier will rack up tens of billions of extra borrowing for our families and will put Brexit negotiations at risk. Jobs will be lost, families will be hit and our economic security damaged for a generation if Jeremy Corbyn and the coalition of chaos are ever let anywhere near the keys to Downing Street.

*   *   *

On Thursday 11 May, the leak did not look like it had bought the Labour Party any breathing space at all. It looked like a disaster for Corbyn, a crisis that simply reinforced his image as a shambling old socialist without

the ability to lead even his own party, let alone the country. The twenty-four hours that followed the leak could
have wiped out the painfully limited progress Labour
had made so far in narrowing the gap in the polls.

The morning headlines were grim. The *Daily Mirror*
had played it straight: 'Corbyn Will Nationalise Energy,
Rail and Mail.' But almost every other paper was hostile. The *Daily Telegraph*: 'Revealed: Corbyn's Manifesto To Take Britain Back To The 1970s.' The *Daily Mail*
followed suit: 'Labour's Manifesto To Drag Us Back To
The 1970s.' The morning news was full of debate about
the calamitous leak and Labour's internal crisis.

At the emergency meeting the night before, Andrew
Gwynne drew the short straw and was sent out onto
the early morning radio and television shows to defend
the manifesto. His task was daunting: he had to resist
confirming that what had been leaked really was the
manifesto, while at the same time avoid appearing to
distance himself or the party from the ideas within the
document. First came ITV's *Good Morning Britain*, then
Sky News, *BBC Breakfast* and finally the *Today* programme on BBC Radio 4.

Gwynne's performance is still talked about in the
leader's office with almost childish gasps of delight. It
cemented his reputation as one of Corbyn's best media
performers – a role he relished in the campaign, taking
on Boris Johnson in two memorable skirmishes during
the televised leader's question-and-answer programmes.

'He had the incredibly difficult task of not confirming anything and not commenting on anything which
had been leaked, while rejecting the idea that these were
outlandish ideas and saying this is where the majority of

the British people are,' says one of Corbyn's senior aides. 'There was no backsliding.'

Gwynne was sticking to the plan: when presented with the choice of playing down their radicalism or playing up to it, they would always choose the latter.

One senior Corbyn aide explains:

You can say, this is not actually that radical, it's only a small change – that's the normal approach, which we were definitely not going to do. The other approach, which is what our campaign was all about, was to demonstrate that this is where the overwhelming majority of people are. It's not that it isn't radical because it's piecemeal, it's that these things are where people's common sense is.

CORBYN GETS HIS PLATFORM

At just before 11 a.m., Labour MPs and officials began to assemble at the Institution of Engineering and Technology in central London. The occasion was to be critical in shaping the party's offer to the electorate. It was the so-called Clause V meeting of the National Executive Committee and other senior Labour figures, and their job was to sign off the final draft of the manifesto. As they walked through the media scrum outside, reporters shouted questions including: 'Is it a shambles?' and 'Are you embarrassed?' It was not going well. And then Jeremy Corbyn ran over a journalist.

On the way to the meeting, the Labour leader's car, driven by Special Branch, was in a collision with BBC cameraman Giles Wooltorton, who was left in agony on the side of the road with a foot injury that required a trip to hospital. Adding to the sense that everything was falling apart, Unite's Len McCluskey later fell down the stairs of the building where the talks were taking place.

Inside the meeting there was condemnation of the leak. 'The Clause V meeting deeply regretted that at the highest levels of our party, there are those who are completely disloyal and who are a total disgrace,' NEC member Peter Willsman wrote shortly after.[177] The blame game had begun. Labour's factions were at war and the appearance was of a party imploding. Ian Lavery and Andrew Gwynne told the gathering that work was needed to turn the polls around. Nobody knew that the work was already under way.

Despite the crisis, Corbyn's inner circle began to feel things were not working out so badly after all. Schneider discussed with the Labour leader how the leak was being reported. 'There was rolling coverage of our manifesto. Fifty-odd journalists desperate for a live of [backbench Labour MP] Keith Vaz going into a meeting. At this point, because we're not saying our policies are scandalous, we thought "this is going our way",' says one aide close to Corbyn.

The Labour leader was happy – he had emerged from the party meeting clutching an undiluted Corbynite prospectus for government. 'He owned it,' says the Corbyn aide.

He was supremely confident. He came out and stood there for about twenty seconds before he said anything. Then he spoke for forty-five seconds, the perfect amount

to go on the news, and then went back in. He looked like
a leader with a plan and the confidence to implement it.
That moment sealed that day as being positive.

The manifesto itself was indeed radical, adding up to a
prospectus for a 'fundamentally different economy' according to the Institute for Fiscal Studies. Taxes would
rise on businesses and the wealthy in order to pay for
billions of pounds worth of extra day-to-day government spending, including an £11 billion pledge to abolish
tuition fees – the most expensive and symbolic policy in
the document.

At the heart of the manifesto there was a strategy:
populism. A shopping list of policies for ordinary Brits
paid for by somebody else. It was expressly 'antagonistic', explains one of Corbyn's closest advisers. 'It wasn't
just about Labour doing something nice. It was Labour
doing something nice – paid for by somebody else.'

DEAD CAT

The impact of the leak was dramatic. It dominated the
media coverage of the election for days. But rather than
provoking a full-scale meltdown in Labour support, the
episode refocused the national debate on the party's policies, moving it away from the Tories' preferred topics of
Brexit and the contrast between May and Corbyn.

Conservatives are convinced the leak was a deliberate
move to win publicity – not least because such a move
comes straight from his own campaign manual. By dic-
tating the news agenda, Labour had damaged the Tories,

who until that point had been dominating the air war. Instead of discussing Brexit and the leadership qualities of May and Corbyn, journalists moved onto a debate about schools, hospitals, universities and nationalising the railways. This was the territory on which Corbyn's team thought they could win. Reflecting on the episode, Lynton Crosby says: 'The Labour manifesto I assume was leaked deliberately, which was very smart. It took the focus off Brexit.'[178]

Another senior figure who sat in the morning and afternoon Tory planning meetings says: 'They handled the manifesto well. We thought it was a very clever leak. They got back into the race because it changed what people were talking about. The salience of Brexit came down. The salience of their issues came up.'

The leak bought Labour 'a modest movement' in the polls, a senior Tory insider explains. When it happened, the Tories still did not see it as a game-changer because the polling movement was not decisive: 'It would have meant a catastrophic defeat not a double catastrophic defeat,' the Tory says.

But it was the beginning of the brake on the Tories' seemingly inevitable march towards a crushing victory. Labour had succeeded in shifting the ground on which the rest of the election battle would be fought.

*   *   *

Andrew Fisher, the manifesto's author, is a controversial figure in the party. He was briefly suspended shortly after joining Corbyn's team in 2015 over messages he posted on Twitter, urging voters to back a hard-left candidate

standing against Labour's Emily Benn, the granddaugh-
ter of Corbyn's ideological hero, Tony Benn.

Even though Fisher wrote the document, the manifesto was fundamentally a product of Milne's political
philosophy. It was written in open defiance of the 'establishment' media commentariat, who Milne and others in
his team believe are out of touch with the reality of life
outside of central London. Corbyn's inner team argue
that Britain is fundamentally a left-wing country that
has been starved of the policies it wants. One senior
Labour aide close to Corbyn explains:

> Politically there is huge support for this stuff and no
> one has been offering it. You just have to look at the
> polling, in terms of support for higher levels of taxation
> on the wealthy, public ownership of core utilities, these
> are all hugely popular and have been for thirty years.
> These things have been incredibly popular for decades
> and nobody in mainstream politics has been allowed to
> say them.

Even sceptical members of Corbyn's shadow Cabinet
believe there is something in this. 'We were talking
about things that people turned out to be genuinely
excited about,' says Gwynne, who before the election
feared Corbyn would not cut through with ordinary
working-class voters.

Another shadow Cabinet minister, the shadow Health
Secretary Jonathan Ashworth, says the manifesto was
'aspirational' in that it wasn't just about social justice
but appealed directly to lower-middle-class families who
wanted their children to get on in life. It was accidentally

Blairite, offering policies that enthused the young, middle-class families, not just students and the poor.

Ashworth says:

> Policy wonks can argue whether or not it's a bung to the middle classes or about whether the money could be better spent elsewhere, but to parents who want their own kids to go to university, they're thinking 'How am I going to afford it?' The tuition fee pledge was really important and it was perceived as aspirational.

SUCCESS

How much of the Labour surge that followed the leak was due to the popularity of the manifesto's policies and how much of it should be attributed to the transformation in the Tories' campaign is impossible to answer precisely. Corbyn's aides are clear on this matter, as one official close to the leader says:

> Imagine if the Tories had run a more traditional campaign. Imagine they had come up with some tax cut or hadn't been so presidential on the basis of someone who obviously couldn't handle it – a major strategic miscalculation. Let's say that none of that had happened; would there have been a Labour surge? I think there clearly would have. If you look at the factors driving it and the excitement around the policies – the huge popularity of those policies and the nature of the campaign around Jeremy – all those things would've been happening anyway. It's very difficult to argue that the huge

mobilisation of young people was all the response to the Tories' fuck-ups. It's obviously not. They did self-harm but our success would've happened anyway.

Corbyn offered the electorate neat Corbynism. Forty per cent voted for it. That success means the man and his movement are here to stay. It was an outcome the Tories were certainly not expecting as they put the finishing touches to their own manifesto – a document which would soon go on to achieve even greater notoriety than Labour's.

CHAPTER 12

GIANT CHALLENGES

'Nothing has changed.' Tired and frustrated, Theresa May raised her voice. 'Nothing has changed.' Everything had changed.

It was 22 May and the Prime Minister was holding a press conference in Wrexham, only 50 miles away from Dolgellau, the pretty town in north-west Wales where she had reached her decision to call the election during her Easter holiday six weeks earlier. It must have seemed like a lifetime ago. May was tetchy, her voice hoarse. She stumbled over her words and shook her head at journalists who dared to ask impudent questions.

May had just become the first party leader in recent memory to have scrapped a flagship manifesto pledge, just four days after announcing it in the middle of an election campaign. Reporters gathered for the press conference were not kind about her decision to reverse the policy on social care. The BBC political editor Laura Kuenssberg accused her of 'panic in the face of opposition'. Channel 4's Michael Crick said May looked 'weak and wobbly', not 'strong and stable'. Another reporter described her blueprint for government as a 'manifesto of chaos'.

May was forced into her U-turn on Tory plans to reform the funding of elderly care in order to quell a rebellion from her candidates and her Cabinet. Instantly dubbed the 'dementia tax', the offending proposal involved ditching an earlier Tory promise to cap the lifetime costs of social care. It is not an exaggeration to say the row derailed May's campaign. Her pitch to voters was based on two things: being a strong, reliable leader, and not being a typical Tory in the 'nasty party' mould. The plan to take vulnerable elderly people's homes away when they fall ill (as it was inevitably portrayed) made May look mean. Her U-turn, and the manner in which she performed it, made her seem weak – and, worse, untrustworthy. That is the honest assessment of some of the Prime Minister's strongest supporters and closest colleagues, including people who toiled during the election on the very manifesto that caused so much grief. These were her loyal aides, party staff who wanted it all to work.

One of those with more distance from May's project was less forgiving. 'The manifesto was a pile of shit,' a leading member of the Conservative operation says. 'I've never seen anything as brick wall-like as this. We hit it and things totally changed.'

*   *   *

How did a single 84-page document inflict so much damage in the space of a few days on a national leader who had seemed politically invincible a month earlier? Who was responsible for drafting such a catastrophically unpopular set of policies and how did they ever get past the supposedly rigorous and restrictive message censorship regime of Lynton Crosby? Why did nobody stop the debacle before it was too late? Just why was an argument on policy details so fatal to May's chances in an age when personality and image are generally thought to count above everything? These were some of the many questions Conservative candidates – and defeated MPs – asked in the days and weeks that followed. To understand the full story of what happened to the Tories during the 2017 election, it is essential to grasp the events that led to what even disappointed party supporters have called 'the worst manifesto in history'.

*   *   *

The Tory prospectus was supposed to be short on detail and long on vague aspirations. Instead, it carried policy programmes ranging from a new digital bill of rights, to a review of the operations of the NHS internal market and a plan for developing the shale gas extraction industry.

When Theresa May called the snap election on 18 April, she told the world the main reason was Brexit. Yet, the UK's withdrawal from the EU was only one of five 'giant challenges' facing Britain that the manifesto sought to address.

Minutes before she stepped out of the famous black door of No. 10 to make her shock election announcement, the PM chaired a meeting of her Cabinet. One after another, ministers told her that the manifesto should really be as vague as possible, leaving the government with more room for manoeuvre, for example to increase taxes, after the election. Philip Hammond, the Chancellor, was said to have been among those

advocating a minimalist approach, after he had been
forced to drop plans to push up National Insurance contributions for the self-employed at the Budget, because
the policy clashed with the 2015 manifesto.

Cabinet ministers and senior campaign officials claim
they were horrified at the scale and detail in the eventual
document a month later. 'Too much went on without
people knowing about it or without it being shared,' one
senior minister says. 'When we had the Cabinet meeting
on 18 April, we decided it was to be a short manifesto,
of broad principles, not detailed policy. When the manifesto came out, it was detailed on areas we hadn't talked
about.'

Some ministers harked back to the days of Margaret
Thatcher's relatively brief, 9,000-word manifesto from
1979. 'Those nostalgic, with long memories, pointed
back to the 1979 manifesto for what it should be,' one
of those present recalls.

> Others made the point that one of the problems we had
> in government was that the previous manifesto was full
> of commitments that we never expected to deliver be-
> cause the Lib Dems would stop us in a new coalition.
> Cabinet wound up with what seemed to be clarity that it
> was going to be a thin, principled manifesto.[179]

A senior figure explains why the final 2017 document
was more than 30,000 words long: a thin prospectus in
modern politics is no longer possible. Government has
moved on from 1979 and the Tories need an explicit
mandate in order to instruct the civil service on developing policies, and to persuade an obstructive House of

Lords, where the party has no majority, not to block key legislation. The NHS alone requires detailed contractual proposals for any reforms to be set out in the manifesto. While ministers at that Cabinet meeting in April recall a broad discussion about keeping the document short, no formal decision was made on that point.

*   *   *

As the man who hated – but could not escape – being called 'Theresa May's brain', Nick Timothy was the obvious candidate to oversee the 2017 manifesto. He was the PM's chief policy adviser – creative, energetic and with total authority over the Downing Street machine. Timothy began by picking his team. First he spoke to Ben Gummer, the young Cabinet Office minister who had become a trusted member of May's inner circle. He told Gummer he wanted him to start leading on the manifesto process about a week before May called the election, bringing the young minister into the small group of advisers who were trusted with her secret.

Gummer, who was defending the marginal seat of Ipswich, was deeply sceptical at the prospect of an early election and told Timothy he did not like the idea. He did not believe the large poll lead meant the Tories were in an unbeatable position and worried that political volatility in 2017 made it impossible to guess the eventual result. After raising his concerns, which Timothy understood, Gummer agreed to take on the role of manifesto writer. The two men are friends. They rate each other's abilities and remain close, despite the election result. In government they agreed on most things, though

Gummer was a staunch Remain supporter and Timothy a fervent Brexiteer. This, said one witness, made for a healthy 'creative tension' around the table.

Next, Timothy turned to the No. 10 Policy Unit, led by John Godfrey and his deputy Will Tanner. Tanner was on holiday when May announced the snap election but the PM's chief of staff wanted him to coordinate the process and ensure there would be a full set of briefing materials for every major policy.

Gummer had early meetings in No. 10 to discuss a conventional manifesto structure, in which the document would be divided into familiar sections such as 'stronger economy', 'fairer society' and 'global Britain'. Timothy felt it was not ambitious enough. As they mulled it over, Timothy and Gummer realised the manifesto was a rare chance to be bold. They could use the election to address the big, long-term problems the country faced. 'We're about to go through this very significant change to Britain's relationship with the world and if you're going to do that, we wanted to use this as an opportunity, given the settled position of the country, to work through these big challenges,' a senior figure close to the process says. 'That's why we came up with the "five giant challenges". We didn't settle on five because it was a nice echo of Beveridge but it ended up being a nice echo of Beveridge.'[180] No doubt an allusion to the founding father of the welfare state also appealed to the authors' sense of history and ambition. When Gummer and Timothy presented their idea to May, she loved it.

Gummer had been making the case to the Prime Minister for the best part of a year that she was in the perfect position to rebuild trust in politics. The Brexit vote, as he saw it, was not simply about Britain's relationship with Europe, but its relationship with its entire political class. Voters feel used and manipulated and only by painstakingly earning back their trust, through honesty and directness, will that ever change, he said. It was in this spirit that he, Tanner and Timothy, in particular, approached the manifesto.

'It is an upbeat document,' one source says. 'It says, we've got a great future but it's going to be a challenge to get there. If you're going to go down that line, you have to have a campaign which really focuses on taking difficult decisions and the honesty to level with the public.'[181]

*　　*　　*

Once Parliament had been dissolved, Timothy, Gummer, Godfrey, Tanner and the rest of the No. 10 Policy Unit moved into Matthew Parker Street. As well as the war room on the ground floor, the party hired the fourth floor of the building, where the manifesto team took up residence. Although the manifesto team occupied the quieter part of the building, it was not quite quiet enough for Timothy. He wrote the introductory chapter of the manifesto away from CCHQ.

The chief of staff's responsibilities for overseeing the development of the document came at a cost. Senior Tories were used to Timothy taking control of the full range of May's workload. While he still attended the 6 a.m. and 6 p.m. daily meeting of the top brass, policy development and designing the intellectual architecture for the next five years of government were Timothy's passions and some

Tories sensed he was taking a step back. 'All Nick wanted to do was write the manifesto and he went off and did that. So he wasn't really central to a lot of the decision making for the campaign,' one Conservative says.

The drafting process itself was highly secretive. Gummer liaised with his ministerial colleagues, meeting secretaries of state and other senior ministers to discuss their ideas, but none of them were allowed access to the full document. Some ministers, like Sajid Javid, the Communities Secretary, and Matthew Hancock, the Minister for Digital, impressed the manifesto authors with their creative and incisive contributions. In Hancock's case, this was a political feat. As George Osborne's right-hand man and a loyal disciple of the former Chancellor, he had been tipped for the sack but his ambitious plan for creating the first 'digital bill of rights' dazzled sceptics, including Timothy. Javid, another minister who was rumoured to be on the way out at the next reshuffle, made friends by delivering a timely intervention on council housing policy. While the experienced Defence Secretary Sir Michael Fallon submitted a chapter that went in virtually unchanged, some of his Cabinet colleagues' contributions were thin and disappointing – and their shortcomings were noted.

Timothy drafted the first chapter, which on publication was instantly regarded as the bible of Mayism. Gummer took the lead writing the chapters on policies that followed. Then, in consultation with ministers and Mark Textor's focus group team, the policy details were refined and amended repeatedly until a near final draft was produced. At that late stage, chapters were shared in full with the relevant secretaries of state. Timothy believed this was exactly the same protocol as was followed during the 2015 campaign. The authors and the campaign chiefs were worried that the document could leak. There were only five copies, which were numbered. 'Labour's manifesto had obviously been leaked, we were genuinely worried about the same thing happening to us,' one source on the manifesto team says.[182]

Not everyone understood. Two of May's most senior ministers were said to be annoyed that they were locked out of the manifesto-writing process. 'No one expected to read the whole thing, other than the Chancellor and Boris,' said a senior figure.[183] Philip Hammond was 'frustrated' at his lack of access and the fact that he had been virtually banned from appearing in the media during the campaign. Boris Johnson, the Foreign Secretary, repeatedly demanded access to the full manifesto text. He was told he could not have it – he was not deemed to be trustworthy. 'No doubt Boris wanted to leak it, so he wasn't going to see it,' the senior Tory says. 'No one was going to see it.'[184]

*   *   *

The manifesto was being written in a Google Doc – a document stored online which can be shared among a group when the original author gives permission. Only Timothy and Gummer had editing rights to the document, although it was visible in its entirety to John Godfrey, Will Tanner, Douglas McNeill, May's chief economic adviser, and latterly Chris Wilkins, the director of strategy and May's chief speechwriter. May herself was kept fully informed as the plans evolved.

At the start of the campaign, Gummer and Timothy sat down with the PM and talked her through what they were proposing. She was 'content' with some of the most controversial policies – such as scrapping free school lunches for all but the poorest primary-aged children to fund bigger teaching budgets, and means-testing the winter fuel allowance for the elderly. Both of these cuts became problems almost as big as social care. 'Nick was seeing her every day, more or less. He was having conversations with her every day and trying ideas out on her.'[185] Towards the end of the drafting process, Timothy found himself flying around the country to meet up with May. He travelled to Northern Ireland to speak to her about the emerging shape of the manifesto and read extracts to her in the back of the official car during spare half-hours on the campaign trail.[186]

Timothy and Gummer took the approach that they did not want to censor themselves – they felt they should include as many ambitious policies as possible during the drafting process and haggle with their internal critics later. Among their more radical ideas – ultimately left out – was a plan to abolish stamp duty, proposals drawn up by McNeill and the Policy Unit behind the Chancellor's back.[187]

Throughout the campaign, Lynton Crosby had been warning that detailed, policy-rich manifestos could be a problem. Though he expressed this in a light-hearted way, there was a serious point to Crosby's comments on the manifesto as it evolved. 'Bloody manifestos, wish we didn't have them, I hate policy, it only causes problems,' he would say, according to those present.

The chief authors of the document, Gummer and

Timothy, were expecting the Australian consultants Crosby and Textor to demand that many of the most potentially problematic plans be cut. Crosby and Textor's team were running focus groups with voters and larger polls on key policies to test the public responses to some of the more contentious policies in the plan. Textor, who ran the research and fed the findings back to Timothy, asked for wording to be changed on various subjects including fox hunting, though he did not say the social care plans – as he had seen them – were likely to be fatally toxic. 'All the way through, Nick was really surprised that Lynton and Tex were happy. He said, "I'm amazed, they aren't asking for stuff to come out,"' one campaign insider says.[188]

The feedback from CTF research was that the policy caused a few alarm bells to ring but May's team believed they could handle it. 'What we found from social care in focus groups was that no one really understood it anyway.' The manifesto team were not particularly worried because they believed the main thrust of their plan would be popular. 'We saw it as a good policy in a "retail" sense. We didn't expect all the things that happened next.'[189]

SONNING

By the weekend of 6 May, Gummer and Timothy had their draft. Gummer spent the next week revising it, while Timothy took the full document to show to May for the first time. Then, after revisions and refinements, came the crunch meeting. On Sunday 14 May, a bright but chilly spring day, Gummer drove to meet Timothy, Fiona Hill and the deputy No. 10 chief of staff JoJo Penn at the Mays' house in Sonning.

The document was due to go to the printers on Tuesday 16 May – ready to be presented to the world's media at the official launch on the Thursday. This was the last chance to make major changes. As the group gathered around the dining room table, Philip May poured mugs of tea, produced some biscuits and then left his wife and her advisers to their meeting at the dining room table.

Gummer pointed out some of the most dangerous areas: means-testing the winter fuel allowance, ending the triple lock pension guarantee from 2020, and social care. 'These are the toughies – I don't know which one will be trickiest,' he said. Gummer guessed that restricting the winter fuel allowance might be the most difficult, but Hill and Penn were nervous about the social care reforms.

*   *   *

The funding of the care system for elderly and disabled adults in England is complicated and opaque: very few people who have not been directly affected understand it properly. Earlier government research found most people believed it was free and provided for by the NHS. Successive attempts to address the looming crisis of an ageing population that will need help with daily tasks such as washing and dressing have met with insurmountable political difficulties. Before the 2010 general election, the Tories branded a Labour plan for funding the care system a 'death tax'.

May's government had been planning social care reforms for months. Godfrey was instrumental in leading
the process, along with Gummer and officials inside
the Cabinet Office. Sir Jeremy Heywood, the Cabinet
Secretary, was also fully aware of the development of
the policy, which was very close to the plan that finally
made it into the manifesto. All the way through, however, Fiona Hill was said to have had doubts. According
to colleagues, she worried that the reform of elderly care
funding was a potential political minefield.[190]

The two most difficult parts of the manifesto policy
were abandoning an earlier plan to cap the total amount
anyone would have to pay for residential care home fees
in old age at £72,000. This was devised under David
Cameron, in response to recommendations from the
economist Andrew Dilnot, as a way to guarantee no one
would have to sell their home to pay for care in old age.

The second problematic aspect was that for the first
time the value of a person's home would be included in
the means test to receive state assistance at home. This
would have affected thousands of people and represented a significant tightening in the state's offer.

The good news, as Gummer and Timothy saw it, was
that more of people's assets would be protected overall.
Under existing rules, people needing care are expected to
run down their own wealth until they have only £23,000
left. This figure includes – for those in residential care –
the value of their homes. Under the manifesto plan, this
'capital floor' would be raised to £100,000 – meaning
nobody would lose the last £100,000 of their assets.

This policy was clearly generous in one sense: it meant
people would be able to keep up to four times as much

of their money and assets safe from being eaten up by care fees. For anyone looking to pass on an inheritance to their children or grandchildren, this should have been straightforward good news. But it was still perplexing in its complexity and laborious to explain. Hill, among other top campaign officials, did not understand the policy fully. As the communications director for the campaign, she was meant to be selling it.[191]

* * *

On that Sunday afternoon in Sonning, Hill suggested removing the details from the care section of the manifesto, prompting an intense bout of soul-searching. There was no argument about the policy itself, only the political implications of how to present it. May and her four advisers discussed whether it would be better to give only a cautious outline of the policy in the document: they could promise to deal with care funding without detailing everything they had in mind. Timothy and Gummer disagreed. They wanted the manifesto to be as direct and straight with voters about their plans as possible. Gummer was especially strong in his view, according to one source. 'This is a difficult call,' he told the meeting. 'We've promised to fix social care. Secondly, given this is what we know we're going to do, it's dishonest to leave it out. It would do everything we say we're opposed to doing in politics.'

May was 'very receptive' to this argument, which Timothy also supported, according to those present. 'The question is how much do you describe at this stage and the PM, unsurprisingly, was on the honesty-and-directness side, as was Nick,' one source says. May decided that giving more detail rather than less was the right thing to do. That would mean keeping the care policy in full. But the agonising was not yet over.

*   *   *

On Monday 15 May, Stephen Gilbert, the veteran campaign chief, appeared on the fourth floor of Matthew Parker Street and asked for two printed copies of the final draft. Will Tanner, who had been coordinating the logistics, checked with Nick Timothy that this was permissible under the regime of strict secrecy surrounding the document. Full copies were restricted and Cabinet ministers had been shown drafts of only their own chapters. Gilbert took the copies downstairs to the ground floor and sat with Lynton Crosby. The first thing they noticed was that it was far longer than they had expected – too long, in fact, to digest properly in the short time they had available. The document was due to go to the printers the following day. The pair went back up to the fourth floor to see Timothy and demanded that he talk them through the manifesto. 'You tell us what the political stuff is in here,' they said. Timothy provided a list of ten policies, including school funding, the cuts to universal free school lunches, social care, the pensions triple lock, the winter fuel allowance and looser language on low taxes (to provide room for increases in the future).

Crosby and Gilbert were 'very concerned' and made their own list of what they saw as the most difficult issues, which included social care and school meals. Gilbert was especially worried about abolishing free lunches for pupils at primary school. 'It was an attempt to sort out the issue of school funding, which was a big concern for voters on the ground,' one senior Tory recalls. 'We said we would sort school funding in the manifesto. Both Lynton and Stephen said: "Look, this will not be about school funding, it will be about cutting school meals and there is no communication plan that will convince anyone that you have sorted school funding."' Timothy replied that scrapping free lunches for all primary school pupils was the only way to find the cash to make the plan work.[192]

Crosby's and Gilbert's concerns with the social care plan were that it was both 'massive' and incomprehensible. They feared the reform was too dramatic to be dropped into the middle of an election campaign, and raised their worries with Hill and Timothy. Hill again expressed doubts, but Timothy had the trump card and he deployed it: he told Crosby and Gilbert that all these issues had been discussed with the Prime Minister; she understood the risks and wanted to keep the policy. Crosby and Gilbert had no answer to that. One source says: 'At the end of the day, the content of the manifesto is signed off by the people running the party. Lynton has always said that the one thing the campaign director doesn't decide is the manifesto. The party leadership decides the manifesto. That's why you stand for election.'

There was yet another eleventh-hour wobble. Fiona Hill was still unhappy. Her strong instinct for spotting political danger, which had helped keep May out of trouble for six years at the Home Office, was telling her that launching the social care plan was too big a risk to take in the middle of an election campaign. Another tense conversation took place, this time inside No. 10 without Ben Gummer. Hill, Timothy and Penn talked through the issues a final time with May, just hours before the manifesto went to print. It was difficult. Hill tried to get the details of the care plan watered down again – and again Timothy resisted. In the end, May made the final call. 'I want to go with it,' she said. If there was a single decision that cost her the majority, this was it.

*   *   *

Outside Westminster, Tory ministers and candidates were delighted with how the campaign was unfolding. The polls at that time were still giving the Conservatives a mouth-watering lead of up to twenty points over Labour. 'We'll get a majority of something like 120, I'm sure,' one minister confided privately at the time. 'Labour will easily lose more than forty seats. It's ours to fuck up – but you've really got to fuck up massively for it to go wrong from here.'

Inside CCHQ there was an air of disarray as the manifesto launch approached. The operations team were trying to find a venue that would be suitable. Two days before the launch, the options May's team shortlisted included an event in the centre of Newcastle, which was deemed too risky, and a speech at an air museum packed with Second World War planes. Timothy felt that presenting the manifesto on the eve of delicate Brexit negotiations with the Prime Minister surrounded by Spitfires, Hurricanes and other warplanes would send an unfortunate signal, but Crosby apparently liked the proposal. In an email to Timothy, Hill and others, he said: 'I don't think the second world war issue is relevant or a problem ... and you won it. Nice contrast with the anti-defence Corbyn.'[193]

When this was abandoned, the logistics team spent hours in a frantic search for a venue in Middlesbrough that could handle large numbers of journalists, television equipment and the security requirements of accommodating the entire Cabinet and the Prime Minister in one place. None could be found. There was no obvious rationale for Middlesbrough other than it was a target seat. Only on Wednesday 17 May, the day before the launch, did CCHQ find a conference venue in another apparently random town in the north: Halifax.

As the hours ticked down to manifesto day, Chris Wilkins, May's director of strategy, had to write her speech for the launch. He finished a draft and sent it to Crosby, Timothy and others. When Timothy saw it, he was not happy. He told Wilkins he had picked the wrong policies to include in the speech. Wilkins replied: 'Those are the policies that Lynton says we should be talking about.' Timothy responded: 'No, we want to be talking about these policies.' In the end, Wilkins had to include both sets, and May's speech contained a long list of issues, half of which came from Crosby and the other half from Timothy. 'We should probably have known then that there was a problem,' Wilkins says.[194]

Hill and her press team briefed the social care reforms overnight for inclusion in the morning papers on launch day – and the early signs were what might be called in media crisis handling circles 'just about manageable'. Papers such as the *Daily Mail*, which had run campaigns calling for better care for the elderly, were willing to go along with May's idea. 'The reviews were amazing,' one of the manifesto team recalls. However, Ben Gummer, who was known for being cautiously pessimistic by nature, was worried. He feared that if the *Mail*, *Times*, *Sun* and even *The Guardian* were all impressed at the same time, the story would only go one way.

*   *   *

There was already one darkening cloud on the horizon: Andrew Dilnot, the usually sunny-tempered economist and statistician and the man to whom David Cameron's government had entrusted the design of a new social care funding system. Bright, academic and likeable, Dilnot's favourite description of himself is 'Pollyanna-ish'. His relentless optimism was tested when the Cameron government shelved his 2011 proposal for a cap on the lifetime costs that anyone would have to pay for their care in old age or adulthood. When civil servants in the Cabinet Office and No. 10 began working on their own social care reforms, under the guidance of Godfrey and Gummer, Dilnot – who was not directly involved – would tell anyone who asked that he regarded a cap on costs as essential.

The truth is nobody in the Conservative policy team drawing up the manifesto had even read Dilnot's report. They were working from the basis of George Osborne's proposals, which adapted Dilnot's but were less generous. May's manifesto team believed even Cameron and Osborne realised the Dilnot plan would not work because it was essentially unfair. One Tory explains:

You're asking low-paid people in the north to subsidise
the inheritance of middle-aged people in the south. It's a
wicked idea, actually. If it created an insurance market
then you could kind of explain it away but it didn't even
do that. It's hopeless. We realised that. George realised
it, that's why it was all put on ice. It just didn't work.[195]

Nevertheless, the night the policy was briefed, ahead of
the manifesto launch the next morning, the Tories decided it would be worth giving Dilnot a call to ensure he
knew what was coming. This was partly out of courtesy,
but mostly because they wanted to avoid any unfavour-
able commentary from the respected and independent
economist who would be the media's first point of call
for a reaction to the fact that the Prime Minister was
formally abandoning his recommendations.

Jeremy Hunt, the Health Secretary, was given the task
of calling Dilnot. Hunt himself had only been shown the
social care passage of the manifesto hours earlier. While
he had helped write the NHS parts of the document
with his special adviser Ed Jones and Downing Street
health aide James Kent, the minister was not involved in
drafting the care funding proposal.

Before he called Dilnot, Hunt was warned to take
care by an aide. 'Andrew's really not happy,' the adviser
said. In fact, he was incandescent, having already found
out the Tory plan to axe his cap from a journalist. A
senior campaign figure explains the shock and anger
that Tories felt at Dilnot's private and then his public
reaction: 'When Jeremy Hunt rang him up to brief him
about what we were doing, we expected him to say
"OK". Apparently, he just exploded.'

Sure enough, BBC Radio 4's *Today* programme interviewed Dilnot the morning of the manifesto launch.
He did not sugar the pill in his criticism of May's new
plan, warning that people would be unable to prepare
for their own futures in old age. 'There's nothing you
can do to protect yourself against care costs, you can't
insure it because the private sector won't insure it, and
by refusing to implement the cap the Conservatives are
now saying they're not going to provide social insurance
for it,' he said.

> So people will be left helpless knowing that what will
> happen is if they're unlucky enough to suffer the need
> for care costs, they'll be entirely on their own until
> they're down to the last £100,000 of their wealth in-
> cluding their house.
>
> The analogy is a bit like saying to somebody you can't
> insure your house against burning down, if it does burn
> down then you're completely on your own, you have to
> pay for all of it until you're down to the last £100,000
> of all your assets and income.

By 7.10 a.m., the backlash had begun. Dilnot's early
morning intervention gave the left-wing papers, among
others, the excuse they needed to get their teeth into the
policy. Tim Farron, the Liberal Democrat leader, branded the plan an 'unspeakable' tax on frail, elderly people,
adding: 'For the first time you'll be asked to cash in your
home when it comes to paying for your care and your
treatment.'

The worst thing, to my mind – let's say you're the wife

of a husband who has to go into a nursing home because of dementia, the reality is your house, the house that you still live in, the family home, will have to be cashed in now under the Tories' heartless dementia tax.[196]

CHAPTER 13

NOTHING HAS CHANGED

Dean Clough Mills is an imposing complex of towering Victorian buildings in Halifax and was once the largest carpet factory in the world. Sprawling over half a mile, it is the sort of place that could have inspired the novels of Elizabeth Gaskell or Benjamin Disraeli, whose portrait of the social chasm between the lives of the rich elites and the misery of the working poor in the nineteenth century gave rise to 'One Nation' Conservatism. Now the site houses art galleries, cafés and other local businesses, including spaces that can be hired for large events. It made a dramatic setting for the launch of Theresa May's election manifesto, which was titled 'Forward, Together'.

On the morning of Thursday 18 May, a small but noisy protest was under way in the street outside the main factory gate. Activists brandishing 'Socialist Worker' placards lined the pavement as May's team and the media arrived for the manifesto launch inside. At the back of the building, May's campaign battle bus had been ambushed by a protest unit from the Unite trade union, who unfurled a huge white banner that stretched the full length of the coach. The banner demanded: 'End Zero Hours'.

'Tories at a mill in Yorkshire – you couldn't make it up,' the man leading the demonstration bellowed through his loudhailer. 'It's not back to the 1970s, it's back to the 1870s.'

Members of the Cabinet filed into the conference centre to take their seats in the main hall and wait for the Prime Minister's speech launching her prospectus for a landslide. Before they went in, a party press officer warned them not to flick through the manifesto in front of the TV cameras as if it was the first time they had seen it – but it was.

For the manifesto team, the media management problems had started much earlier, back in London. Ben Gummer was alarmed at how badly successive BBC reports had managed to mangle the detail of the social care reform, while Jeremy Corbyn also appeared not to understand the policy.

At the start of the week, the plan for the launch event had been for May to make a speech and then take questions on camera from the media. Afterwards, Fiona Hill, as the Tory communications director, would brief reporters in a 'huddle' and answer any follow-up questions off camera.

On the morning of the launch, however, the plan suddenly changed. Timothy and Hill decided that she should not do the huddle with political correspondents herself. Shortly after 6 a.m., Timothy turned to Will Tanner, the trusted deputy head of the Downing Street Policy Unit, to fill her shoes. Tanner knew all the policies in the manifesto and had prepared media briefing notes for most, so was theoretically the best man for a difficult job.

Timothy's logic was blunt: 'If Fi does it and she gets it wrong, it will become a big story,' he said.

Horrified, Tanner put his head on the table. It would

have been a daunting responsibility even for an experienced spin doctor, but he did not even have time to prepare.

A few minutes later, Hill spoke to Tanner: 'Has Nick told you? We'd quite like you to do the huddle. It will be fine.'

'I'm really worried,' Tanner replied. 'I think the social care policy is going to unravel.'

'Of course it's going to unravel,' Hill said. 'All of these things unravel. But it will be fine.'

Tanner had no time to argue. He had to catch a plane to Yorkshire.

TROUBLE AT T'MILL

At the launch event, Brexit Secretary David Davis, who pushed May to go for an early election, introduced the Prime Minister to applause from the rest of her Cabinet and activists gathered in the bare-brick walls of the conference room. As journalists abandoned their coffees and cakes to speed read the 84-page document in a race to be first with the headlines, May began her speech:

> Today, as we face this critical election for our country, I launch my manifesto for Britain's future. A manifesto to see us through Brexit and beyond. A plan for a stronger, fairer, more prosperous Britain. A plan to seize the opportunities ahead and to build a country that our children and grandchildren are proud to call home.
>
> It is a detailed programme for government – rooted in the hopes and aspirations of ordinary working people

across this land. But it is more than that. It is a vision for
Britain: a portrait of the kind of country I want this nation
to be after Brexit as we chart our own way in the world.

For at this defining moment for the United Kingdom – as
we embark on this momentous journey for our nation – we
have a chance to step back and ask ourselves what kind
of country we want to build together. I believe our United
Kingdom can emerge from this period of national change
stronger, fairer and more prosperous than ever before.

During the question-and-answer session, May kept faith
with her script of election messages. Only once was
she nudged off course, when BBC *Newsnight*'s Nick
Watt asked if the manifesto represented the set text for
'Mayism', as a rejection of Thatcherism.

'There is no Mayism,' the Prime Minister replied with-
eringly, with the weary air of a disappointed grammar
school headmistress. 'There is good, solid Conservatism.'

Afterwards, to Tanner's relief, the Conservatives can-
celled the 'huddle' with political reporters on the advice
of the Tories' head of press, Robert Oxley, who knew
the assembled hacks – and the perils of handling them –
from his time working for Vote Leave in the EU referendum campaign. Instead, Oxley acted as the chaperone
for Tanner and Douglas McNeill, May's economic adviser, as they briefed journalists individually, rather than
in a potentially more dangerous hunting pack.

*   *   *

At 8 p.m., Will Tanner's long day still wasn't over. Philip
Hammond was in a rage and it was left to Tanner – a

thoughtful policy expert with the manners of a diplo-
mat – to calm him down. The source of Hammond's
displeasure was a decision from the manifesto team
not to publish a separate costings document itemising
how each pledge would be paid for. For the Chancellor,
wedded to steering the economy safely through the tur-
bulence of Brexit, this amounted to economic degenera-
cy. How could he credibly argue that the Conservatives
were fiscally responsible?

The campaign leadership had ruled that publishing
the party's internal calculations could backfire, and so
they decided not to do it, even though the document
existed internally.

'If we have to prove our fiscal credibility then we have
a problem,' Tanner told Hammond. 'Labour clearly has a
problem. We don't.' The Conservatives decided that
publishing a series of detailed spending plans would
simply give their opponents something to unpick.

Tanner spent forty-five minutes on the phone, talking
the Chancellor through the decision. In the end, Hammond resorted to role play. Tanner had to pretend to be
Hammond, while Hammond took the part of a hostile
TV interviewer, demanding to know why the Chancellor
of the Exchequer had failed to publish policy costings
alongside his manifesto, when Labour had done. Once
Hammond understood and accepted that the position
was not going to change, he was supportive.[197]

Hammond's frustration had been simmering for
weeks. He had been locked out of the manifesto process,
despite being the manager responsible for the government's economic policies. He felt he should have had
a bigger role in the 'air war' media campaign and he

should have been asked to approve the public spending plans earlier. Critically, he wanted to make sure the document did not tie his hands at future Budgets. He had been among the ministers calling for a thin, principle-based manifesto at that early Cabinet meeting in April, his Budget U-turn on National Insurance contributions fresh in his mind.

The problem was that Hammond had clashed too many times with Nick Timothy, and the relationship soured badly after the National Insurance row. The Prime Minister's own view of Hammond was only a little better, though she was careful how she expressed it. The closest she would get to venting her frustrations at the Chancellor would be to raise her eyebrows at the mention of his name during campaign meetings, according to one senior figure. No. 10 aides regarded Hammond with suspicion, and at times contempt, for what they saw as a lack of political nous and a tendency to talk too much out of turn. One senior Tory says of the relationship between May and Hammond:

> It wasn't the George and David relationship, it was a much more traditional relationship. The fact is that Philip and his special advisers talk too much. The story about a source close to Hammond saying No. 10 was 'economically illiterate' caused enormous bad blood. I believe it wasn't Philip who said that himself. It was someone close to Philip. It's sad because Philip is a decent person but he can't help himself. He tends to speak as he thinks.

Timothy did not want Hammond to see a full draft of the manifesto until May herself was happy with it.[198]

The Chancellor was eventually allowed to see the document hours before it went to the printers. 'He got it later than he would have liked – but he did get to see it.'[199]

With Hammond excluded, Timothy and Gummer consulted his deputy, David Gauke, the Chief Secretary to the Treasury, and he was brought into the circle of trust from an early stage. Now a full Cabinet minister in his own right, Gauke was seen by May's inner team as loyal, reasonable and completely competent. 'David saw the whole manifesto earlier than anyone,' one senior Tory says.

> He saw the whole first draft because the whole thing was costed very closely. Douglas McNeill, who's the PM's chief economic adviser, was doing all the sums on it. David was helping and because David was responsible for public spending, he had to be content with every single public spending pledge.

Thanks to Gauke, McNeill and latterly Hammond and his advisers, the Tories costed their manifesto fully, to within tens of millions of pounds. One of those responsible says the bill for the entire policy package was less than £1 billion – minimal in overall public spending terms. 'We were able to find savings so it was cost-neutral, it was completely consistent with our need to be economically restrained,' a senior official involved says. 'The requests coming from secretaries of state were considerable – there's a huge spending commitment within the manifesto – and we managed to pay for it.'[200]

*　　*　　*

In the end, the row that blew up from the Tory manifesto was not about costings – at least, not the cost to the public finances. It was about the menu of misery that the manifesto had become in the public imagination. One of the biggest frustrations for Timothy and Gummer was that the document's more appealing 'retail' offers – those electorally attractive policies that candidates could use as selling points on the doorstep – were never promoted properly by the communications team, which Fiona Hill led, although they do not blame her. Their theory is that the problem stemmed from Crosby's edict that the campaign had to be about May as a strong, stable leader, rather than about policy details. The result of this, the manifesto authors believe, is that no real effort was put into publicising policies that would have been popular.

Whatever the cause, the implications of the social care reform dominated the election debate over the next four days. It came up repeatedly on the doorstep. As voters struggled to understand the complexities of the policy, they told candidates they feared they would lose their homes to pay huge care costs for themselves and their frail or disabled relatives. Over the weekend of 20 and 21 May, Tory MPs and ministers were shocked by the scale of the backlash they encountered. Voters were spontaneously emailing candidates to raise their fears.

'It takes a lot to force someone to be bothered to write, and I had a dozen emails in one morning from people on this – mostly worried that they were going to lose their homes,' one minister said at the time. Another angry minister blamed the tightly controlled culture of May and her two chiefs for such a glaring loss of touch. 'Too much is being decided in the centre without enough political nous,' the minister said at the time. 'I had emails today from constituents who think their house is going to be taken away if it's worth more than £100,000. People in clever little offices in Downing Street don't see this.'

It was little wonder that voters did not understand the policy – nor did many staffers in the Tory war room, including Hill, the woman who was in charge of communicating it effectively to the world. Two days after the manifesto was published, on the Saturday afternoon, Hill said to a colleague: 'Wait, I thought our social care policy was to cap the cost to individuals at £100,000.' It was the opposite of what the party was proposing.

Inside Matthew Parker Street, the phones were ringing off the hook. Lynton Crosby was receiving calls from experienced MPs warning him that the manifesto was a huge problem. Cabinet ministers rang to demand that the care plan be scrapped. 'There was a barrage on Saturday evening and Sunday in particular from Members of Parliament and candidates saying it was catastrophic,' one of the senior campaign officials recalls.

The previous weekend they'd been to the local market square and people had been coming up who'd never voted Tory before – they were positive and warm and were definitely going to vote Conservative. That stopped. Conservatives were very angry. One candidate – an excellent campaigning MP – said they'd been out canvassing in an area they knew well and somebody had taken down a Conservative poster and torn it up in front of them. That weekend we had, anecdotally, but from a huge variety of sources, a sense of just how serious this was.

The impact of the manifesto had apparently been to alienate Labour voters in the north and the Midlands. Until that point, people who had in the past supported Labour in these areas had been switching directly to May's Tories, according to internal Conservative polling and canvass data. The manifesto also 'scared the horses' and infuriated the party's own base, those loyal Conservative voters who turn out every time, according to numerous accounts from senior officials inside CCHQ. 'A lot of MPs were saying their own supporters were really turning angry,' one senior campaign official says.

> Then the people who'd never voted Tory before, who were prepared to give the party the benefit of the doubt, who were overwhelmingly older people, suddenly thought, 'I'm going to lose my winter fuel allowance, my grandchildren aren't going to get free school meals and they're removing the triple lock. We don't understand what it is but it doesn't sound right. And they're not prepared to make commitments on taxes.'

After three days of this, the campaign team held a crisis meeting inside CCHQ on Sunday evening, with Crosby, Textor, Gilbert, Hill, Timothy and Penn. Jeremy Hunt and Gummer were also closely involved. They talked through their options as a group and three emerged: the first was to do nothing.

Gummer believed strongly that a U-turn would be a disaster for May's brand and would undermine the entire campaign. He told Timothy and Hunt that they should weather the storm and with a few more days it would settle down. He argued that May should admit the policy was tough but insist she was only being honest with voters, while Labour was lying. However, the scale of the problem meant doing nothing did not feel viable to those fielding calls from terrified candidates around the country. Gummer's plan was rejected.

'The second option was to do a straightforward values-driven rebuttal, attack Labour and say: "Look, trust me, I'm going to put this right. This is all about being on your side," but then not to specify a cap,' one of the officials involved recalls. 'The third was to do that, but also to say there would be a cap [on lifetime social care costs]. It was a U-turn – we wouldn't say it was a U-turn – but we wouldn't deny that there had been a change.'

Hunt and Timothy were among those arguing strongly for a U-turn and to introduce a cap on the total amount anyone would have to pay for social care. Fiona Hill worked through various formulations for the wording that May could use to announce the humiliating reversal while minimising the damage. After the meeting, they called May and told her what her campaign advisers were thinking.

Timothy says they had no option but to reverse the decision: 'My sense was that it was coming from Tories in safe Tory areas. To be honest, I don't think we had very much choice but to clarify and insert the cap because we would just have had a big rebellion on our hands, I think.'

Yet the way May handled the crisis was troubling in itself. One veteran Conservative who had worked on previous campaigns noted that Cameron and Osborne would have gripped the problem sooner and taken personal control of the situation rather than leaving it to advisers. 'David would have done things differently. David would have called a meeting on the Saturday and chaired that meeting himself. She talked to Nick and Fi. They operated in different ways.'

*   *   *

On Monday 22 May, the Prime Minister rose early and prepared to travel to Wales to launch the Conservatives' Welsh manifesto. At 7 a.m., she held a conference call with her campaign chiefs, who had just finished their morning meeting. They told her that she would have to reverse the social care plan and tell the world the Tories would put a cap on lifetime care fees after all. The Prime Minister was displeased. 'She wasn't overjoyed because she believed in the proposition in the manifesto – and having given a position, she doesn't really like changing it very much,' one aide recalls. 'But I think she accepted there was a lot of pressure to change.'

The decision was taken. May would make her announcement at the press conference to launch the party's manifesto for Wales in Wrexham later that morning.

Strategy director Chris Wilkins felt largely sidelined during the campaign. He was frustrated that Crosby had taken over the role of setting the strategic direction for May's public agenda and disagreed strongly with the decision to stand on a platform of 'strong and stable leadership', rather than one of embodying the changes he believed voters wanted in their lives. Wilkins is Welsh and decided that he wanted a day out of the office. So he travelled to Wrexham for May's press conference.

The *London Evening Standard*, now edited by George

Osborne, got wind of the U-turn and the former Chancellor tweeted the news that would later appear on his front page minutes before May got to her feet at 11.35 a.m. When May started to speak, Wilkins could not believe what he was hearing. The Prime Minister made clear that a cap would be part of the consultation she had always planned on the social care reforms after the election. She was simply 'clarifying any doubt about our social care policy and the family home'. May attacked Corbyn for making 'fake claims' about the Conservative plans in an attempt to scare the elderly. 'These are good and sensible plans – they provide the beginnings of a solution to social care without increasing taxes on younger generations,' she insisted.

Under hostile questioning, though, May seemed rattled. She held out both arms, gesticulating in frustration and shaking her head, before almost shouting the now infamous words: 'Nothing has changed. Nothing has changed.'

An adviser recalls that she was genuinely angry after the press conference: 'What annoyed her most was the broadcasters grandstanding. They don't care about finding out the answers, all they care about is performing so the evening news can show a clip of them taking on the Prime Minister.'[201]

For Wilkins, however, May's refusal to admit the change in policy was baffling and devastating. 'People don't mind you doing U-turns if it shows you're listening and if you explain what you're doing – so to change the policy and then claim you're not changing it was devastating to the brand. At that point, you're just another politician.'[202]

Other officials watching May in CCHQ did not expect her to deny that there had been a change. Technically, some Tories believe May had in mind a detail of the policy proposal that never made it into the manifesto. They were considering an option which would have had the effect of limiting the costs of care fees, like a cap. But it would not have been a taxpayer-funded cap of the Dilnot model.

An outline of the draft plan was sent to Mark Textor for testing but it was left out of the final manifesto because the policy was not deemed to be ready. The draft said: 'For younger people, we will introduce a new social care insurance system, backed by a British sovereign wealth fund, so that everyone – no matter where they live and how much they have earned – can be promised a secure and dignified old age.'[203]

One Tory close to the process says:

> There are various ways of getting people to insure themselves at retirement age. Given the fact that a cap limits your liabilities, you can get a premium which does the same thing. It's not a Dilnot premium, because that doesn't work because there's no market – but you can get the state to back it and it's a slightly different thing. There are fairer ways of doing it.
>
> In the wonderful way that these cock-ups unravel, she was being honest when she said, 'Nothing has changed.' Some of this was already in train but only about five people knew that. The rest of the population thought, 'Oh, not only are you weak but you are also lying.'
>
> Voters didn't understand the bloody policy, and the bit they understood the least was the cap. What they

did understand was that she had changed her mind, and
looked shifty doing it. She looked ghastly. No longer
'strong and stable', but 'weak and wobbly', and a bit
dodgy to boot. The sad thing is, it's completely the opposite of what she is.[204]

The result of the policy and U-turn combined was devastating. Research by the British Election Study shows
that social care dominated the final weeks of campaigning until the terrorist attack at London Bridge took
place on 3 June.

THE ASHES

In the smouldering ashes of the election debacle, a row
ignited over who was to blame for the failure of the Tory
campaign, dividing Conservative officials largely into
two camps. It has taken on some of the character of the
oldest feud in May's beloved sport of cricket: the battle
between England and Australia.

Nick Timothy and his allies were batting for a vision of
an England they believed May was the perfect person to deliver. Now they blame the Australians Lynton Crosby and
Mark Textor (and also Jim Messina, the American strategist) for missing the extent of the Labour Party's surge in
support, and for forcing May into a campaign straitjacket
that made her the candidate of the establishment, rather
than the radical leader of the Brexit revolution, embodying
the change they believed the country wanted.

The other side blames the manifesto for crashing the
campaign into a self-made wall, alienating the core Tory

vote with a lot of painful and scary policies that made
people question May's good intentions.

Crosby has many fans and friends in the broader
Tory family and is a longstanding Conservative supporter. One ally says he could not understand why the
Conservative manifesto failed to focus on Brexit. 'If you
want to have an early election, Brexit has got to be the
reference point. Which then begs the question, why have
a manifesto which talks about something completely
different?'

During the campaign, Gummer and Timothy argued
their radical, policy-packed blueprint for the next five
years of Conservative rule would only work if the core
election messages matched it. They wanted to build the
party's offer on the platform of being straight, strong
and fair: 'Theresa May: honest about the challenges,
strong enough to be able to deal with them, and fair in
the way she approaches the future of the country.'

As part of the manifesto development process, CTF,
Crosby's firm, ran focus groups to test the reactions of
members of the public to particular policy ideas and
arguments. On 25 April, only a week after May's announcement of the snap election, and before the official
campaign had even begun, Timothy sent Textor an email
setting out 'some of the slightly more controversial' policies he was proposing for inclusion. There were twelve
in all. They included 'scrapping the winter fuel payment
for all but the poorest of pensioners'; ending the 'triple
lock' guarantee for state pensions after 2020; social
care reform along the lines of the plan that eventually
appeared (though less generous);[205] and abolishing free
lunches for primary school children except the poorest.

Other policies outlined in Timothy's email covered housing, the NHS, a digital bill of rights and ending future state subsidies for renewable energy.[206]

Timothy himself is clear that everyone at the top of the campaign knew the risks of the policies they were putting forward before the manifesto was launched. He says:

> Lynton and everybody knew all the controversial content in advance, they tested everything. He saw the final draft in printed format. That version he would have seen only several days before it was published because that version only existed several days before it was printed. Social care was tested. Winter fuel payments was tested. Free school meals was tested. It was all tested. The answer that came back from Tex was, 'There's a risk in this but it's a manageable risk.' Clearly we didn't manage the risk very well on the social care stuff. But that's how it worked.[207]

However, one ally of Crosby's says Timothy never provided enough detail on the policy proposals – because May's team wanted to have maximum flexibility in designing their reforms once they had won the election.

> It is true that some of the ideas in the manifesto were tested but they weren't the policy detail. It was like: 'We should reform social care so the burden doesn't fall on younger people and we have a more sustainable programme for the future.' Well, fine, 70 per cent will support that. They did put some of this stuff to the test in quantitative and qualitative research, but the problem was they wouldn't be specific.

For example, the means-testing of the winter fuel allowance. Lots of MPs were saying, 'Why can't we just spell out that anyone on the basic state pension will still get it?' The answer was because most people were going to lose their winter fuel allowance. They had actually costed it all so it would only be the very poorest of the poor who would get some of these things. The lack of detail made people nervous and they were right to be nervous because the lack of specifics was quite deliberate – they wanted the flexibility.

The CCHQ plan was to handle the risks inherent in some of the manifesto policies as well as possible. The prize, for May, would be a government with the authority to deliver its programme of reforms. 'The point of a manifesto is to have a mandate to govern the country,' Timothy says. 'It's not just about winning.'

Ultimately, this conflict between winning and governing became a battle between the consultants – especially Crosby and Textor – and May's 'true believers', led by Timothy, but at various times including Hill, Gummer and Tanner. It was a conflict that remained unresolved, with severe consequences for the Conservative campaign.

CHAPTER 14

MANCHESTER

At 10.31 p.m. on 22 May 2017, a young British man stood in the foyer of the Manchester Arena, waiting for the fans of the American pop star Ariana Grande to start making their way home for the night.

He was carrying a home-made bomb, packed with metal nuts and screws. When Salman Abedi detonated his device, he became the first suicide bomber to strike on British soil since 2005, killing twenty-two people, including children as young as eight. More than 100 others were injured. The attack devastated all those who lost loved ones that night.

It also disrupted the general election, with consequences few expected. Theresa May and Jeremy Corbyn suspended their campaigns. In public, the party leaders expressed their grief and anger at the atrocity. Behind the scenes, they argued over when to restart the election, while their own teams fought among themselves over how to handle the politics of the tragedy.

After three days of high emotion and low calculations, the Labour Party had reached 38 per cent in the polls, and Corbyn was closing in on May.

THROUGH THE NIGHT

The Prime Minister was working late in No. 10 when she heard about the attack.

But her key advisers, Nick Timothy and Fiona Hill, were not with her. As political aides, rather than permanent civil servants, they had handed in their Downing Street security passes when the election campaign began and had no formal role in government. They were strictly Tory campaign workers now.

That night, Timothy was recovering from a difficult day and a stressful weekend. On a trip to Wrexham earlier, May had publicly ditched the Tories' social care plan in the face of a growing rebellion from candidates and activists. The U-turn had fatally damaged the credibility of the manifesto he had spent weeks lovingly writing.

Around 2 a.m., a weary Timothy noticed a message on his mobile phone. It was from James Slack, the senior civil servant and former *Daily Mail* journalist who runs the Downing Street press office and serves as the Prime Minister's official spokesman. Slack told him he was needed back in No. 10 immediately. When Timothy made it into the office, he found Hill was already there. May had ordered the civil service to draft them both back into government temporarily so they could be by her side during the emergency. Reunited in Downing Street, the trio began their grim task as the distressing details emerged.

'I have been involved in the government after terrorist attacks and other incidents,' recalls Timothy. 'That was truly terrible.'[208]

At 2.20 a.m., the No. 10 press office issued a short

statement to the media, confirming the worst – the incident was being treated as an act of terrorism. It was the second terrorist massacre in May's short tenure as Prime Minister, after the Westminster Bridge attack in March, and it would not be the last.

At 4 a.m., the Prime Minister asked for a call to be put through to Jeremy Corbyn. Their conversation was brief. May updated the Labour leader on the details of what was known about the attack and he agreed to halt the campaign.

For May, there was no debate. 'The enormity of it was clear,' says one senior government adviser. 'By the early hours of the morning it was quite clear the campaign needed to stop. It was just obviously the right thing to do.'[209]

Hill and her Labour counterpart, Karie Murphy, would speak later that day to discuss the practicalities of pausing the campaign. Their phone call was not easy to arrange, as two of the most combative figures in British politics did not have each other's number. It fell to Patrick Heneghan in Southside and Stephen Gilbert in CCHQ to put the two backroom operators in touch.[210]

If any political calculations were being made, they were not being made by the Prime Minister in No. 10 that night, according to officials who saw May working first hand. 'In these moments the campaign just disappears and she is the PM and that is all she is,' says one. 'The politics of all these things were never discussed. It was: "What do we need to do? What do the police need? What do the security services need? Have they got everything they need?" It was awful, really awful, but she just dialled back in. She was totally in charge.'[211]

NOT CAMERON

May was locked in rolling meetings and calls throughout the night, as MI5 and the police scrambled to get
a grip on the emergency. Who was the attacker? Were
there any more terrorists in his cell preparing another
bombing? The security apparatus of the state had been
caught cold and it urgently needed to get up to speed.

For the Prime Minister's advisers, thoughts turned to
what she would say to the country. The priority was to
act responsibly, according to officials who were with
her that night. Above all, they did not want to mislead
the public or say anything that would stoke fears at a
time when the facts were not clear. It was typical of the
caution May displayed in reaching all her decisions. She
and her aides wanted a clear understanding of what had
happened before she spoke to the nation in any form –
in a formal statement or via social media.

Their approach came at a cost. It took almost four
hours before the first official statement from Downing
Street emerged – at 2.20 a.m. In the meantime, senior
officials in the Conservative campaign were baffled and
grew increasingly exasperated. How could the PM sit
in silence at a time like this? With the death toll still
rising and children unaccounted for, Twitter filled with
statements of grief and condemnation from thousands
of people both famous and ordinary. May's rivals and
other politicians – including Jeremy Corbyn – shared
their thoughts and expressed sympathy with the victims.

Officials in Tory HQ were desperate for May to make
a short, strong statement on Twitter, setting out what
she was doing to get a grip on the crisis. They insisted

it was not about politics but about showing 'national leadership'. The public needed to be reassured and must not be left in the dark for hours. The trio of May, Hill and Timothy refused.

'There was a huge row,' reveals a senior Tory strategist. 'There were things they said they wouldn't do because "that's what David Cameron did" – and reacting quickly on Twitter was one of them,' the senior Tory says.[212]

That night, Timothy and Hill were adamant. They would wait until after the government's emergency Cobra committee of security officials had met, and make a statement when the facts were in order. They told the campaign team: 'We're not going to tweet, we're not going to put anything up on Facebook. We're going to have the Cobra meeting and then she'll make a statement outside No. 10. We do things differently. This is serious.'

The position infuriated CCHQ insiders and their frustration boiled over. 'There was an exchange of views,' another Tory official admits.

> Yes, it is a serious event but it is also happening now and the public are looking for it. I just thought, 'For fuck sake.' Everything became, the playbook is not Dave. I think Nick and Fi felt No. 10 under Cameron talked too much, announced too much and put gimmicks first and governing second. They didn't want to govern by Twitter.

Downing Street aides loyal to the two chiefs of staff flatly reject the idea that they were following an anti-Cameron agenda that night. At a time when emotions are running high, it is more important than ever to be clear and responsible about communicating the facts, rather than stoking the crisis with ill-considered comments simply to satisfy the internet, they say.

Timothy himself rejects the charge – and is clear that they were simply being true to May's method of governing and communicating, pointing out that he worked for years in Cameron's government and bore no animosity towards the former Prime Minister.

> Consistent with our longstanding approach to responding to terrorist attacks, we believed it was right to a) wait for the facts to be confirmed from the police and intelligence agencies and b) make a proper statement to the country rather than tweet in the early hours of the morning. This is exactly how Theresa May responded to incidents as Home Secretary and as Prime Minister outside the election context.[213]

Fiona Hill did not respond to requests for comment.

PRIME MINISTER

At 11.04 a.m., May finally emerged from No. 10 to speak to the waiting cameras. After chairing an hour-long meeting of Cobra on Tuesday morning, she confirmed the twenty-two fatalities. 'It is now beyond doubt that the people of Manchester, and of this country, have fallen victim to a callous terrorist attack,' May said. 'This was among the worst terrorist incidents we have ever experienced in the United Kingdom. And although it is not the first time Manchester has suffered in this way, it is the worst attack the city has experienced, and the worst ever to hit the north of England.'

The reference to Manchester's past experience of terror was a nod to the IRA's 1996 bombing of the city. Labour suspected the Prime Minister was sounding a dog-whistle to anyone who had forgotten about Corbyn's connections to Irish Republicanism in the 1980s. It was a theme the Tories would return to throughout the campaign, even though there were signs it was having limited success.

May's closest advisers believe she spoke for the nation that morning, striking a balance between disgust and defiance. 'All acts of terrorism are cowardly attacks on innocent people, but this attack stands out for its appalling, sickening cowardice – deliberately targeting innocent, defenceless children and young people who should have been enjoying one of the most memorable nights of their lives,' she said.

At terrible moments like these it is customary for leaders, politicians and others to condemn the perpetrators and declare that the terrorists will not win. But the fact that we have been here before, and the fact that we need to say this again, does not make it any less true.

For, as so often, while we experienced the worst of humanity in Manchester last night, we also saw the best.

The cowardice of the attacker met the bravery of the emergency services and the people of Manchester. The attempt to divide us met countless acts of kindness that brought people closer together.

And in the days ahead, those must be the things we remember.

The images we hold in our minds should not be those

of senseless slaughter, but of the ordinary men and women who put concerns about their own safety to one side and rushed to help.

Of the men and women of the emergency services who worked tirelessly to bring comfort, to help and to save lives.

Of the messages of solidarity and hope of all those who opened their homes to the victims.

For they are the images that embody the spirit of Manchester and the spirit of Britain – a spirit that, through years of conflict and terrorism, has never been broken. And will never be broken.

There will be difficult days ahead. We offer our thoughts and prayers to the family and friends of those affected. We offer our full support to the authorities, the emergency and the security services as they go about their work.

And we all – every single one of us – stand with the people of Manchester at this terrible time. And today, let us remember those who died and let us celebrate those who helped, safe in the knowledge that the terrorists will never win – and our values, our country and our way of life will always prevail.

This was May as Prime Minister first and Tory election leader second, grappling with a national crisis after a night without sleep. Even her critics inside the Conservative campaign saw that May was at her best.

THE POLITICS OF TERROR

Unlike the reticent May, Jeremy Corbyn reacted quickly to the news of the attack on Monday night, posting a message on Twitter at 12.06 a.m. when the scale of the atrocity was clear. 'Terrible incident in Manchester,' he wrote. 'My thoughts are with all those affected and our brilliant emergency services.' Later that morning he recorded a TV clip stressing the need for unity.

Inside the Labour leader's office, however, they were frantic. A strategy meeting was called and it was agreed that Corbyn should go to Manchester that day. The leader's office began making calls to Andy Burnham, the newly elected mayor of Manchester, Richard Leese, the leader of the council, and Lucy Powell, the Labour candidate for Manchester Central, where the attack took place. According to those involved, the calls became 'incessant' and Burnham and Leese were beginning to lose their patience. 'There was a feeling that some people saw it as part of the general election campaign and that was something we just didn't want to deal with at that time,' says one Manchester Labour source.[214] They had a major attack to handle.

Burnham had been up since the early hours of the morning, making a joint statement with Leese, before travelling to Greater Manchester Police headquarters to join May's Cobra meeting via a conference call to London.

By Tuesday morning, Burnham understood the horrific scale of what had happened inside the arena – hosting Corbyn was not at the top of his list of priorities. He had been in the mayor's job less than three weeks. It was a role that also put him at the top of the police structure and he had a live operation to oversee. Leese was also overwhelmed by the practicalities of the ongoing situation.

At first, Powell, Burnham and Leese wanted Corbyn to delay coming to Manchester until the following day, but the leader's office insisted he must visit immediately. According to one government official, Corbyn's office repeatedly contacted No.10 that morning requesting that the two leaders coordinate a joint visit to Manchester. When May announced she would make a trip north, it was inevitable that Corbyn would too.

The tension between Labour officials in Manchester and the party leader's office escalated into open confrontation. The Manchester-based group were immediately worried on Tuesday morning – 23 May – when they discovered Corbyn was bringing with him his chief of staff, Karie Murphy, and his election coordinator, Ian Lavery. 'Why is the election coordinator coming to the scene of a terrorist attack?' asked one Labour figure still upset with the leader's office.[215]

Corbyn's office said they wanted him to do a TV clip from St Peter's Square, behind the town hall, surrounded by the city's Labour Party candidates. The leader's aides apparently suggested that the emergency services' first responders should also be there.

Senior figures in Corbyn's office insist that no such request was ever made formally, and that even if it was floated as an option by someone in the leader's office, it was not done with the knowledge of Seumas Milne, who was ultimately responsible for such decisions. There is no suggestion that either Milne or Corbyn was personally involved in the plan or supported it.

However, the claim that people in Corbyn's team wanted the leader to appear with Labour candidates and emergency responders was made by two sources, both of whom said they received the request directly.

The idea shocked Labour's Manchester contingent. 'It

was completely inappropriate to have a photo-op with the first responders to a terrorist attack literally the day after it had taken place,' says one Labour source from the city. 'Some of these first responders were deeply affected by what they had seen or what their friends had seen and many of them were still immensely busy.'[216]

Corbyn's office were told 'absolutely no way'. A host of other options were then presented by Corbyn's team – all of which were vetoed by senior Labour figures in Manchester over similar concerns. 'Their first concern was how can they make sure Jeremy is involved and "owns it". There is a line. It was the wrong end of that,' says another Labour source involved that day.[217]

VIGIL

Corbyn arrived in Manchester and went to sign the book of condolence in the town hall. A vigil was planned for the evening. Burnham and Leese were keen to ensure politics did not encroach on the sombre event. They agreed that no national or local politicians would speak – and told Corbyn's office. But the leader's aides were not ready to give up. 'They were still making unrealistic, slightly misjudged suggestions about what could happen,' says one source.

The clash of priorities burst into an argument when the two sides met at Manchester's Midland Hotel. According to witnesses, angry words were exchanged before the situation overwhelmed Leese, who broke down in tears as he gave them the latest details on the attack.

'It was only then that they [Corbyn's team] thought:

"Oh shit, this isn't about us and the general election,"'
says one witness. 'Leese was crying, he was telling them
that it was hard to identify the bodies of children because of their injuries.'

During her visit, the Prime Minister met Greater
Manchester Police chief constable Ian Hopkins, made
a private trip to Manchester Children's Hospital and
signed a book of condolence in the city's town hall.

Labour complain that the Tories' behaviour that day
also left much to be desired. Corbyn's officials say May
broke an agreement that neither party leader would be
pictured signing the condolence book.

The Prime Minister then travelled back to London
to chair another emergency Cobra meeting that
evening. She missed the vigil and sent Home Secretary
Amber Rudd in her place. By skipping the vigil, May
allowed her critics and opponents to insinuate that
she was aloof and out of touch and that – literally, at
least – she did not want to stand with the people of
Manchester.

As May sped back to London, Corbyn joined the vigil
in Albert Square. 'Tim Farron was there, Andy Burnham
was there, Jeremy was there and Theresa May was there
fifteen minutes before,' recalls Andrew Gwynne.[218]

> She signed the book of condolence, she met privately
> with the police and the council leaders and then she left.
> It was Amber Rudd who went on the stage. That was a
> mistake because she [May] was there and people knew
> she was there. Nobody would have been hostile in the
> circumstances. She'd have probably got a round of ap-
> plause for being there.

Instead, the atmosphere was hostile to the government, represented by Rudd. 'It turned nasty, and she got booed. It was like a Corbyn rally,' says Gwynne.

AUSTERITY

It was not the reaction Labour strategists had expected. The party was convinced that the terror attack was going to reinforce the public's doubts about Corbyn's record on security, in contrast to a Prime Minister looking resolute and in charge during a crisis.

Instead, questions began to be asked about how the attacker got through the net. Had the government gone too far in forcing austerity on the police? If the Home Secretary who oversaw the cuts to police and who was now Prime Minister had taken different funding decisions, might the twenty-two victims still be alive? To some, the deployment of troops onto the streets in support of the police later that night reinforced the point. Were troops needed because there were no longer enough police officers to keep the public safe?

'It became very apparent that people were hostile towards Theresa May. They blamed Theresa May for cuts to the police when she was Home Secretary,' says Gwynne. 'That [the attack] brought it home to them.'[219]

Labour campaigners were as surprised as anyone that May was not benefiting politically from the attack. 'I hadn't factored that in,' admits Gwynne. 'I felt the opposite would be true – she would come out all prime ministerial, the embodiment of strong and stable, taking on the terrorists. It was a real turning point.' Gwynne recalls: 'People were saying, "She made us unsafe, she cut our police" – and with hostility.'[220]

The reaction exposed an underlying advantage for the Labour Party – they were not the government. After seven years in the Cabinet, May had a record to defend. She had overseen cuts to the police and had even built a reputation for taking on the Police Federation, who had opposed her austerity plan. In 2010, Greater Manchester had over 8,000 officers. By 2017, it had just over 6,000, a 25 per cent decrease. The Labour Party were campaigning for 10,000 extra police officers nationally, paid for by putting up tax on the rich. The Tories were offering more 'tough choices', a euphemism for cuts.

A two-year-old video of a Greater Manchester police officer challenging May about police cuts was quickly picked up by the media. Damian O'Reilly, British community police officer of the year in 2010, publicly warned the Home Secretary that frontline police cuts had increased the chances of a terrorist attack.

'I have worked in inner-city Manchester for fifteen years,' O'Reilly told May at a Police Federation conference in 2015. 'In 2010, I had to leave. I couldn't take it any more because the changes that have been imposed have caused community policing to collapse. Intelligence has dried up. There aren't local officers, they don't know what's happening.'

He added: 'Neighbourhood policing is critical to dealing with terrorism. We run the risk here of letting communities down, putting officers at risk and ultimately risking national security, and I would ask you to seriously consider the budget and the level of cuts over the next five years.'

*   *   *

On Tuesday evening, May arrived back in Downing Street to chair Cobra, emerging at 9.42 p.m. to inform the country that the terrorism threat level, as determined by the intelligence agencies, had been increased for the first time since 2014, rising to 'critical'. This, in the jargon of MI5, meant another attack was 'expected imminently'. May announced that almost 1,000 armed troops would be sent onto the streets, under an emergency plan known as Operation Temperer. In a statement from inside No. 10, she explicitly linked the deployment of soldiers to freeing up armed police so they could counter the terror threat. 'Armed police officers responsible for duties such as guarding key sites will be replaced by members of the armed forces, which will allow the police to significantly increase the number of armed officers on patrol in key locations,' she said. The following day, soldiers armed with SA80 rifles were guarding Parliament, Downing Street and Buckingham Palace.

SPECIAL RELATIONSHIP

Amid the carnage, devastation and creeping politicisation that followed the attack, another row was brewing.

Hours after the Manchester Arena bombing, details from the investigation had started to leak to media in the US. Before official confirmation in the UK, American TV networks were already reporting the number of casualties. Official irritation over the leaks was put to one side as May addressed the country and the names of the

dead slowly emerged throughout Tuesday. But at 4.30
p.m. that day, prior to any confirmation from the British
authorities, CBS and NBC, two American TV networks,
announced the name of the attacker. The revelation infuriated Greater Manchester Police, who had hoped to
keep Abedi's name secret for thirty-six hours in order to
give them a head start rounding up his associates.

Amber Rudd called her counterpart in the US, Secretary of Homeland Security John Kelly, to demand an
end to the leaking of intelligence that Britain routinely
shared with its ally.

Her warnings were ignored. The *New York Times*
published images from the crime scene showing in graph-
ic detail the bloodied detonator, ripped backpack and
pieces of shrapnel found inside the foyer of the arena.
The newspaper's accompanying report even set out the
preliminary conclusions of the police investigation that
was still ongoing. NBC then revealed that Abedi's family
members had warned UK security officials about him
and had described him as dangerous. Downing Street
was incensed.

A statement from 'a senior Whitehall source' – diplo-
matically concealing the identity of the very senior official
– condemned the US. The images 'from inside the American system' were 'clearly distressing to victims, their families and other members of the public', the source said.
'Protests have been lodged at every relevant level ... They
are in no doubt about our huge strength of feeling.'[221]

By Thursday morning, the Prime Minister was under
growing pressure to tackle the issue directly with President Trump. The pair were due to meet at the NATO
summit in Brussels later that day. Her desire for a close

relationship with the US President was becoming a burden in the election campaign – another stick for Momentum and others to beat the Tories with online.

Before she set off for Brussels, it emerged that Greater Manchester Police had taken the extraordinary step of suspending intelligence sharing with the Americans. The suspension lasted less than twenty-four hours but sent a message.

When it came, on Thursday 25 May, May's protest to Trump was minimal, delivered as they waited for a photograph to be taken. Her spokesman said she told Trump that British–American information sharing was 'hugely important', but should be safeguarded. In a statement released from Brussels, Trump promised to 'get to the bottom' of the leaks.

That night, *The Times* ran a poll on its front page under the headline 'Tory lead cut to five points as Corbyn closes in on May'. The YouGov research put Labour on 38 per cent, up three points from the previous week, and the Tories down one point to 43 per cent. If the picture was replicated across the country in the election, the Conservative Party would lose seats and see its majority cut from seventeen to just two, the paper reported. If May's team thought the terrorist attack would move the debate on from their troubles, they were wrong.

COMBATIVE CORBYN

Corbyn was anxious for the campaign to restart. The Labour leader discussed the issue with the Prime Minister in a phone call on Wednesday 24 May. They agreed local campaigning should begin again at midday on Thursday, after the nationwide minute's silence at 11 a.m. The full national election campaign would resume on Friday.

It was the first conversation between the pair since the early hours of Tuesday morning, shortly after the blast. According to senior figures in the Labour leader's office, May tried to extend the suspension of national campaigning until Monday. 'By the end of the week, we wanted to resume but she didn't,' says one of Corbyn's staff. 'There was direct discussion with her about that. We effectively forced the issue. At that stage she still wanted to bring back local campaigning over the week-end and restart national campaigning on the Monday.'[222]

Corbyn's team suspected May was looking for a political advantage. 'She wanted to continue it as long as possible. Although the terror attack in itself was not to their advantage, the suspension of campaigning was. It halted our advance because people weren't talking about social care and the dementia tax.'

In a final phone call between the pair, on Thursday 25 May, according to the Corbyn aide, the Labour leader took a firm line with her about the campaign needing to restart, having gained the support of other parties before speaking to her. Corbyn took the call from the Prime Minister, putting it on speakerphone so his aides could listen from the room in Southside where they had assembled.

Labour insist they did not speak to UKIP – who had by that stage already promised to restart campaigning – but had spoken to other parties. 'Suspending national campaigning was tough for us because our campaign was about policy announcements, which you can't make; Jeremy being on TV all day long, which you can't do; and having tens of thousands of people knocking on doors – because we're a mass-membership party – and you can't do that either,' says one aide close to Corbyn.

'For the Tories, it's different. They don't have a story of the day. They aren't having Theresa May on TV all day going from rally to rally. And they don't have thousands of people knocking on doors. Their thing, which is the presidential thing, carries on.'[223]

CORBYN SPEAKS

Theresa May was out of the country for two days in the middle of the election, discussing security at a NATO summit in Brussels and then how to combat international terrorism and online extremism with the G7 in Sicily. To Labour, it looked like another ready-made public relations coup for the Conservatives' 'President May' campaign.

On Friday 26 May, while the Prime Minister was at the G7, Corbyn chose his moment to intervene. UK military action overseas had made the British people less safe at home and 'we must be brave enough to admit the war on terror is simply not working', he told an audience in London.

Many experts, including professionals in our intelligence and security services, have pointed to the connections between wars our government has supported or fought in other countries, such as Libya, and terrorism here at

home. That assessment in no way reduces the guilt of
those who attack our children. Those terrorists will for
ever be reviled and implacably held to account for their
actions.

But an informed understanding of the causes of terrorism is an essential part of an effective response that
will protect the security of our people, that fights rather
than fuels terrorism. Protecting this country requires us
to be both strong against terrorism and strong against
the causes of terrorism. The blame is with the terrorists,
but if we are to protect our people we must be honest
about what threatens our security.

It was a speech crafted by Milne, setting out what he and
Corbyn had always believed. It was also written painstakingly, to avoid overstepping the mark, repeating that
terror can never be excused. It was a speech anticipating
the coming response.

At 5.57 p.m., that response duly came from the Prime
Minister, speaking in a press conference at the conclusion of the summit in Taormina, Sicily, before flying
back to London that night:

I've been here at the G7 working with other international leaders to fight terrorism. At the same time, Jeremy
Corbyn has said that terror attacks in Britain are our
own fault and he's chosen to do that just a few days after
one of the worst terrorist atrocities we have experienced
in the United Kingdom. I want to make one thing very
clear to Jeremy Corbyn and to you – and it's that there
can never, ever be an excuse for terrorism. There can be
no excuse for what happened in Manchester.

Corbyn had his debate. On Friday evening, he defended his speech, pointing out that in drawing attention to the links between foreign policy and terror, he was expressing views previously set out by the likes of Boris Johnson and the former head of MI5.

* * *

Blaming British military action for terrorism just days after an attack that killed children at a pop concert was clearly a risky move from Labour. It allowed May to claim Corbyn was holding Britain accountable. If her critique had worked, it would have undermined the progress Labour were making in the polls. Why take the gamble? The reason is simple and revealing: because Corbyn's argument was popular – and he was running a populist campaign.

The speech fitted Milne's strategy – to say things that are politically controversial but popular and feed off the row that follows. It is a theory imported from Donald Trump and only works with the oxygen of publicity provided by your opponents' outrage. 'Received wisdom is that in such situations you can't talk about how these terrorist attacks come about and why they come about,' says one of Corbyn's most senior aides. While Corbyn's argument 'was obviously controversial ... the majority of the population think that there is a link with the wars Britain has been involved in'.

> Because we made such a strong case on police cuts and firefighter cuts, the Tories were on the back foot and it didn't play in the way they had hoped. It's another

example of how the campaign broke all the rules. The whole orthodoxy of elections is based on a previous political era and a much less volatile political culture.[224]

Corbyn was certainly defying expectations. He had taken Labour from 24 per cent in the polls to 38 per cent in five weeks. Every time he looked to have made a damaging mistake, Labour closed the gap with the Tories even further.

In the midst of a terrorism crisis, the traditional party of law and order was losing ground to a man who had voted against every piece of anti-terrorism legislation since he was first elected to Parliament in 1983. Written off at the beginning, Corbyn was suddenly in the game.

CHAPTER 15

OFFICERS' MESS

'Every White House is a reflection of its leader.' The maxim from Jim Messina, President Obama's former aide and a key adviser to the Conservatives, could apply as much to an election campaign as to the West Wing. The issue of leadership is critical to understanding the snap election campaign of 2017. It dominated the public debate, thanks to the media's tendency to focus on personalities and to the Tories' initial branding of Theresa May as the 'strong and stable' leader the country needed.

The question of who was in charge inside the rival campaign teams was also a live and vital one for those directly involved. Who ran the Conservative machine, who was setting the strategy, directing the troops and making the final decisions? Were the leading Tories more or less effective than Corbyn and his allies? In the end, the answers reveal how the contrasting characters of the individuals running for office can permeate everything their parties do and shape politics in dramatic and unexpected ways.

LEADERSHIP OR DICTATORSHIP?

From the moment she called the election, Theresa May made it clear that she would not be taking part in any head-to-head television debates with other party leaders. It was a break with a tradition, albeit a young tradition. Incumbent Prime Ministers appeared on panels with rival party leaders at the 2010 and 2015 elections. May faced an immediate onslaught. Jeremy Corbyn said the premier's decision was 'rather strange', adding: 'I say to Theresa May, who said this election was about leadership, come on and show some. Let's have the debates. It's what democracy needs and what the British people deserve.' Liberal Democrat leader Tim Farron added: 'The Prime Minister's attempt to dodge scrutiny shows how she holds the public in contempt. The British people deserve to see their potential leaders talking about the future of our country.'

May's opponents did not relent. Every day, they accused her of hiding and treating voters in an arrogant manner. They had willing accomplices in the media, especially among broadcasters, who were desperate to secure what would make box office television viewing with audiences of millions. A *Mirror* journalist dressed as a chicken followed her everywhere she went, to emphasise the point.

May's refusal to take part in the debates contributed to a narrative that proved even more damaging – the idea that she, personally, was overly controlling, an automaton and unwilling or perhaps unable to engage in genuine, open conversation. The nature of her stage-managed stump speeches – repeating Crosby's mantra of 'strong and stable leadership' – added to the sense that the Prime Minister was more a political robot than a human being. When journalists complained on Twitter that Tory press officers were trying to vet their questions to the PM in advance, their drizzle of discontent fell on fertile ground.

To the Conservative communications team, the broadcasters were so obsessed with trying to get May to debate Corbyn face-to-face that they failed to notice how much more controlled Labour's media operation was. But the truth is that most journalists and editors believed the election contest was so one-sided that Labour's behaviour was inherently less newsworthy. They needed a story from somewhere. A visit to the southwest in early May gave the media what they wanted.

On 2 May, the Conservatives were accused of hiding from residents on a Bristol housing estate and shutting reporters out of a factory visit in Cornwall. The Bristol residents were not allowed inside the room where May held her stage-managed rally with its audience of party activists holding CCHQ-approved placards. Earlier, a local press reporter complained on Twitter that he had been locked in a room unable to watch May's visit to a driving equipment factory in Helston, Cornwall. 'I've had better visits. This was me, shut in a room, while Theresa May was in #Cornwall,' the journalist Graeme Wilkinson said, posting a picture of a locked wooden door on Twitter.

The Conservatives insist that the reason Wilkinson was not allowed to be with the PM was because he wanted to run a 'liveblog', in which her movements would be documented in real time, minute by minute, on his paper's website. The party claims revealing the Prime Minister's movements in real time presented a clear security risk. Nevertheless, the cartoonish impression of a control-freak dictator locking up the free press spread rapidly online. The story gained coverage from the BBC, the *Telegraph*, *The Guardian* and *The Independent*, among others.

'The reception, especially in the media, was much more hostile to Theresa May than I thought it was going to be,' a senior adviser to the party says. 'The regional media were playing odd games. Their aim now seems to be to maximise online hits and the way to do that is to get themselves a national story and promote it online. The easiest national story was "Here is Theresa May looking like a tit."'[225]

After the flurry of criticism about the way they were conducting the process of the campaign's media events, May's team changed tack. They went for what another adviser describes as a 'masochism strategy' of inviting questions from any random journalist who turned up at her campaign rallies. 'All we achieved with that was the Prime Minister being beaten up on TV every day,' the adviser recalls. Corbyn, by contrast, refused to take questions from newspaper reporters during his routine campaign events – but nobody noticed, the Tory complains.[226]

YORK

On 2 June, Theresa May travelled to York for her most important television appearance of the election: the *BBC Question Time: Leaders Special*. She and her team prepared for the event at a hotel in the city where BBC staff were also staying. Her team included Mark Textor, Nick Timothy, Fiona Hill and Tom Swarbrick, the head of broadcast media at No. 10. Carefully, they coached the PM through the likely subjects that would come up and how best to handle hostile questions – and heckling – from the audience.

Wearing a beige jacket over a red dress, May stepped carefully onto the stage to face her first question. 'You said you wouldn't call an election,' Abigail, a young audience member, told the PM. 'You are here calling an election and refusing to take part in debates, refusing to answer people's questions, refusing to talk to Jeremy Corbyn, and you've backtracked on your social care policy and your entire manifesto has holes in it – and everyone else can see that.'

'First of all,' May began but she was interrupted by applause. 'Can I just say, I'm not refusing to take part in debates because I'm here answering questions from you, this audience this evening.'

May thanked the audience members for turning up to what was an important part of the election campaign, but the crowd would not be charmed. An angry and very animated young man, who didn't give his name, told her: 'Just face it, you called the election for your own political gains.' It was not about Brexit but about boosting the Tory majority, he said.

'No, it's not, sir,' May bluntly replied. It would have been 'the easiest thing in the world' to carry on as PM for another couple of years, but the British people deserve to have a say over who they want to lead Brexit negotiations, she said. This was a slightly different way of putting her original argument for the snap election, which was that she needed a stronger hand to overcome opposition at home and to show strength to Brussels.

The well-mannered vicar's daughter then threw an

extraordinary counterpunch as she tried to go toe to
toe with her young opponent. 'I had the balls to call an
election,' she said, perhaps thinking this macho display
would win her some credit.

But the young man interrupted, jabbing his finger in
the air as he spoke. 'Your party called a European referendum for the good of the Conservative Party,' he shouted.
'You've called a general election for the good of the Conservative Party and it's going to backfire on you.'

David Dimbleby, the veteran *Question Time* presenter, tried to put May on the spot about her social care
policies but his line of questioning did not hit the target
as well as a disabled audience member, Derek Griffin.
He asked how he could be sure he and his wife, who is
also disabled, would not be bankrupt in old age.

Other questioners tackled the Prime Minister on
austerity and mental health, as well as pressing her for
details of her bottom lines in the Brexit talks, which she
refused to divulge. Perhaps most damagingly of all, May
invited fury when she told a nurse who had not received
a pay rise for eight years: 'There is no magic money tree.'

THE RED BUTTON

With May's forty-five minutes up, Jeremy Corbyn took to
the stage. While May received polite applause, the Labour
leader was cheered by enthusiasts in the audience as he
entered the studio. The BBC selected the York crowd
carefully and split it into equal thirds to ensure it wasn't
biased in one direction or another: one third were Tory
supporters, a third Labour, and a third were undecided or

backers of other parties. When he got his chance, Corbyn pressed home his advantage over May for at least showing up to the previous leaders' debate in Cambridge.

'Thank you for inviting me here tonight and I'm very sorry this is not a debate, this is a series of questions. I think it's a shame the Prime Minister hasn't taken part in a debate,' he said, to applause.

Corbyn was tackled over how he would conduct Brexit negotiations but immediately seemed more relaxed than May in front of the audience. He was fluent, where May stumbled over her words. He let fly a volley of crowd-pleasing comments about deploring Donald Trump's climate change policies, and fighting to win a majority so he could implement Labour's 'amazing' manifesto, which he held aloft for the audience to see.

A small business owner asked why he should vote for Corbyn, who was proposing to hike corporation tax. The Labour leader confirmed that while the smallest firms would be protected, it was right to fund schools and hospitals properly. Corbyn became animated, as he warmed to his theme. 'So yes, we are asking the very biggest corporations to pay a bit more,' he said.

> But I tell you what, I think it's worth it. It's worth it so that any young person can go to university and not leave with debt. It's worth it to make sure school head teachers don't have to collect at the school gate in order to pay the teachers' salaries. I think it's worth it for a better society in which everyone can achieve something.

Cue more applause and more cheering from Corbyn's fans in the crowd.

It was a startling, undiluted left-wing argument from a committed socialist. The Labour leader spoke to the audience in the studio and at home with passion and a personal conviction that was impossible to fake. It was Comrade Corbyn unchained. 'Poverty is a waste,' he said. 'People who can't get the education they want and the qualifications they want – we all lose. It's a question of whether the community gets together to support everybody or we just let the rich get richer and the rest suffer.'

The Labour leader didn't have it all his own way. He was asked why he hadn't thrown his left-wing colleague and former London mayor Ken Livingstone out of the Labour Party for his allegedly anti-Semitic remarks; he was challenged over whether his policies were 'realistic' or 'just a letter to Santa Claus'. The worst passage for Corbyn came towards the end, when the audience pressed him on national security.

'If Britain were under imminent threat from nuclear weapons, how would you react?' Corbyn initially dodged the question. He would do 'everything' possible to resolve the dispute peacefully through negotiations before it reached the stage of a nuclear conflict, he said. When pushed for an answer about whether he would ever pull the nuclear trigger, the Labour leader said: 'The weapon is there and I would say no first use of the weapon.' It was not fashionable or popular with the audience – he was heckled repeatedly and jeered – but it was authentically Corbyn.

When another audience member said it would be better to have the option of nuclear weapons but never use it, than not to have it at all, Dimbleby asked Corbyn if he wanted to respond. Astonishingly for a show like

Question Time, especially days before an election, Corbyn declined the chance to give his answer, shaking his head and muttering 'no'. It was a bizarre moment and provoked laughter from some in the studio. Corbyn's campaign advisers knew they had to find a way to neutralise what his opponents saw as weakness on national security but the Labour leader himself seemed sure of his own logic. 'If we did use it, millions would die,' he said.

As Dimbleby drew the programme to a close, Corbyn joked: 'But I've got so much more to say.' His fans in the studio audience cheered just as passionately as when he arrived.

*   *   *

Although Corbyn's appearance was more dramatic, May survived her *Question Time* encounter without a disaster, and gained in confidence as she went on. Afterwards, there was a rare chance to unwind before continuing with her campaign the next day. In a hotel bar in Leeds that night, she was drinking wine with her team when a group of women arrived. They had been attending a church group meeting during the day and May crossed the room to meet them. After chatting for a few minutes, she joined in with a group prayer.[227]

MILITARY INTELLIGENCE

For Seumas Milne, the priority that night was to find an antidote to the poisonous issue of Corbyn's opposition to nuclear weapons. He boarded the 10.20 p.m.

train from York to London King's Cross and took his
seat, knowing that questions over Labour's record on
national security could be deeply damaging at a time
when the country was under attack from terrorists. As
he sipped a small white wine, he decided to call Corbyn
to talk through how they should handle the issue next
time Trident was raised.[228]

Gareth Milner was in a drunken daze. He had taken
a day off from his job as a Tory staffer in the party's
media monitoring unit to attend his brother's wedding
near Durham, and had celebrated the occasion in the
traditional ale-fuelled manner. As he slumbered in his
seat on the train home, he suddenly became aware that
the person sitting in front of him was discussing politics
on the phone, first with someone called 'Ed' and then
with someone else called 'Jeremy'. Forcing himself to
his senses, Milner concluded that the passenger must be
Milne. Then his army training kicked in. The Labour
strategy director had sat within earshot of a Tory staffer
who had completed two tours of Afghanistan, including
a spell working in military intelligence.[229]

Milner immediately set about trying to confirm
Milne's identity. He staggered to his feet, switched his
phone onto video mode and strolled casually past the
Labour man. After capturing a 'still' image from the
video, he sent it in a WhatsApp message to the Conservative press office group, who confirmed to him that his
target was indeed Milne. Then the former military spy
went to work, recording Milne's side of the conversation
with the Labour leader.

'Without looking defensive, we need [to] seal down
the Trident thing so it doesn't keep intruding in the next

few days,' said Milne. 'We just need a form of words ... to shut down the nuclear question.' The recording, in which Milne laughed at the idea that using nuclear weapons would be a viable retaliatory 'second strike', was passed to the *Mail on Sunday* newspaper and written up twenty-four hours later in the front-page article under the headline MAY GOES NUCLEAR.

The Prime Minister received a boost last night from a sensational leaked conversation between the Labour leader and his Left-wing spin doctor Seumas Milne. In a phone call two hours after Mr Corbyn was heckled by the audience in the BBC's Question Time Leaders' Debate on Friday for refusing to say if he would use nuclear weapons, the two men agree that launching such a strike would be 'bonkers'.[230]

FIELDS OF WHEAT

Aside from the television set-piece events, May's aides tried to give voters an insight into her character and personality during the closing stages of the campaign. She had done a number of profile interviews – with *Vogue*, for example – since becoming PM. On 5 June, three days before polling day, ITV News broadcast a personal portrait of the Prime Minister in an interview with Julie Etchingham. In it, May was asked to name the naughtiest thing she had ever done. 'Oh goodness me,' she said, clearly stumped. 'Do you know, I'm not quite sure.' Eventually, she said: 'Well, nobody is ever perfectly behaved, are they? I mean, you know, there are times when – I have to confess – when me and my friend, sort of, used to run through the fields of wheat, the farmers weren't too pleased about that.'

May's remarkably tame tale of young rebellion was an instant source of joy to Twitter users fond of political mockery. Social media was in full ridicule mode, as far as the formerly 'strong and stable' Prime Minister was concerned.

There was a serious and even more revealing section of the interview. May described her 'tremendous shock' at the death of her father in a car crash, and also what sounded like a somewhat lonely life growing up as an only child.

'You can't get away from the fact that I was a vicar's daughter,' she said.

> I was quite, sort of, bookish as a child; I enjoyed going to school; I enjoyed reading books; I enjoyed learning. I was an only child, so of course I didn't have brothers and sisters who I was playing with and so I obviously had friends but sometimes had to just go out and, sort of, do things on my own.

Psychoanalysing politicians based on the details they choose to reveal in media interviews is unlikely to reveal the full, unvarnished truth. Even so, there's something in the portrait of May's almost reclusive childhood – shut away with books, or spending time on her own – that seems consistent with her very closed life and her model of leadership of the Conservative Party. She made few friends, never gossiped or played the game that other MPs play in Westminster pubs and bars.

She was cautious and trusted few people with her confidence. When she did find people to trust, she kept them close.

STATE OF PLAY

During the 2015 election, Lynton Crosby was in total command of the Tory campaign, running the war room with a mix of iron discipline and personal charisma. The nerve centre inside No. 4 Matthew Parker Street was unquestionably his domain. David Cameron said so, and George Osborne told anyone who would listen: Lynton's the boss. As the contest wore on, Crosby invited a series of conservative speakers to address the troops inside Tory HQ. John Howard, the former PM of Australia, gave a speech, while Sir John Major, who was at the time the last Tory leader to win a majority, issued an inspirational rallying call to the staff to keep faith that they could beat Ed Miliband despite the deadlocked polls. And of course there was Cameron himself.

Wind the clock forward two years and there was hardly a sign of Cameron's successor. In the aftermath of the manifesto debacle, Theresa May was not only refusing to take part in televised head-to-head election debates with Corbyn, she was also avoiding her own activists toiling at CCHQ. Timothy and Hill were worried about her health, in case she should be struck down by a virus before polling day. 'She didn't come into the office very often because it was basically a pit of germs,' a Tory source says. 'Stephen and Lynton got quite ill during the campaign – there were quite a lot of germs flying around.'[231]

But May's absence came at a cost to staff morale and Crosby, Timothy, Hill and Gilbert were all told the troops needed their leader.

'After three or four weeks, people are working hard. It's a bit dysfunctional managerially in here, just get her in,' one staffer recalls saying. 'Get her to rally the troops. They haven't heard from her. They are fighting for someone they've never spoken to, they've never seen.'

When she did emerge and address the war room, it was hardly the rousing battle cry the staff required.[232]

One witness described May's address as simply a repeat of the stump speech everyone in the building had heard her make dozens of times already. 'It was all "strong and stable" and the risks of Corbyn's "coalition of chaos". I couldn't believe it,' the witness said. 'This was the Prime Minister of the United Kingdom talking in the middle of an election to her own campaign staff and she couldn't even hold the room. People were checking their phones.'[233]

For the final three weeks of the election, the Conservatives needed their leaders to take control. The manifesto crisis and then the Manchester attack badly disrupted the flow just as the campaign reached its most critical point – what Jim Messina regards as the ten golden days before the vote, the period when people are making up their minds. The poll numbers were not good.

In the aftermath of the social care U-turn, Messina predicted just 304 seats for the Conservatives, a catastrophic fall in the party's ratings since his early – and seemingly wild – projection of 470 at the start of the

campaign. Internal Tory polling showed the party with a
ten-point lead straight after the launch, which fell quickly to six points, then two, and then nothing. Corbyn was
on course for Downing Street. 'The campaign then was
all about clawing it back, trying to regain the agenda to
recover the lost votes,' one strategist says.[234]

* * *

Lynton Crosby never personally provided May or her
team with a forecast number for how many seats they
were on course to win. His fear is that people stop working if they think victory is a certainty and he always
takes the view that defeat is possible. Expectations were
too high at the start of the campaign – and now the
Tories' plummeting ratings were showing how over-
hyped those predictions had been.

Although she had never led a national campaign,
May was an experienced MP who had successfully
fought five parliamentary elections in twenty years. She
apparently had an instinct for what was happening to
her campaign. According to one senior figure: 'She was
very worried. She would take it all on herself, saying,
"I'm going to lose this election."' May was frustrated
by Crosby and Textor's refusal to share data with her.
Another senior member of her team said she was ac-
customed to having all the polling and canvass data at
her fingertips during her own constituency campaigns
over the years. 'Why am I not seeing any of this data?'
she asked during a strategy meeting for an upcoming
speech. 'I don't know what we're doing, or how we're
doing.' May's adviser says: 'She found the campaign

incredibly frustrating from that point of view. She just put all her faith in the people running it and believed the numbers were there, and she was doing what their strategy told her she should do.'[235]

Nevertheless, May remained resilient, despite the pressures of her first major national campaign and the see-sawing polls, a Tory says. 'We kept her going. She carried on campaigning. She knew the manifesto had caused a change but she got out there and did a job.'[236]

In truth, nobody in the Tory team – or in Labour HQ, for that matter – really understood the true picture in the country, or how bad their situation would become. The opinion polls published in the papers varied wildly. Some pollsters gave the Tories healthy double-digit leads all the way until election day. Not everyone got it wrong, though. On 25 May, YouGov ran a poll in *The Times*, cutting the Tory lead over Labour to just five points. It was the first clear sign that a real change could be happening but was widely dismissed by commentators and analysts as unrealistic. Five days later, YouGov produced something even more dramatic: a seat projection model that said the Tories were on course to lose their majority in a hung parliament.

Jim Messina and Mark Textor did not believe it. Sitting inside CCHQ, Messina composed a message on Twitter: 'Spent the day laughing at yet another stupid poll from .@yougov. Hey .@benleet do you want to bet for charity? I'll take the over.' Messina showed it to colleagues and asked if he could tweet it, before doing so. Textor later joined in with his own tweet.

Messina now admits he should never have sent the 'stupid' message, but Tory MPs are unlikely to forget any time soon. 'Obviously he's laughing out the other side of his face now,' says one disgruntled former MP who lost his seat.[237] The YouGov findings were unusual. Most polls agreed that the Tories would get a bigger majority. 'There was nothing that we knew, or the Labour Party knew, that was substantially different to the polls, which showed that we had taken a knock but we were still ahead,' a Tory campaign official says.[238]

Gradually, though, candidates on the ground in seats around the country started to worry. As it became clearer that all was not well, the Tories started scaling back their ambitions. They knew Wimbledon, Hastings, Kensington, Putney and Battersea were all at risk. The most ambitious targets in Wales and the Midlands had to be abandoned.[239]

HAM YARD

Arranged around a garden filled with trees, the Ham Yard Hotel in the middle of Soho claims to have 'an urban village feel'. It was here, in the cool cocktail bar, that Messina had arranged to meet Fiona Hill. He wanted to warn her that he feared the campaign was going wrong.

The former White House deputy chief of staff – now an international election consultant for hire – is a giant of world politics. Credited with masterminding Obama's re-election campaign in 2012, he had been hired to work for Cameron in 2015, where his ability to analyse a vast range of data in order to pinpoint the precise concerns of different types of voters became legendary.

Passionate and plain-speaking, he earned a reputation as a political fixer for Obama in 2008, telling the *New Yorker* magazine at the time: 'I handle what people on the campaign call s**t sandwiches. If it goes wrong, I have to deal with it.'[240]

Messina, forty-seven, believed he was in just such an unpalatable situation once again as May's campaign hit trouble at a critical time. After the Manchester Arena bombing, public anger at police cuts had started to bite into the Tory lead; the issue would rise to the top of the agenda in the final days of the election after the second terrorist outrage at London Bridge. Messina's seat projection model had already told him the party could fall short of an outright Commons majority. Jeremy Corbyn was dangerously close to power, the strategist believed.

Messina's team had been working on a piece of analysis known as 'social listening'. This involved dissecting the conversations voters were having on Twitter and other social media outlets. It served as an additional way to measure the momentum in the contest, based on what people were discussing. According to Messina's evidence, the conversations were all about the manifestos – and 'Theresa May's police cuts'. To Messina's intense frustration, Timothy and Hill did not seem interested. They were not fighting back against Corbyn's increasingly resonant anti-austerity message that you can't protect the public 'on the cheap'.

'They just sat on the defensive and got pounded for the cuts, which is ridiculous, because suddenly we were on the defence on security – when was the last time Labour has been [on] the offensive and the Conservatives have been on the defensive on security?' one campaign insider recalls.[241] Crosby, Textor, Messina and others could not understand why it was taking Hill and Timothy so long to rebut the argument. As a former Home Secretary, the issue of cutting police budgets was squarely in May's domain, making Labour's attacks all the more telling. Messina called a meeting.

'Social [media] was just being dominated by the police cuts issue but No. 10 wasn't making any decisions. I tried to warn them,' Messina says.[242]

Initially, Timothy and Hill agreed to meet Messina at CCHQ but then Timothy was diverted elsewhere. Hill then told Messina she would meet him for a drink at the Ham Yard Hotel. He arrived at the bar at 7.30 p.m., armed with a folder of charts to show May's co-chief of staff his worrying analysis of the internet chatter. At 8.30 p.m., Hill said she was 'on her way', according to Messina. At 10 p.m., he left the bar after sitting there for two and a half hours waiting in vain for Hill to show up. 'I've never been treated like that professionally before,' he says.

THE VOID

The story of the second half of the Tory campaign was one of a loss of grip by its leaders, who, in different ways, were all absent. The only thing they ultimately had in common is that none of them wanted to be in charge.

In the final weeks of the election, Hill and Timothy – who could have been calling the shots – lost control, according to senior CCHQ insiders. Hill had apparently fallen out with Crosby and Textor, and was not responding to Jim Messina. According to people in the room, Hill raised her concerns in a meeting late in the campaign. She said the Crosby–Textor strategy had failed to capture the real Theresa May – and feared that it was going badly. By this point it was too late to change course. The consultants did not thank her.[243]

Timothy, meanwhile, was said to have been preoccupied by the horrifying thought that his cherished manifesto could have fatally harmed his boss's chances of winning a bigger majority. 'After the manifesto, Nick was terrified for the rest of the campaign. He realised it could all go wrong and he kept seeking reassurance,' a senior campaign figure recalls.[244] Staff complained that it was difficult to get decisions signed off by Timothy and Hill. It would take two days to agree to a media line rebutting Labour attacks on police cuts, for instance. Worryingly, even Mark Textor, Crosby's hard-working long-term business partner, was said to be taking a step back. When press releases needed approval against Textor's research, which helped to fashion the language of the party's key messages, he would normally respond within minutes. Towards the end of the campaign, staff could wait days without answer. 'Structurally, it was chaotic,' admits one leading member of May's inner circle.

> Strategically, it was chaotic and disastrous but it was also just structurally chaotic. So it was completely unclear actually who was supposed to be doing what. Everything had to go through a clearance process, which was Stephen Gilbert, Lynton Crosby, Mark Textor, Nick and Fi. And it was never clear who actually would sign things off. It was

basically whoever came back first that would sign it off. It was completely unclear what the structure was.[245]

Before the election began, Crosby was adamant he did not want to be the campaign director, friends say in part because he didn't know Theresa May. Crosby was also overseas for the first few days of the election. In his absence, the mild-mannered Stephen Gilbert took on the role, though he has told friends that he was not ever formally appointed campaign director. Patrick McLoughlin, the veteran party chairman, also ran a few staff meetings. 'In HQ, the biggest failing was the way four groups of people were thrown together and there was no attempt to integrate them,' one Tory staffer says.

On the ground floor, you had CCHQ staffers who had been there for years, and suddenly the invading hordes came in. You had CTF in the form of Lynton, Tex and also their team, who were basically put in one corner. You had Edmonds Elder, who came in and were put next to CTF but in a different bank of desks. And then you had government advisers who were not just special advisers but also former Conservative Research Department staffers.

Nobody ever introduced these different groups to each other. I found that weird because if you are trying to embark on a joint endeavour, you need team spirit. It's actually quite an easy thing to engender, especially in an election, where it's 'us' versus 'them'. You don't have to fake that.[246]

Crosby is a natural leader, a man who is close to incapable of standing aside and watching people wilt under pressure when he knows he can give them a boost. In the 2015 campaign, he made it his business to ensure everyone in the war room had fun while working hard and long hours. The quality of his leadership made Cameron's campaign HQ a tough yet rewarding place to be. But he had two years to prepare and Cameron's blessing to arrange everything exactly as he wanted it.

When he arrived in late 2017, Crosby effectively took over the management of the war room, according to numerous witnesses, but without ever explicitly taking on the role of campaign director. In a conversation with Gilbert, Crosby agreed he would take over chairing the twice-daily strategy meetings. It was what Gilbert had always wanted anyway.

WAR WEARY

After the manifesto crisis, Crosby refocused the campaign onto Brexit and Labour's threat to the economy and national security. First, though, he needed to pick the rest of the team up and restore the war room's fighting spirit. He revived an office game he had played with the campaign teams he had led in the past: awarding prizes each day to workers who have gone beyond the call of duty for the cause. Awards could be given for ambushing a Labour Party photo-call with placards or Corbyn masks or for discovering some damaging information that would hurt the Labour campaign, or merely for putting in long hours on a major announcement, such

as the manifesto. During Boris Johnson's mayoral campaigns, Crosby gave someone a pink cardigan to wear
for the day. In the 2015 election, it was a cuddly koala
or kangaroo. For May's 2017 campaign, the trophies
were cardboard cut-outs of Jeremy Corbyn, or masks of
Corbyn, Nicola Sturgeon or Tim Farron.

Although he has a fearsome reputation as a political
operator, Crosby is personally charming, softly spoken
and passionate about theatre. One of his favourite activities in London is to go to the theatre with his wife,
Dawn, and when he was younger he even raised money
for the Liberal Party in Australia by staging musicals.
When, on Sunday 28 May, the Conservative Friends of
India released a catchy song for the election – in Hindi –
Crosby was delighted. He was so thrilled that he played
it repeatedly throughout the remaining week and a half
of the campaign – at top volume on his laptop – to the
amusement (or irritation) of anyone trying to work in
the war room. The song, 'Together with Theresa', includes the lyrics: 'Let's join hands with Theresa May,
for a strong, stable government. She will bring growth
and prosperity for us all, Theresa May will support us
always.'

One Tory staffer says:

Lynton is a battlefield general who wants his troops to
see him. He will be there, he will gee you up and tell you
it's all going well. So, even on a Saturday, other people
would flake out but he would be there just to show his
face. In fact, he'd be largely getting in the way and being
annoying, playing that idiotic Indian Theresa May song
on his laptop. Once he'd found it, he loved it and he'd

play it all the time. You'd just be trying to get something done and all of a sudden it would pipe up.[247]

Crosby and the other senior figures in CCHQ were trying to keep spirits up amid the drudgery of a seven-week campaign which had unexpectedly ground into the mud of a Labour Party austerity debate. The Australian duo of Crosby and Textor also invested in a Nerf gun, a toy weapon that fires foam darts. Their chief target was the cardboard cut-out of Jeremy Corbyn that was installed in the office. Sometimes, though, they would take aim at colleagues on the other side of the war room. After a period of sustained attack, Rob Oxley, the head of press during the campaign, bought another Nerf gun so he and his team could return fire. Campaign staffers working on desks between the two opposing sides would have to take cover as foam ammunition flew overhead. The fun and games helped team morale but they could not overcome the structural flaws in the campaign that were ultimately the source of the anxiety. CCHQ was leaderless at the very top – and heading for disaster.

Tory high command provided breakfast and dinner for staff working early and late during the week in the catering area downstairs. Lunch was laid on for those working at weekends, with menus such as pasta, pies and chicken. The long hours meant few in the campaign were able to go out for dinner or drinks with friends or partners outside the campaign team for the duration of the election. There were rumours of office romances starting up and socialising among staff in the bar of the St Ermin's Hotel, a short walk away, where many of the

Tory top brass stayed for the duration of the election, at considerable expense.

The team battled on, working debilitating hours, having fun when they could. But just as nobody was formally and fully in charge of the war room, the party had also lost control of the election agenda. Corbyn was making waves with his big-spending, populist policies, and Theresa May's personal ratings were in freefall. After her manifesto U-turn, May's promise of 'strong and stable leadership' was no longer a compelling election message but a punchline to someone else's joke.

AGE OF DEFERENCE

Despite appearances, Crosby has insisted he never wanted to be in charge of the Tory operation and never was. Timothy and Hill were sure it was not their role either. Hill had her hands full running a communications team, while Timothy was largely preoccupied with the manifesto process and they were both still providing critical advice to their boss every day. Now, Timothy says the trio deferred too much to Crosby over the campaign strategy.

One thing seems brutally clear. The strategists with seats at the power pod – Crosby, Gilbert, Hill and Timothy – were all willing to defer when it suited them.

The culture of deference arguably started at the very top. May herself delegated and often deferred on some issues to Timothy and Hill in government and then, during the campaign, the chiefs bowed to the strategy of Crosby and Gilbert, except when it came to the manifesto. The trouble was, neither Crosby nor Gilbert really wanted to lead that snap election campaign. But the people who called it and hired them to run it didn't either. 'I think it's a bit unfair that Nick and Fi are getting criticised,' one senior strategist says. 'At the end of the day they are working for somebody. Either she condoned the way they operated or she didn't know, but either way who really is at fault?'[248]

Another says:

I think the PM deserves a bit of blame. In the end, campaigns are a reflection of the leader. She acquitted herself well, she stayed on message, but the problem comes when you have a government which is really only you and your two people and no one else matters. You can't run an election campaign like that.[249]

May, Timothy, Hill, Gilbert and Crosby. In the end, this was the quintet in the wheelhouse of the unsinkable Tory ship. They all stared out of the window into the icy night – but no one was actually at the helm.

CHAPTER 16

THE UNION

At 9.15 a.m. on 18 April, Ruth Davidson's phone rang. It was Theresa May.

The Scottish Conservative leader was one of the last senior figures in the party to learn that the Prime Minister was going to call for an early election later that morning, but she didn't care. 'She was absolutely cock-a-hoop,' says one of her closest aides. 'She could see immediately that it was great for us.'[250]

The general election in Scotland was unique and distinct from the contest taking place elsewhere. It was also critical to the national outcome: without the success of Davidson's Scottish Tories, Theresa May would have found it far harder to cling on to power. The contest in Scotland was a fascinating tangle of the threads of populism, identity and revolt that were running through the election across Britain. It also lent a tartan tint to the debate about the one issue that hung over the entire election: Brexit.

More than anything, the British general election of 2017 was the Brexit election. It was fought in a political climate transformed by the momentous vote to leave the EU in June 2016. That turbulent decision split the UK down the middle, and stirred up unpredictable storms a year later that buffeted the Tories, put wind in Labour's sails and all but sank the smaller vessels of UKIP and the Liberal Democrats.

More than any other strategic question facing the party leaders, how they responded to Brexit would determine how they fared when the country went to the polls on 8 June. It was a question that was felt in every corner of the United Kingdom.

SCOTLAND BLUES

For Ruth Davidson, the biggest open goal of her political career had suddenly appeared in front of her. She knew that the battle in Scotland would be shaped not by one referendum, but by two.

The 2014 independence vote was an earthquake. It erased the political map of Scotland and replaced it with a country painted almost entirely in the yellow of the Scottish National Party. Although voters rejected independence, the general election of 2015 saw the SNP sweep the board, winning fifty-six of the fifty-nine available seats in an upswell of support almost unparalleled in British history.

For a time it seemed that Sturgeon could do no wrong, but Brexit was to change all that. The EU referendum saw 62 per cent of Scots vote to Remain, but their wishes were outweighed by the millions of Eurosceptics living in England and Wales. Sturgeon felt it was unsustainable for Scotland to be dragged out of the EU, and its single market, against the clearly expressed wishes of its people. Her radical, but predictable, solution in March 2017 was to announce plans for a second referendum on independence. Let the people decide whether they want a 'hard Brexit' or an independent Scotland, Sturgeon said. The problem was that the people had had enough of making decisions. In the ten years since 2007, Scottish voters had taken part in five Westminster and Holyrood elections and three referendums.

Private polling and focus groups conducted for the Conservatives found voters were sick of being asked to adjudicate on huge constitutional issues and wanted the Holyrood government to get on with its day job.

In response to Sturgeon's gambit in March, May chose her words carefully. She said 'now is not the time' for a new independence campaign, which implicitly did not rule out another referendum at some point in the future. Davidson and Fiona Hill had devised the nuanced position in order to avoid fuelling the independence movement with an outright rejection of a new vote. Nevertheless, it allowed Davidson to attack Sturgeon for reopening old wounds and gave the Scottish Conservative leader the chance to establish herself as the voice of the 55 per cent of Scots who voted No to independence in 2014. It was to prove a masterstroke, as opposition to a new independence referendum became the central pillar of the Tory offer to Scottish voters at the general election.

Craig Elder, the Scot running the Tory digital operation in London, says the party had already road-tested its strategy in Scotland during the 2016 Holyrood elections:

We worked on the 2016 Scottish elections as well, so we were already familiar with how best to use Ruth's popularity, the issue of a second referendum and voters' frustration with the SNP's lack of focus on day-to-day

issues as part of a successful digital campaign. We focused on the seats where the constant threat of a second
referendum was a key issue, and the voters who trusted
Ruth to stand up for them on that key issue.[251]

Sturgeon realised the Tory attacks were hitting home
and tried to separate the election campaign from the
question of another independence referendum. 'The
election won't decide whether or not Scotland becomes
independent,' she said within a week of May's announcement. 'The issue at this election campaign is quite clear
– how do we make sure we have strong voices arguing
Scotland's corner at Westminster?'

Sturgeon's attempt to park the constitutional issue
failed. For the next seven weeks, the Tories relentlessly
beat the drum against another vote on Scottish separa-
tion. 'They were obsessed by it,' says the SNP MP Tommy
Sheppard, referring to the Tories' focus on independence.

> They literally talked about nothing else. They achieved
> this bizarre trick where they made the public think it was
> the SNP who was obsessing about a second independence
> referendum when in fact we rarely talked about it. It was
> constantly Davidson in attack mode saying, 'Say no to a
> second independence referendum.'[252]

SEPARATION ANXIETY

The local elections in May gave Davidson a shock. Conservative HQ in London had set a modest goal for the
party north of the border: keep its one MP and seek

to gain two more, according to one influential Tory.[253] When Davidson's aides analysed the local council results ward by ward, they found the party was on course to win fifteen seats on 8 June. 'To win fifteen would have been absurd,' explains one senior Scottish Tory.

Faced with the shock numbers, Davidson threw caution to the wind and released the findings to the media – she wanted to show voters that even though the Conservatives had only one MP in Scotland, they were a viable choice again. She needed to convince the public that they had to turn to the Tories if they wanted to get rid of the SNP. Then she took the fight to the nationalists directly. 'Let's go to Salmond's patch,' Davidson declared. The Scottish Tory leader turned up to make an impromptu campaign speech in Inverurie, in the Gordon constituency of Alex Salmond, the godfather of the independence movement. 'She was showing that she's ballsy enough to go for his seat,' one source says.

It was bold, and typical of Davidson. Even before the general election, the Tory leader in Scotland had transformed the party's fortunes. Voters warmed to her determined and passionate opposition to Sturgeon's government and the SNP's quest for independence. In 2016, Davidson made an appearance on the national stage, famously taking on Boris Johnson in an EU referendum TV debate. A former BBC journalist and army reservist, she relishes performing in front a crowd. Her wicked sense of humour often comes at her colleagues' expense – although it is just as often at her own. She once described herself unflatteringly as 'a short-haired, flat shoe, shovel-faced lesbian'.

Some Tories in London were suspicious of Davidson's

rise and saw her as a potential rival to May. Although
Davidson had worked with Fiona Hill on formulating
the party's position on a second independence referendum, the pair were at odds during the election campaign
itself.

Davidson was fighting an entirely separate campaign
to the strategy directed from CCHQ in London. She
was taking aim at Sturgeon on her own terms, rather
than deploying the presidential 'Theresa May' message
devised by Lynton Crosby and Mark Textor. On 8 May,
the Scottish Tory leader gave a speech inviting voters to
'cut the SNP down to size'. The headlines made their
way to London. 'Instead of pats on the back, people
weren't happy because it hadn't been cleared [i.e. signed
off by the campaign chiefs in CCHQ],' a senior Scottish
Conservative says. 'We got a call saying Ruth needed
to come down to London immediately. Fiona wanted a
word.'[254]

CCHQ wanted Davidson to stick to the script about
Theresa May's 'strong and stable leadership' and to
put May's picture on all her campaign leaflets. When
Davidson arrived at Matthew Parker Street on Friday
12 May, however, Hill was not there. It was left to
Crosby and Textor to discuss the options with her.
Once the Australians had seen Davidson's polling, they
agreed that she should carry on with her own campaign, and fully accepted that the messages they were
using in England would not work north of the border.
There, they could clearly see, independence coloured
everything. 'I completely understand,' Crosby told her.
'Crack on.'[255]

LABOUR'S LESSON

By the time Theresa May called the election, Scottish Labour had realised that it too needed a clearer stance on independence. Labour saw its working-class base switch to the SNP after it opposed independence in the 2014 referendum. At the election the following year, Labour paid the price of campaigning with the Tories to keep the union together, losing forty of the forty-one seats it had won north of the border in 2010.

After dismal Holyrood elections in 2016, when Labour finished third, the party's Scottish leader Kezia Dugdale realised she could no longer stay out of the fight. If it was going to survive, Labour had to pick a side, and that side had to be against independence. 'That summer we made a conscious choice,' says one of the party's chief strategists in Scotland. 'We started to focus on our long-term strategy and to make sure people were aware we opposed IndyRef2.' Then trouble hit.

Jeremy Corbyn was asked for his view on Sturgeon's plan for a new independence referendum straight after she announced it in March. Instead of signalling his implacable opposition, he said he would be 'absolutely fine' with another vote, if it was what the Holyrood Parliament wanted. Scottish Labour politicians were incensed. Corbyn, whose leadership was a laughing stock at the time, had trodden all over the Scottish Labour Party's carefully prepared plan.

Nobody was more astonished than Dugdale's team when Corbynmania spread north from England in the final weeks of the campaign. Sturgeon's SNP government

had begun to come under pressure for its record on running the country. A nurse garnered headlines for the anti-
austerity campaign that Labour was running when she
took on the First Minister during a TV debate, claiming
her low pay forced her to use food banks. Labour research found Sturgeon herself was becoming unpopular.
'People were saying to us, "What are you going to do
about that woman?" It was a bit of a wake-up call for
us,' one of Labour's senior figures in Scotland says.[256]

Corbyn had been making the same arguments about
austerity for weeks to TV audiences and mass rallies in
England. The Corbyn surge in England and Wales then
broke through the border to the north, and began to
hurt the SNP. 'Initially, Corbyn was a figure of ridicule,'
says the SNP MP Tommy Sheppard, who felt the change
in his constituency in Edinburgh East.

> As the campaign got to the finishing line and the polls
> began to narrow and television programmes began to
> accept the possibility that Jeremy Corbyn might win
> without the attendant ridicule – then suddenly people
> thought, 'I'll have some of this.' It then became quite
> infectious. I could feel the support shifting.[257]

He says Corbyn's message of 'imagine a different world'
appealed to the same instincts in the electorate that
fuelled support for independence in the 2014 referendum. Like Alex Salmond's 'Yes Scotland' campaign in
2014, Corbyn's 'For the many, not the few' was the battle
cry of a revolutionary. 'The reason people voted Labour
who hadn't done before was because of Corbyn, with his
message of let's get on the radical train,' says Sheppard.

Opposition to independence had stabilised the Labour campaign, but the shift in the end had little to do with the party's views on independence. Corbyn had cut through in Scotland to become the only political figure in British politics with a truly national appeal.

The SNP saw the change coming but could do little to stop it. On 2 June, Sturgeon said she would help Corbyn become Prime Minister by ordering SNP MPs to support him on an 'issue-by-issue' basis if there was a hung parliament. A few days later, the party ran an article in the *Daily Record* headlined: 'If you want a Labour Government in Westminster you should vote SNP.'

'By the time we were sure, we were only a week from the poll,' says Sheppard. 'It was too late.'

Corbyn's surge northwards would have been impossible without Labour first having neutralised the question of Brexit by taking up an ambiguous position that could appeal to both Leavers and Remainers. The party in Scotland then had to take a firm position against another independence referendum to avoid becoming bogged down in arguments. With these two constitutional issues largely cleared – despite the Labour leader's stumble over independence – Corbyn had the space to build his campaign on austerity.

WALES

Wales, with its spectacular landscape, provided the setting in which Theresa May's election dream was born. It was also the graveyard where her manifesto was buried six weeks later in Wrexham.

As they plotted their strategy at the start of the campaign in London, however, Conservative officials believed that Brexit had opened the door to parts of Britain that had, at previous elections, slammed it in Tory faces. In the EU referendum in 2016, Wales voted to Leave by 52.5 per cent to 47.5 per cent. The Tories believed the collapse of UKIP gave them a historic opportunity to sweep into a working-class Labour heartland that had been off limits for decades.

Throughout the election, Wales would act as an extreme barometer of the national mood, a canary in the coal mine, warning both parties of the perils they faced. In the days following May's snap election announcement, it was clearly the Labour Party that was in gravest danger, not the Conservatives.

On 24 April, one of the most astonishing polls of the campaign was released. It showed Corbyn facing catastrophe in Wales. Carried out by YouGov for ITV Wales and Cardiff University during the three days after May's election announcement, the Welsh Political Barometer survey put the Conservatives on 40 per cent, ten points clear of Labour. 'Wales is on the brink of an electoral earthquake,' wrote Cardiff's professor of political science Roger Scully. According to the poll, the Conservatives were on course to win a majority of Welsh parliamentary seats for the first time since 1918.

The Tory momentum reflected, in part, the death of UKIP as a relevant force in national politics, but that was only half the story. Labour was losing voters directly to the Conservatives. The poll suggested a revolution was under way. The Tories were on course to win twenty-one seats – an increase of ten on their already impressive performance in 2015 – with the Labour total falling to just fifteen, down ten. The findings landed like a bomb-shell in Westminster and reverberated well beyond, even warranting coverage in the *Times of India*.

BREATHING SPACE

Against this backdrop, Labour was braced for disaster in the local elections. But the catastrophe never came.

When the results emerged, a pattern was clear: Labour had taken a few jabs, but the Tories did not have the power to land the knockout blow they hoped for. Labour lost control of Blaenau Gwent and Bridgend councils, as well as its council leader in Merthyr Tydfil. But it also held on in seven councils including Cardiff, Swansea and Newport. The Tories had a good night but there was no blue revolution.

Amid heavy losses elsewhere in the country, it was Wales that gave Corbyn his most obvious source of hope. The Labour leader congratulated the Welsh party for 'defying the pundits'. That did not stop Welsh Labour MP Stephen Kinnock condemning the leadership with a warning that the results were 'simply not good enough'. YouGov, which can make a good case for being the most reliable of the pollsters during a difficult election for the industry, charted Labour's slow fight-back in the weeks that followed.

In May, three dramatic events combined to fuel a Labour surge in Wales that was even more powerful than those seen in either England or Scotland.

First, on 17 May, the popular former Labour Welsh

minister Rhodri Morgan died. It was a moment of national reflection and a reminder, one of his admirers in the Conservative Party says, of the country's Labour heritage: 'It reminded people of the Labour they knew.'

Immediately following Morgan's death came the Conservative manifesto – a disaster in Wales as much as it was in England. May had called an election as a different type of Tory, one for whom it was socially acceptable to vote in parts of the country where for generations it had not been. In the weeks running up to the manifesto launch, Wales had been more open to this pitch than any other former Labour heartland. It was on the brink of turning blue.

The manifesto shattered May's reputation. The change in the Prime Minister's standing was doubly damaging because, unlike in Scotland, where they were running a separate campaign, the Welsh Tories had hitched their wagon to Theresa May. 'It was lost with this absurd idea you can run the same campaign in all four nations of the kingdom,' says one minister. 'I was in Newport West handing out Theresa May leaflets, "strong and stable" and all of that. It just didn't work.' One problem for the Tories was a dearth of local talent: 'We haven't got a Ruth Davidson in Wales,' the minister says.[258]

Four days after the manifesto came the U-turn on the so-called dementia tax. The social care debacle was the lowest point of the Tory campaign; that it happened in Wales only reinforced its impact there.

*   *   *

In the final poll before election day, Labour moved thirteen percentage points clear of the Tories, with 47 per cent of the vote. Something dramatic had happened on the ground.

On Corbyn's final day of campaigning, he travelled to Colwyn Bay in the heart of one of the Tories safest Welsh seats, Clwyd West. Waiting for him on the promenade were thousands of supporters, ready to greet their hero like a rock star. Children had been given permission to skip school to see him. The crowd cheered every campaign promise and chanted his signature anthem 'Oh, Jeremy Corbyn. Oh, Jeremy Corbyn...'

In Leave-voting Wales, not even Brexit could save the Tories from the rising red tide.

NORTHERN IRELAND

As Theresa May contemplated calling the election in April, one part of the country was weighing on her mind as a potential problem: Northern Ireland.

The province was once again mired in a political crisis of which most people in London were only dimly aware. Fresh assembly elections had failed to break a stand-off between Sinn Féin and the DUP after the collapse of the power-sharing executive in Stormont in January.

As Theresa May left for her walking holiday before Easter, there was little sign of a breakthrough. When she returned, and resolved to go to the country, one of the first ministers she needed to talk to was her Northern Ireland Secretary, James Brokenshire. He was trying to work for a deal to restore power sharing and his job was about to get harder.

'This election is the worst possible thing to do,' warned

the director of Belfast's Institute for Conflict Research Neil Jarman, shortly after the announcement. 'You are having negotiations to bring the parties together and now you have elections pushing them apart. Nobody knows when, or how, to bring them back together.'[259]

Brexit added an extra sectarian kick to the mix. While the province had voted against it, the Democratic Unionist Party was strongly pro-Leave and Sinn Féin equally strongly pro-Remain. Sinn Féin was arguing for Northern Ireland to have a special status in the EU, but the DUP wanted a clean break. Into this mix came the upheaval of the snap election.

SECTARIAN HEADCOUNT

For unionists worried by the rise of Sinn Féin, there was little choice but to vote DUP. In return, some nationalists, who were alarmed at the prospect of a hard border with the Republic that could result from leaving the EU, had little choice but to fall in line behind Sinn Féin. Northern Ireland had been tripped into an unexpected sectarian headcount – in part thanks to Brexit – just when the country needed to come together.

The forces dragging each community apart became quickly apparent when Sinn Féin made it known that it was seriously targeting Belfast North, a DUP stronghold that had never elected a nationalist. Sinn Féin's candidate was John Finucane, whose father, Pat, was murdered by loyalist paramilitaries in 1989 in one of the most infamous killings of the Troubles. In the end, Finucane finished just 2,000 votes short of causing a historic upset.

*   *   *

All across Northern Ireland, support for the larger parties soared as the smaller, more moderate UUP, SDLP and Alliance were squeezed.

Overall, the DUP increased its share of the vote by ten percentage points, helping the party finish the night with a record ten MPs. In some respects, Sinn Féin's performance was even more striking. Even though the party does not take its seats in the House of Commons, its vote share increased by five percentage points to 39 per cent, topping the DUP's tally of 36 per cent across the province.

While Northern Ireland had long been split along sectarian lines, the divisions were hardening around the two parties. The divide was even becoming geographical. A map of Northern Ireland after 8 June 2017 is a picture of sectarian division, split in half, unionist orange and republican green. Every constituency along the border with the Irish Republic is now represented by Sinn Féin. Apart from an enclave of rock-solid nationalism in west Belfast, the country is now divided by a diagonal line running north-west to south-east. For the first time there is no nationalist presence in Westminster at all.

This was a campaign that took place outside the national British conversation in almost all respects and yet the big issue lurking in the background was the same: Brexit. Theresa May called the election at the worst possible time for Northern Ireland and on an issue that risked further deepening the divisions within the province.

Ultimately, the polarisation of Northern Irish politics gave May her route to power. Having lost her majority, she sent Gavin Williamson, her Chief Whip, and Damian Green, the First Secretary of State, to talk with Arlene Foster, the DUP leader, and her team. After weeks of slow progress, the two sides eventually struck a deal. With more funding for the DUP's priorities, May was told she could count on the votes of their ten MPs in the Commons.

May's Brexit election pulled Northern Ireland further apart. The payoff for the Prime Minister, when her gamble backfired, was the chance to survive.

CHAPTER 17

COLLATERAL DAMAGE

LIBERAL DEMOCRATS

For Tim Farron, the 2017 election was a long and personally dispiriting campaign. The struggle to reconcile his politics with his personal faith ultimately proved a battle too far. He would resign as Liberal Democrat leader afterwards. Electorally, too, Farron's campaign had fallen flat. By the final week of the contest, it was clear that Brexit was not the boon for the party that Farron and his team had hoped at the outset it would be. The prospect of a Lib Dem resurgence on a wave of anger over the EU referendum had faded.

In an election about Brexit, the one issue on which they had something clear and potentially popular to say, Farron's party was largely ignored. But so too were the other small parties with clear messages on the EU. Plaid Cymru and the Greens were squeezed on the left, while UKIP was all but eliminated as an electoral force on the right.

More than any other single factor, the divisive EU referendum of 2016 created the conditions for the two main parties to swell, blocking out the light the smaller parties needed to grow, or even, in the case of UKIP, to survive. In the daily storms of the contest, the issue appeared to recede from view as questions of austerity, social care, police cuts and terror dominated. And yet Brexit was always there, like a low-lying cloud hanging over everything, even if it was sometimes possible to forget about it.

YELLOW HOPES

On 18 April, Farron was waiting in the departure lounge at Manchester airport when he got a text from his spokesman Paul Butters saying a snap election looked like it was on. It was approaching 11 a.m. and the podium had been brought out from No. 10 without the prime ministerial crest.

Inside Liberal Democrat HQ, they were excited. It had been a tough couple of years for the party. They had been all but wiped out in 2015 and were on the long road back to political relevance. Brexit, Farron's officials felt, was potentially their saviour. With Labour's support base split on whether to Leave or Remain, as it had been in Scotland over independence, the Lib Dems saw an opportunity to win back lost ground. Their offer was simple: a second referendum to overturn Brexit. May's decision to frame the election as the coming battle for Britain in Europe could not have been better. As they watched the Prime Minister's statement from Great George Street, the party's London HQ, Farron's aides punched the air. 'When she said it was a Brexit election, I crossed my fingers and thought "maybe",' says Paul Butters.[260]

Farron was waiting for a flight down to the West

Country for the launch of the Lib Dems' local election campaign that day. The media were already waiting for him. It was a perfect opportunity to get the party's message across and yet, within hours, he would be caught up in an apparently obscure row about his personal faith – whether he thought gay sex was a sin. It was an issue that would knock his campaign off course before it had even begun. The Labour Party was the main beneficiary of Farron's troubles. It was also, in a small way, responsible for them.

GAY SEX

Shortly after 12.30 p.m. on the day the election was called, Corbyn and his team had left their office in Westminster to head up to Birmingham for a scheduled event with a group of carers. Channel 4's Cathy Newman was quickly in touch asking for an interview with the Labour leader for one of the lead items on that evening's news. When James Schneider, Corbyn's main press man, said 'no', Newman attempted to up the pressure by saying she still had time to get to Bristol to interview Farron. Unmoved, Schneider said 'fine' and so Newman set off in search of the Lib Dem leader.[261]

'A while back, I asked whether it was true that you believed homosexuality was a sin,' Newman asked Farron in a live interview from Bristol that night. 'Now that you have had a while to consider that question, what is your answer?'

It should have been a straightforward enough question for a politician to handle. Theresa May, who is also

a practising Christian, was asked the same thing later in
the campaign and replied clearly: 'No.' But Farron was
concerned that if he answered one question about his
private religious views, it would only encourage more.
'We talked about it,' says one aide. 'Opinion was split
but lots of us thought, well, what's next, sex before marriage? We wanted to move on.'[262]

Farron attempted to put an end to the discussion. 'I'm
not going to spend the next six weeks talking theology
or making pronouncements,' he told Newman. 'Just because I'm a Christian it would be a bit boring for everybody if we spent the next six weeks trying to get me to
make theological pronouncements. I'm not planning to
do so.'

After seven more days of pressure, he finally acknowl-
edged the issue was not going to go away. 'I do not think
gay sex is a sin,' he said. But the fact that it had taken
so long to answer a simple question damaged the party
irreparably. For Farron personally, the controversy was
acutely painful. 'You've got your family, your church
and your congregation on one side and everybody else
on the other,' says one of his closest allies. 'Of course it
was tough.'[263]

BREXIT SPLITS

Farron later said he felt guilty about the distraction he
had caused. He felt the Lib Dems' message on Europe
was not being heard. In an election about Brexit, only
the Lib Dems offered a second referendum. The truth is,
however, even the Lib Dems were split by Brexit. While

the party was strongly pro-European, much of its traditional heartland had voted to leave the EU in 2016. Some on Farron's side worried that opposing Brexit would make it look like they were ignoring a referendum because they did not like the result – an ill-fitting impression for a party with the word 'democrat' in its name.

The issue came to a head at a bad-tempered all-day meeting on 22 April, held to agree the party's manifesto at its Great George Street headquarters. Farron's chief of staff and the former coalition health minister, Norman Lamb, were among the senior figures there. The most contentious topic: Brexit. Much of the party's manifesto had already been written in expectation that May would go to the country early, although, like Labour, the Lib Dems assumed the election would not be called until at least after the local council contests in May.

Many in the party wanted to take the strongest anti-Brexit line within reason to give a clear message to the public. They proposed a commitment to hold a second referendum on the terms of the final Brexit deal and to campaign for a vote to remain.

Lib Dems close to the leader felt the party needed to carve out a message as distinct as possible from Labour's. Eighteen months earlier, shortly after Farron had taken over, his officials commissioned research in the south-west, London, Scotland and the north of England, asking centre-left voters for their views of the party. The results were dire. People said after the 2010 Lib Dem–Tory coalition they no longer understood what Farron's team stood for. In one question, respondents were asked if the party was 'dead', according to one senior aide. A sizeable proportion said it was and they could never vote for the Lib Dems again.

With the results of the poll in mind, the Lib Dems set out to convince voters that they could be trusted on Brexit. There could be no ambiguity. 'They needed to know when push came to shove where our red lines were,' says one aide close to Farron. But at the meeting to decide the manifesto, the desire for clear red lines collided with the reality of a party trying to win seats in parts of the country that had voted to leave the EU.[264]

Norman Lamb, who had stood against Farron for the leadership two years earlier, refused point-blank to endorse a pledge to campaign for Remain in a referendum on the final Brexit deal before the terms of the settlement had even been negotiated. Lamb argued that the position amounted to dismissing the result of the first referendum and would be seen as such by voters, certainly in his Norfolk constituency, where the Tories were closing in. He said it was an incredible position to take and would be indefensible on the doorstep. According to two sources in the room, Lamb's argument led to one committee member leaving in tears.

SOFT BREXIT, NOT NO BREXIT

The Lib Dems' internal struggle over Brexit exposes the dilemma that faced many pro-Remain parties, from the SNP to Plaid Cymru as well as Labour. Much of the electorate saw Brexit as a process that was already happening and not as a question to be debated all over again, however much some politicians wanted to reverse the referendum result. According to the British Election Study, which interviewed 30,000 voters throughout the campaign, by May 'the Brexit debate was not so much about whether or not to Leave or Remain, but about how to leave the EU'. It was a question of soft or hard Brexit, not whether to Brexit. Labour and the Tories were offering answers to the question on the exam paper. The Lib Dems were still answering the question they flunked last time.

Farron's party also ran up against their age-old problem: the electoral system. When the Tories were comfortably above 40 per cent in the polls, voters who wanted something other than a hard Brexit had little choice in most seats but to back Labour, the British Election Study team found. 'A realisation amongst Remain voters that the Lib Dems could not win in most seats meant they were not the first choice for those favouring a soft Brexit,' the researchers said. The Lib Dems were not offering the country the alternative it wanted. Even if the party had done, the country did not believe Farron was in a position to deliver it.

LAST PAST THE POST

As the campaign wore on, with their poll ratings stalled below 10 per cent, it became clear that the hoped-for resurgence was not to be. In fact, the party was once again in a battle for survival. Inside Conservative campaign headquarters, some speculated that the Lib Dems could end up losing every one of their seats. Farron was being forced to spend more and more time in his own

constituency of Westmorland and Lonsdale to combat
a major Tory push there. In Scotland, they were under
pressure from the SNP, while in the north of England,
Labour was on the march.

The Tory rout of the Lib Dems' heartland in the south-
west in 2015 meant the party was reduced to defending disparate enclaves of territory, dotted around the
country so far apart it was impossible to run a national
campaign. They were fighting in North Norfolk and the
Shetland Isles, Sheffield and Eastbourne and few places
in between. Its final result would be creditable, losing
four seats in the north of England – including Nick
Clegg's – but winning eight others in mainly metropolitan, Remain-supporting areas, to finish with twelve MPs.
And yet even this relatively modest showing manages to
mask a much steeper decline in the party's fortunes. For
the second election running, the party lost its deposit in
over half the constituencies it contested.

It could have been different, but probably not in 2017.
The Tories made one important calculation in deciding
to move quickly. Lynton Crosby and Stephen Gilbert
believed the biggest threat to the Tory majority came
not from Labour but from the Lib Dems, particularly
in the West Country. But they believed that going for an
election early gave them a better chance of managing
this threat. Gilbert in particular argued that the threat
posed by the Lib Dems would only grow as the impact
of Brexit began to be felt. While this assessment under-
estimated Labour's resilience, it probably helped the
Tories trample on Tim Farron's revival before it could
spring into life. Without their knowing it, the Liberal

Democrats were being crushed by Brexit before the election had even been called.

UKIP

The other important Brexit calculation made by Theresa May's closest advisers was more straightforward: UKIP was finished. The party had been over for the purple people from the moment the Prime Minister backed a hard Brexit in her party conference speech in October 2016. What was the point in UKIP if the government was implementing its core policy of withdrawing from the EU anyway?

The last flickering signs of life appeared to have been finally extinguished in February when UKIP leader Paul Nuttall failed in his attempt to enter Parliament at the Stoke-on-Trent by-election that followed the departure of the Blairite MP Tristram Hunt, who left to run the V&A Museum. Stoke was deep in Brexit land and Labour was riven by divisions over both Europe and Jeremy Corbyn's leadership. If Nuttall could not win then and there, he would never win.

Nuttall's defeat followed revelations that he had exaggerated the personal impact that the 1989 Hillsborough stadium disaster had had on his life. In 2012, the UKIP leader claimed he had lost 'close personal friends' in the tragedy, but was forced to admit during the by-election campaign that this was, in fact, not the case. The admission was a reputational disaster that he found it impossible to overcome. 'His confidence was knocked

badly,' his election head of strategy Patrick O'Flynn
says. 'I don't think he was ever really able to become a
compelling leader.'[265]

BAD TIMING

When May's snap election announcement came, UKIP
was the only major political party not to have made any
plans at all, having believed the Prime Minister's repeated assurances that there would not be an election. 'We
were caught completely on the hop,' admits O'Flynn.
Nuttall responded in the only way a party leader can,
by 'welcoming' the opportunity, but it was through
gritted teeth. 'Make no mistake,' he said. The election is
'driven by Labour's obvious weakness, not the good of
the country'.

UKIP's problems were soon obvious. On Monday 24
April, almost a week after the election was called, Nuttall found himself holed up in a room at the Marriott
County Hall hotel near Parliament with a pack of journalists camped outside demanding to know if he would
stand as a candidate. He would not answer the question
for another four days – and even then would not say
which seat he would fight.

In the meantime, the party's former leader Nigel
Farage had flirted with and then rejected the chance
to stand again in Thanet, while Arron Banks, the mil-
lionaire party donor, promised to stand in Douglas
Carswell's old Clacton constituency, only to pull out.

On reflection, Farage, the party's talisman, says UKIP
'ceased to be relevant' in many voters' minds as soon

as Labour and the Tories accepted Brexit and the need for controls on EU immigration. 'UKIP was effectively out of the campaign early on,' he says. 'The really big issue was not being seen to be relevant. The word on the street was we were the party for Brexit but Mrs May says that's happening and so does Mr Corbyn so it's back to two-party politics.'[266]

UNITE THE RIGHT

To the outside world, UKIP looked a mess. Its leaders did not even know whether to fight the election or stand aside to allow the Tories to deliver Brexit unopposed. Different factions quickly opened up. One sizeable group believed the party should get out of the way to give May a clear run at winning a Brexit mandate. 'The party did not want to be blamed for blocking Brexit,' explains O'Flynn. 'That is what we were set up to achieve.'

A different wing of the party, led by its deputy leader Peter Whittle, felt it was important to stand everywhere. A compromise was reached for the party not to stand against Brexit-supporting MPs to insure against accusations that they were putting Brexit in jeopardy.

In the end, even this compromise did not go far enough for UKIP's members, who staged a near mutiny over the prospect of undermining May. UKIP's party executives had proposed not contesting 100 seats, almost all of which were Conservative-held. Honourable exceptions were made for Eurosceptic Labour MPs like Frank Field and Kate Hoey. But a grassroots revolt meant the party ended up fielding candidates in only 378 seats, down

from 624 just two years earlier. Of the 378 seats they contested, they failed to reach 5 per cent of the vote in 337.

When Farage announced he would not stand, 'the
signal went out that it was job done for UKIP', says
O'Flynn. 'Theresa May and to a certain extent the
Labour Party had taken our unique selling point. It
became pretty obvious we weren't going to win any
seats. First past the post killed us.'

The only seat UKIP had even the remotest chance of
winning was Thurrock, where it had a solid presence
on the council, but even there the party could finish no
better than third, with 20 per cent of the vote. In Boston
and Skegness, the constituency with the highest Brexit
vote in the country, Paul Nuttall limped home in third
place with just 7.7 per cent.

Overall, UKIP lost 3.27 million votes in the space of
two years. They went from 12.6 per cent of the national
vote in 2015 to 1.8 per cent, winning just 594,000 votes.
'Most party members just thought the most important
thing was safeguarding Brexit,' explains O'Flynn, who
was tasked with trying to save the party's campaign.
'The worst thing was not being crushed to death, but
being crushed to oblivion – and the Tories still almost
blowing it.'

UNINTENDED CONSEQUENCES

The Tory high command had predicted UKIP would collapse. What they did not expect was that in many seats a
chunk of its support would go to Labour. 'Safeguarding
Brexit' in seats like Peterborough meant standing aside for

leading Eurosceptics such as Stewart Jackson only to see them lose to a resurgent Labour Party. Farage explains:

> Everybody underestimated how much UKIP's rise came directly from the Labour Party. The Tories would never have had a majority in 2015 without UKIP. For a lot of Labour voters, voting UKIP isn't very difficult, but it's almost impossible to vote Tory. Where UKIP stood aside to help Tory Eurosceptics, it actually hurt them.

By embracing Brexit and promising control of immigration, the Tories had united the right, crushed UKIP and found a policy that reached directly into Labour's working-class heartlands. Their one concern – a Lib Dem revival – did not materialise. What Tory high command could not countenance was the idea that Labour could become the vehicle for the 48 per cent who voted Remain in the EU referendum, without alienating its Brexit heartlands in the north of England and Wales. Through its policy of deliberate ambiguity, Labour found a way to pull this off and reach into the centre-ground to appeal to moderate pro-Europeans who had backed Remain but now accepted Brexit.

In the end, more than half of UKIP's 2015 vote went to the Tories, but one in five turned red – a significant proportion. An even bigger slice of the Lib Dem vote from 2015 backed Corbyn, with a quarter jumping ship, according to the British Election Study. Labour's carefully constructed position on Brexit neutralised what could have been a toxic issue for the party. It allowed Corbyn to talk to UKIP supporters about other issues like police cuts and school funding.

Brexit created the conditions to crush the smaller parties as election forces. The referendum split the country and the two halves looked to the two biggest parties to represent their opposing views. It took some clever calculations from Labour and Tory strategists to make it happen, but the Lib Dems and UKIP paid the price. In England, at least, two-party politics was back.

CHAPTER 18

LONDON BRIDGE

With just four days of the campaign left, terror struck once again.

At 10.04 p.m. on Saturday 3 June, three Islamist fanatics from east London began a frenzy of violence that killed eight and injured forty-eight more. The attack on London Bridge was less sophisticated than the Manchester Arena bombing that had occurred only twelve days earlier, but its impact on the election was no less profound.

The killers hit as the first editions of the Sunday newspapers were being sent and terror was finally off the front pages. The *Sunday Times* and the *Sunday Telegraph* led with claims of hidden Labour tax rises, while the *Mail on Sunday* splashed with an op-ed from the Prime Minister attacking Jeremy Corbyn's refusal to say whether he would authorise the use of Britain's nuclear weapons, and including Gareth Milner's tape of Seumas Milne. Both the *Mail on Sunday* and the *Sunday Times* also reported a dramatic tightening in the polls, with Labour narrowing the gap to as little as one percentage point. The Conservatives desperately needed the public to focus their minds on their twin campaign themes: Brexit and leadership.

May's most senior advisers had predicted days after

the Manchester attack that the election would return to its core question – Who do you want in No. 10? – but it had taken a long time to get there. Social care, security and austerity had dominated the agenda for two weeks.

London Bridge stopped everything. With little more than 100 hours until polling, the campaigns would once again be suspended and questions over security would surge back into focus. Most observers assumed it would help May – Corbyn was weak on security, after all – but it did no such thing. Corbyn successfully turned security into a question of Tory austerity.

Labour's response to terror in Manchester was politically adept. Its response to London Bridge would be even more so. The speed with which Corbyn politicised the tragedy sparked disgust inside the highest ranks of the Conservative campaign. But May's own actions stirred anger within the Labour Party too.

DÉJÀ VU

The Prime Minister had just finished dinner at Chequers, just over an hour from Downing Street, when she received the news of the attack on Saturday night.[267] She was immediately driven back to London to begin the now familiar routine of terror and its aftermath.

A statement was released by email shortly after midnight. Again, no tweeting. The Prime Minister simply confirmed that she had received updates from the police and security services and the incident was being treated as 'a potential act of terrorism'.

A Cobra meeting was called for Sunday morning,

with Sadiq Khan, the London mayor, in attendance. As had become customary, the Prime Minister would make a statement outside No. 10 afterwards. It was a routine the country had grown familiar with.

May's first use of social media did not come until 10 a.m. on Sunday, when she tweeted a link to a video of the statement she had made. After the argument in CCHQ following the Manchester attack, Timothy and Hill received no push-back this time. 'We now know it's not appropriate to continue with this line of argument,' says one senior Conservative campaign official involved in the discussions.

Jeremy Corbyn, by contrast, had no qualms about expressing his concern on Twitter. At 12.26 a.m., he wrote: 'Brutal and shocking incidents reported in London. My thoughts are with the victims and their families. Thank you to the emergency services.'

POLITICS

Unlike Manchester, there was no call between the Prime Minister and the Leader of the Opposition that night or the next morning. Having heard nothing from No. 10, Seumas Milne tried to call Hill directly to ensure that the two parties coordinated whatever break in campaigning might be required again. She did not answer or return his call. No doubt Hill, Timothy and May were busy working on the response to the attack. Some Labour officials believe the Tories simply did not want to cooperate. 'They played the second one extremely differently,' says a senior figure close to the Labour leader.

Whereas the first one she was extremely cooperative and collegiate, even though they were trying to push the suspension longer, her approach to it was much more national. The second one was not at all. I think they had decided that they had mishandled the first one, that somehow we had come out better from it and they weren't going to do that again.

The lack of communication between the two parties was reflected in their public statements that morning. The Tories were first to announce that they would not campaign nationally all day. Then, at 8.44 a.m., Corbyn said Labour would stop campaigning 'as a mark of respect' – but only until the evening, when he was due at a rally in Carlisle. 'Those who wish to harm our people, divide our communities and attack our democracy will not succeed,' Corbyn said. Terrorists will not 'derail our democratic process'. Labour were determined to get back to the stump.

At just after 10.30 a.m., May emerged from No. 10 to update the nation. The sight of the Prime Minister sombre, tired and reflecting on tragedy had become all too familiar in recent weeks. But this time May was angrier – and more political. 'Enough is enough,' she said, proclaiming that extremism could no longer be tolerated.

TORY TERROR PLAN

The Prime Minister's statement began conventionally enough. 'Last night, our country fell victim to a brutal terrorist attack once again,' she said, before rehearsing

the sequence of events. Three terrorists had come armed
with knives and fake suicide vests to kill and terrorise
ordinary Londoners out enjoying their Saturday night.
Eight minutes later, all three had been shot dead by
armed police.

May made no attempt to play down the threat Britain
faced from Islamist violence. It was the third terrorist
attack on British soil in three months, but five other
'credible plots' had been foiled in that period alone. It
was time to draw a line, she said. 'We believe we are
experiencing a new trend in the threat we face,' May
declared. Because the terror threat had changed, so too
must the government's response. 'We cannot and must
not pretend that things can continue as they are. Things
need to change, and they need to change in four important ways,' May announced.

First, British values had to be promoted to turn people's minds away from violence. Second, there needed to
be a crackdown on internet providers to 'regulate cyber-
space'. Third, less tolerance of extremism. And fourth,
more powers for the security services and, if necessary,
longer prison terms. To watching Labour officials, it was
clear that the Tory leader was writing a new chapter in
her election manifesto, designed to win votes – at the
very moment she claimed to be putting her campaign
on pause.

May's decision to escalate her rhetoric that morning is
crucial to understanding Labour's next move. A Corbyn
speech focusing on NHS cuts that had been planned for
the Carlisle rally that evening was ripped up. Instead, he
wanted to take on the Tories over terrorism, just hours
after an attack on the capital.

WHATEVER IS NECESSARY

Milne and Corbyn's other senior advisers – including campaign coordinators Andrew Gwynne and Ian Lavery – had pushed hard that morning not to agree to a long suspension in campaigning. They were also confident that, having successfully set the agenda on police cuts after Manchester they could match May's rhetoric with their own on austerity.

A year earlier, Corbyn's operation might have reacted to May's speech with simple opposition, but they had learned on the job. His response that evening would remain unorthodox, criticising the government in the midst of another terrorism crisis. But he would also move to close down any potential areas of weakness that could be attacked. It showed that the reluctant leader of 2015 was serious about winning two years later.

Corbyn began his speech by announcing that he was 'ready to consider whatever proposals may be brought forward by the police and security services' to deal with the increased threat. It was not a commitment to hand over more powers to the spooks, but for a man who had boasted that he had opposed every piece of anti-terror legislation brought forward by a government since entering Parliament, it was a concession.

He then went further, addressing Tory attacks on his equivocation about the power of the police to shoot to kill – the very action that had been necessary to bring an end to the massacre at London Bridge hours earlier. 'Our priority must be public safety and I will take whatever action is necessary and effective to protect the security of our people.' Crucially, this included 'whatever force is necessary to protect and save life' – including shooting terrorists dead.

Having moved to close off points of weakness, he pivoted to attack – demanding an end to police cuts and public sector pay freezes. Suddenly, austerity had become a question of national security.

> We are the fifth richest country in the world – it doesn't have to be like this. The Labour Party will end austerity and lift the public sector pay cap. Our nurses, firefighters, police, doctors and paramedics deserve a pay rise. They cannot just get warm words for their heroism, they deserve our respect every day.

Before finishing, Corbyn opened up a fresh line of attack designed to question the Tories' credentials on security. You can't be tough on terror if you're friends with the Saudis, Corbyn declared. This new front, while almost entirely ignored by most of the biggest-selling newspapers, was picked up and pushed hard by Momentum and other third-party groups online.

The speech in Carlisle was classic Milne, refusing to accept the narrative, but with added seriousness about winning. This was not the speech of a man who had given up hope of taking power.

TRUMP

Jeremy Corbyn's cause received an unexpected boost that day from the unlikeliest of sources – the President of the United States. On Sunday, hours after London mayor Sadiq Khan had made a statement urging Londoners not to be alarmed by the extra police presence in the city over the coming days, Donald Trump took to Twitter to accuse Khan of playing down the terror threat. 'At least seven dead and forty-eight wounded in terror attack and mayor of London says there is "no reason to be alarmed!"' he said.

The London mayor's office responded, saying Khan had 'more important things to do than respond to Donald Trump's ill-informed tweet that deliberately takes out of context his remarks'.

Trump's intervention was to prove a major source of grief for May over the next forty-eight hours, forcing her even further back onto the defensive at a crucial moment, as she was repeatedly asked to condemn his remarks. At a news conference the next day, she was twice probed about Trump's comments before finally being asked: 'What would Donald Trump have to say for you to criticise him publicly?'

Only when she was asked a fourth time that afternoon, in a Q&A following a speech in central London, did May offer even the mildest of rebukes, telling reporters Khan was doing a good job and anyone who said otherwise was wrong, without mentioning Trump by name.

It exposed the same weakness that infuriated Tory campaigners: May was not quick enough to react. In the immediate aftermath of the terror attacks, she had been pushed onto the defensive on police cuts, public sector pay, Saudi Arabia and Donald Trump. Corbyn was getting his usual kicking in the Tory-supporting press, of course, but he didn't care.

AUSTERITY RETURNS

If the test of May's and Corbyn's anti-terror plans was how they were covered on the Monday morning round of TV and radio shows, then the Labour leader was the clear winner. From ITV's *Good Morning Britain* to the *Today* programme on BBC Radio 4, police budget cuts was the dominant theme. It was a disaster for May.

The Tories despatched the former Home Office minister turned Culture Secretary Karen Bradley to speak on their behalf. It started off badly and never recovered.

On ITV, the presenter Piers Morgan pressed Bradley repeatedly on whether armed police numbers had gone up or down. After failing to get an answer, Morgan took a verbal swipe that would help the exchange go 'viral' online: 'Is there any reason why you can't answer the question?'

Bradley pushed ahead. 'Piers, we are here to talk about the attack on Saturday, how we react to that attack and how we make sure on Thursday that we have the right person elected to Downing Street so that we can deal with it.'

'So you just don't want to answer?' Morgan shot back.

The government had, of course, reduced armed police numbers as part of the 18 per cent budget cut to the service during the previous parliament. The number had dropped from 6,976 in March 2010 to 5,639 six years later.

*   *   *

The case against Tory austerity was given an unlikely publicity boost on Monday morning when David Cameron's former strategy chief Steve Hilton accused May of being 'responsible' for the London Bridge attack and called on her to resign. The story gained immediate traction. By midday, Corbyn had weighed in, telling ITV news that he agreed. Asked if he backed calls for her resignation, he said: 'Indeed I would.'

Calling for the Prime Minister to quit three days before the general election might seem absurd, but it was certainly not what the Tories wanted to be talking about. 'Instead of having a week arguing about economics, you have a week defending the indefensible,' one May adviser says. 'And worse – they weren't David Cameron's police cuts, or Iain Duncan Smith's police cuts, they were Theresa May's police cuts. It was uniquely negative for us.'[268]

TOO SLOW

Senior Tory strategists believe May's failure to fight back immediately was disastrous. They argue that it exposed her team's inexperience and unwillingness to listen to advice from outside their tight inner circle. One disclosed that Timothy and Hill refused to take a decision to rebut the Labour attacks or move the debate onto something else. 'They wouldn't respond for forty-eight hours,' the strategist says. Amid mounting alarm, Crosby, Textor and Messina tried to intervene. 'Tex stormed in and said they won't listen to us on the police thing. They won't respond. They don't think it's a big deal,' one witness to a top-level meeting recalls. 'In the age of social media you can't sit there for forty-eight fucking hours. There is just no way you can do that. You've got to respond instantly.' the adviser says.[269]

For his part, Lynton Crosby says the terrorist attacks had a significant impact. 'The terrorist attack in Manchester had a practical influence,' he says. 'It disrupted the election because quite rightly the parties paused their campaigning. That happened at a time when we needed to try to rebuild. Labour very effectively turned the second attack at London Bridge into an argument about police numbers.'[270]

Tory headquarters received feedback from the campaign teams on the ground. One person sent a text message to HQ saying: 'I've just been down an entire street where the only thing anyone said was police cuts and terrorism.'

TOO LITTLE, TOO LATE

Theresa May would spend most of Monday and Tuesday, before the Thursday election, trying to get back on the front foot but never quite cutting through. She tried to drag the question on the ballot paper back to leadership.

'In three days, the British people will choose who they want to lead this country through the next five years,' she said. 'Five years that will define the future of our country for generations to come.' Brexit, she said, remained 'the most critical issue in this campaign' and should not be forgotten in the aftermath of the two terror attacks. 'I want to return to the choice people face in three days' time and to the crucial question of leadership. Because that's what this election is about. It's about which leader and which team people trust to take the big decisions that matter to Britain.'

Tory campaigners are sceptical about whether they could have said anything to put people off voting for Corbyn. One Conservative campaigner says:

> You can say anything you want about Jeremy Corbyn, but it didn't matter. He could have believed in the most socially abhorrent things, but it wouldn't have mattered because no one thought he was going to win. So [in response to our] attacks on him, people were like, 'Yeah, that's right, but he's not going to win, is he?' But for us, any suspicion that we might do something was much more real because expectations were very high.[271]

Jim Messina says he saw the problem as soon as he landed in the UK. 'The very first thing I said when I flew into London was we've got to deal with expectations because you know this race is going to be close and Corbyn is going to rise from a low base. This is still a centre-left country and he was going to get things back.'[272]

Inside May's inner circle, they were also annoyed at the headlines that cast doubt on the Prime Minister's record on security. Hill texted one journalist on Tuesday 6 June: 'Explain to me how Theresa has a mixed security record.'

That morning, *The Sun*, *Mirror* and *Mail* had all splashed on how one of the London Bridge killers, Khuram Butt, had slipped through the net despite featuring on a Channel 4 documentary called *The Jihadis Next Door*, where he had unfurled an ISIS flag in a London park.

In spite of the continuing debate over police cuts and security service failures, the Prime Minister's aides were still unaware of how bad things were getting. 'We are looking good on the ground,' Hill insisted. That night, pollsters Survation dropped another shock set of results, showing the Tory lead over Labour at just one point. If replicated two days later, it would see the Tory majority wiped out.

For almost three weeks, May had been on the defensive, first over the manifesto, then foreign policy and police cuts and finally her record combating terrorism, amid the fall-out from two devastating attacks. It is hard to imagine a worse run into polling day.

*   *   *

As the vote loomed, the two sides went back to basics. May returned to Brexit. Corbyn hit the road to meet his adoring masses. In an eve of poll interview with the BBC's political editor Laura Kuenssberg, May declared: 'Brexit is the basis of everything.' It was a return to the script, but terror still loomed large: 'I support the police shooting to kill terrorists,' she said. 'Jeremy Corbyn does not.'

For her final day's campaigning, May and her husband toured the country from London to Norwich, Southampton and the West Midlands. Corbyn, meanwhile, was back on his bus, sparking scenes of political Beatlemania as he travelled from Scotland to London, finishing where he felt most comfortable – Islington. At his final rally of the campaign, at Islington's Union Chapel, he recited those lines from Shelley's poem, telling the cheering crowd in the hall: 'Ye are many – they are few!'

Outside the building, thousands more crowded onto the pavements, holding up placards, and spilled onto Upper Street, halting the traffic as they waited in the drizzle for a glimpse of their leader. 'Oh, Jeremy Corbyn,' they chanted. There was a carnival atmosphere. Some smoked cannabis. Others drank Malbec. One young man shouted: 'We want our magic money tree!' An older woman fixed a hand-written sign to her head: 'We love you Jeremy,' it said. 'But more than that – we trust you.'

The next day's *Sun* front page flashed up on social media and TV news channels. 'Don't chuck Britain in the Cor-bin', it read, with an image of the Labour leader poking out of a dustbin. Previous Labour leaders might have wept at such a headline on polling day from Murdoch's mighty tabloid, which political leaders have courted for years. But when the front page was passed around Corbyn's most senior advisers, Milne and Schneider burst out laughing.

PART FOUR

THE ELECTION

CHAPTER 19

ELECTION NIGHT

On Thursday 8 June, the Prime Minister awoke to a cool, overcast morning in Berkshire. With her husband Philip, she arrived at the polling station in Sonning shortly after 9 a.m., ready to vote. There to greet them were armed police officers and someone wearing the costume of the *Sesame Street* puppet character Elmo.

As she entered the polling booth, wearing her 'lucky' leopard skin kitten heels, May had reasons to feel confident, despite her natural caution. Her campaign consultants, hired to deliver victory at great expense, had led her team to believe they were on course for a healthy win, though Timothy had confided to friends two weeks earlier that he feared he would get the blame if the landslide did not materialise. The signs from Lynton Crosby and Mark Textor, as well as Jim Messina's unit, were that the Tories would win at least 350 seats, or a majority of fifty or more. Some in May's senior team expected a majority of closer to eighty after the forecast Messina had provided a week earlier, according to an aide. At last, the public polls finally appeared to be moving in the right direction for the weary Conservative campaign. A survey published in *The Times* by YouGov, the company that first forecast a hung parliament, put the Tories on 42 per cent, seven points clear of Labour.

After casting her ballot and smiling for the cameras, May did what millions of voters were doing at the same time around the country: she went to work.

In London, Crosby sent Nick Timothy a text message at 9.25 a.m. The polls had been open for more than two hours and it was a nervous time for all.

'How you holding up?' Crosby asked.

'I feel good thanks,' Timothy replied. 'What do you reckon?'

Crosby's response was positive but contained a note of caution, too. 'We should do well. My hesitation is any Labour ground effort that we are not picking up the impact of. In some seats they sent three or four direct mail letters yesterday – people outside of London even got letters from Sadiq Khan!'

When she arrived at No. 10 in mid-morning, the Prime Minister went upstairs to the flat. Her two chiefs and their deputy – Timothy, Hill and Penn – joined her. They discussed the campaign, and how the results might go over the next twenty-four hours.

For Timothy, anxious about the impact of his manifesto, it was a painful question that had dogged him for weeks. He had been war-gaming different scenarios for the previous ten days and could foresee three possibilities. First, the Tories scrape a majority, but one no bigger or perhaps even smaller than before, 'in which case, we are finished', he told friends. The second was a 'decent' majority to govern but not big enough to justify the risk of calling the election and causing some good MPs to lose their seats. In this case, Timothy confided to one colleague, 'there will be a big debate in the party about what to do next which will be horrible, and really destructive for her premiership'. Result number three was the dream: a good majority, meaning May could enforce her agenda at last and reshape the party, despite opposition from 'traditional Tory opinion'. In this reality, May would have the Conservatives and the country at her feet.

The one scenario the Prime Minister and her aides did not entertain was no majority at all.

* * *

After an exhausting final day on the road, Jeremy Corbyn woke up back where he felt most comfortable: at home in Islington.

Shortly before 9.45 a.m., the Labour leader emerged from his 1960s townhouse to cast his vote. Before entering the polling station at Pakeman Primary School, around the corner from Arsenal's Emirates stadium, he stopped to chat to some of his constituents milling around outside.

In a message to the waiting cameras, Corbyn played it safe. It was 'a day for democracy', he declared before adding: 'I'm very proud of our campaign.' The final YouGov polls, which found a late dip in support for Labour, led some in the party to worry the race was turning against them. The pollsters at Survation were more positive for Corbyn, but their result was an 'outlier', forecasting the narrowest of Tory wins, 41.3 per cent to 40.4 per cent.

* * *

In Ipswich, Ben Gummer, the co-author of the Tory manifesto who had been tipped for promotion in the post-election reshuffle, was working with his campaign team to get the vote out. The signs were that his marginal seat would be a close call again. Turnout was up. Friends reported a strong surge for Corbyn, while, during the afternoon, there were worrying indications that more young people – who overwhelmingly supported Labour – would be voting this time than in the past. Parents were turning up armed with proxy votes in numbers that Gummer's team had not seen before. There were also more middle-aged people asking for directions to polling stations so they could vote for the first time. Gummer's experience was replicated in marginal seats across the country. Brexit-supporting members of the government, like James Wharton in Stockton South, or Stewart Jackson, aide to David Davis, in Peterborough, were watching anxiously too.

One Tory recalls: 'Polling day is always bloody awful because you interpret every averted gaze or smile as an omen.'

* * *

At 5 p.m., Corbyn and his advisers met at a hotel near Vauxhall Bridge in central London to plan the night ahead. Seumas Milne chose the obscure venue for some privacy, away from the cameras and reporters gathered at Southside.

In the room, the group went through four potential outcomes, based on the recent polls, which showed them between 1 per cent and 13 per cent behind the

Tories. The picture from Labour's own pollsters BMG was pessimistic. For most of the campaign, BMG had been forecasting a Tory majority of 150. On election day, they thought May was on course for a majority of 80.[273]

John McDonnell was lined up to give the first reactions live in television studios, as the exit poll figures flashed up at 10 p.m. He needed to have his lines ready to go. Labour's most optimistic plan was based on a hung parliament. The other three involved outright defeat.

Scenario one was denying the Tories a majority. Scenario two was an increase in the vote that did not translate into more seats. The third outcome they considered was worse: Labour's share of the vote increases but so does the gap between the two main parties. This was the central forecast of most pollsters. Under Labour's imagined scenario, they would be on around 35 per cent, with the Tories on 43 per cent. This would probably mean an increased majority for May, Corbyn was told, but would also represent a share of the vote for Labour last seen in 2005 under Tony Blair. This would be good news for the leader and his socialist supporters.

The worst-case scenario the party prepared for was a crushing Tory landslide. It was called the 'we are wrong and everyone else is right' outcome, one aide recalls. For Corbyn, this would have meant the end.

*   *   *

At a secret location in London, Professor John Curtice from the University of Strathclyde and his team of psephologists worked all day on the exit poll research. They analysed interviews with 30,000 people who had just voted, at a sample of 144 polling stations around the country. The exit poll would give the first clear signal of how Britain had voted.[274]

The research team hid away in three rooms in the corporation's basement, accessible only to a handful of people whose names were on a list given to a security guard manning the entrance. There was a room for the researchers, a room for the three broadcasters who pay for the poll – the BBC, ITV and Sky – and a separate room for catering.

Throughout the day, dumps of data arrived for the academics to analyse. At around 4.30 p.m., Curtice himself got to work on a whiteboard, where he started writing the raw figures before adding seat projections. His team of psephologists then started to apply their modelling to take into account local factors that might explain anomalies in the numbers.

When the academics had remodelled the numbers, Curtice wrote the first tentative forecast on the board for the select few in the room to see. More 'data dumps' came in after 5 p.m., allowing him to adjust his figures further. The entire exercise was conducted in the tightest security and secrecy. 'There's never a leak,' says one of those who has seen the process up close. The figures are market-sensitive. BBC staff fear that any deliberate breach of the strict secrecy rules could be treated as a form of market manipulation. 'It would be a very big deal,' says another senior broadcaster who has been involved in the process several times.

* * *

For almost the first time since entering Downing Street eleven months earlier, Nick Timothy found himself with little to do. He tried to sleep, knowing he would be working through the night. By mid-afternoon, he had given up on resting and called in at 'central office', as he still likes to call Conservative campaign headquarters. The operations team gave him an update and the signs were still positive.

Teams in the field believed the Conservatives were well-placed. 'Turnout is high in our areas, there's evidence people in more traditional working-class Labour areas are voting for us,' Timothy was told. Target seats in the East Midlands, Birmingham and the north of England were looking good. Even Bolsover, the seat of the veteran Labour MP Dennis Skinner, looked potentially to be turning blue. Campaign chiefs were also positive about the picture in Scotland, though there was some superstition that previous elections had been a false dawn for the party, which had had just one MP north of the border since 2001. The picture in the south-west, where Cameron and Crosby had swept away the Liberal Democrats in 2015, looked solid.

Tory hopes had been boosted by an unusual phone call to party headquarters. It was from Barack Obama. The former US President knew someone who had a friend working on Labour's campaign. Obama heard that Corbyn's team expected to lose twenty or thirty seats. This would leave Labour further from power – but the result would not be bad enough to force Corbyn out. As the election drew to a close, Obama rang a friend on the Tory side to pass on the encouraging message: Labour are likely to lose a few seats, meaning the Tory majority will go up. And even better – the disastrous Corbyn is here to stay.

When the evening came, Timothy, Fiona Hill and JoJo Penn went out for dinner to take a break from the office. They could not afford to stray far, so chose the Caxton Grill, a restaurant attached to St Ermin's Hotel, where senior campaign staff were staying. The three friends chatted over wagyu beef burgers, fried onion rings and glasses of wine, trying not to think too hard about the night in front of them. Outside and around the country, the evening rush was picking up at polling stations, as millions of voters called in to cast their ballots on their way home from work.

* * *

By 9.30 p.m., John Curtice had his final exit poll forecast. Ten minutes later, he briefed a handful of the most senior journalists and executives at the BBC, assembled in a room behind the studio where David Dimbleby would present the election night coverage, starting with the exit poll announcement at 10 p.m. Those listening to Curtice as he revealed his results included Dimbleby, the BBC political editor Laura Kuenssberg, James Harding, the director of news, and Tony Hall, the director general, who joined the meeting by phone.

* * *

Just over 250 miles away, in the small Cumbrian village of Milnthorpe, Tim Farron clambered over a neighbour's fence into his garden after a final day of door-knocking

in his constituency. It was just before 10 p.m. He was
tired and could not face speaking to the reporters
camped outside his front door. Farron just wanted to
get home to put his children to bed. He asked his neighbours if he could use their garden to avoid walking past
the media scrum. Creeping in through the back door, he
found his wife Rosie and their four children waiting for
him to come home.

Farron's chief of staff Ben Williams was inside, braced
for the exit poll. They were not optimistic but felt they
had done all they could. Farron's own seat of Westmorland and Lonsdale was on a knife edge and could fall to
the Tories for the first time in sixteen years. Three days
earlier, the Lib Dems feared they could be left with just
three MPs.

*   *   *

In the war room on the ground floor of No. 4 Matthew
Parker Street, the mood among Conservative staffers
was a jittery mix of excitement and nerves. Upstairs
on the fourth floor, where Timothy and Gummer had
orchestrated the ill-fated manifesto, a party was being
prepared. Blue balloons attached to white sticks were
strewn around the open-plan room, with quiche, dips
and sandwiches from Waitrose laid out for party food.
Bottles of white wine and rosé were put on standby,
along with some beer. A few staff had brought their own
supplies of sherry and scotch.[275]

All were waiting for one thing: the polls to close at
10 p.m. and broadcasters to release the official exit poll
results.

Shortly before 10 p.m., Fiona Hill's phone buzzed. It was Andrew Marr, the BBC presenter and political journalist. He had the exit poll result and wondered if Hill had any comment on whether she thought it was right. Hill immediately grabbed Nick Timothy and pulled him into a side room off the main floor.

'I've just heard the exit poll – they're predicting a hung parliament,' Hill said.

'Are you winding me up?' Timothy asked.[276]

*   *   *

Corbyn was at home in Islington waiting for Seumas Milne and Karie Murphy, who were due to watch the exit poll with him. Milne was cutting it fine as he drove from Southside, but thought he had just enough time to grab a couple of bottles of Peroni from the off-licence before knocking on his boss's door. Corbyn almost never drinks alcohol but his director of strategy was planning ahead, in case of an emergency. Milne arrived at 9.50 p.m. and found Corbyn and his wife Laura Alvarez with their friend Carmel Nolan, the Stop the War activist who had worked on the first leadership campaign. Corbyn and Alvarez had been out for dinner at a restaurant in Islington earlier but they had made food for their guests – Mexican tortillas with egg.

The Labour leader asked everyone in the room to guess what the party's vote share would be. Each had to write a number on a piece of paper and hand it in. Corbyn and Milne were close in their prediction. Neither expected to be walking into No. 10 the next day, but both thought the party would do well. Murphy was the most optimistic. 'Karie was definitely getting ready to take over in Downing Street,' says one who was there.[277]

Even then, with one poll putting them within a single percentage point of the Tories, Corbyn and his closest advisers were not debating seat numbers. They were not calculating their chances of forming a government. Corbyn's team were only thinking about one thing: winning a big enough share of the vote to make it impossible for his opponents to justify ousting him as leader.

As the clock approached 10 p.m., Corbyn, his wife and three of his closest political operatives crowded round the TV. Murphy was bouncing with excitement, sure they were going to pull off something extraordinary. The rest were nervous, but trying to stay calm.[278]

*   *   *

As the seconds ticked down to 10 p.m., Tory ministers including Defence Secretary Michael Fallon were waiting in broadcasters' studios for guidance from Hill on what he should say. Hill and Timothy called Alex Dawson, another No. 10 aide who ran the Tory research department, to join them in the Derby Room just off the main open-plan war room. They discussed the script that ministers like Fallon and other party spokesmen should use in response to the avalanche of media questions that was about to come. They played it straight: it's only an exit poll, let's wait and see.

Hill approached Will Tanner and hugged him. 'It is all going to be OK,' she said. 'Something's funny with the exit poll, don't worry about it.' Then she broke away to take a call. The chiefs stepped into the VIP room where

Crosby, Textor and Gilbert were waiting for the official announcement.

*   *   *

As Big Ben struck 10 p.m., Theresa May couldn't watch. Instead, she asked her husband Philip to watch for her. She wanted to hear the news from him, not the TV. Philip waited in silence at the home they shared in Sonning as the exit poll predictions flashed up on the screen.

'And what we're saying is: the Conservatives are the largest party,' intoned Dimbleby, the veteran BBC election night presenter. 'Note – they don't have an overall majority at this stage.' The number 314 appeared next to an image of May's face, a forecast loss of seventeen seats – and twelve short of a majority. Labour were up thirty-four seats on 266, with thirty-four for the SNP and fourteen for the Liberal Democrats.

Philip went to find his wife. He told her the news and he hugged her. It took a moment for her to understand the scale of the disaster. When she did, a devastated May broke down and wept.[279]

*   *   *

On BBC TV, Marr came on screen to discuss the astonishing exit poll. 'Well, the reaction of senior Conservatives – and I've talked to a few – is that they flatly don't believe it.' Defence Secretary Michael Fallon told the BBC: 'Let's see some actual results. These exit polls have been wrong in the past. In 2015 they underestimated our vote.'

On the international markets, the pound tanked, falling 1.3 per cent against the dollar in two minutes.

Inside CCHQ, it was as if all the air had been sucked out of the room, according to those who were present. Scores of campaign staff stood in complete silence, staring at the central bank of TV screens in the war room as broadcasters described how the poll would mean the Prime Minister's gamble had spectacularly failed.

Timothy quickly collected his papers and laptop, caught Will Tanner's eye and winked at him. 'Don't worry about that, it's all fine,' the chief of staff said briskly. 'Nothing we've seen says anything like it.'

Crosby and Messina couldn't understand the results, telling colleagues they thought it could be an epic blunder, and Hill said she did not believe it. Mark Textor was quiet. Stephen Gilbert feared the poll was right.

Then May called. She was clearly shocked, but she remained calm and asked Timothy's view. 'Obviously this is bad if it's true, but it's only an exit poll so let's see,' he told her. 'It doesn't match what anybody expects or what we've been told through the day.'

In the war room, nobody had moved since Dimbleby had read out the figures. Crosby eventually decided someone had to cheer up the staff for the long night of work that was still ahead. 'There are 150 people out there who don't know what's going on. Somebody has got to do something,' he said. 'Fuck it, I'll do it if no one else is going to do it, I'll do it. I don't mind.' So Crosby came out of the VIP suite and walked among the desks, joking with people and slapping them on the back. 'The BBC's never been right about anything in their lives,' he said.

*   *   *

In Uxbridge, west London, Boris Johnson had finished his burger and was sipping a pint of Young's ale in the Conservative club in his constituency. The exit poll flashed up on a projector screen in the club's bar. 'His reaction was the same as everyone else in the room – crushing surprise and astonishment,' says one Tory watching with Johnson and his wife Marina Wheeler that night.

Despite his shock, the Foreign Secretary knew the focus of attention would rapidly shift to him – and his chances of replacing May in No. 10. He had been in this situation a year earlier, in the aftermath of the Brexit vote.

'Right, ignore your phones. No one talks to anyone,' Johnson ordered his aides. He knew any answer from his office to any question from a journalist about the Tory leadership could be twisted or exaggerated into a story. 'People have accused him of being on manoeuvres that night, but he was incredibly disciplined,' one source says. Johnson's own majority was cut in half.

*   *   *

In Islington, Corbyn smiled broadly. 'They under-estimated me,' he said. It was a moment of personal vindication, though expressed with typical understatement. 'He's not a very demonstrative character but he was definitely pleased,' according to an aide who was with him. 'He felt it was an achievement.'

Almost immediately, the phone started ringing. Corbyn spoke to John McDonnell and answered calls and texts from his friends and family. Milne and Murphy also talked to officials in Southside. The Labour leader was anxious that excited colleagues should not give in to 'euphoria' before the real results started being declared. 'In Jeremy's house there was quite a lot of caution,' says one witness.

*   *   *

At Southside, Labour's most senior executives gathered on the eighth floor, with a team of thirty from the election chief Patrick Heneghan's results unit. The rest of the Labour staff were on the second floor celebrating.

No one in the building received a tip-off about the exit poll, but rumour reached at least one of the party's most senior officials that the Tories had been leaked the result and it was 'shocking'. They quickly weighed the possibilities. Labour's own pollsters had forecast a Tory majority of eighty to ninety so they braced for two things: a Tory landslide or a hung parliament.

When the result was announced, people were stunned. 'We all looked at each other with raised eyebrows,' says one. They had been burnt in 2015 when the final tally of seats ended up worse than first forecast for Labour. The cheering was muted.

*   *   *

Back in the Lake District, Tim Farron watched the exit poll figures flash up on screen from his living room with his wife and chief of staff. Lib Dem HQ warned him the result looked 'too high'.

* * *

Nicola Sturgeon was with her husband Peter Murrell at home in Glasgow. If it was a shock for the Prime Minister in Sonning, her counterpart north of the border was just as taken aback. The exit poll forecast the SNP losing twenty-two MPs. The Scottish First Minister would soon face calls to sack her own husband as the party's chief executive.

* * *

The early results seemed to bear out the Tory optimists, who included Jim Messina. Peter Kellner, president of YouGov, one of the more pessimistic of the pollsters about the Tories' chances during the campaign, said the real results in Sunderland and Newcastle were not as positive for Labour as the exit poll suggested they should be, if Curtice's calculations were to prove accurate. If this pattern was replicated across the UK, May could still get her landslide, Kellner said. Other commentators pointed out that the exit poll included seventy-six seats that were 'too close to call', and did not include postal votes, which could also help the Tories.

Then, at 11.30 p.m., Ben Gummer's phone rang. It was a close friend calling from Gummer's count. Although the result was not yet official, it was clear from looking at the piles of ballot papers that Gummer had lost by about 1,000 votes. At that point, he feared the exit poll would be right. Gummer texted Timothy, who was distraught for his colleague, and for what it signalled for the party.

'Are you absolutely sure?' Timothy asked.

'I trust my team. They know how to do this,' Gummer replied. Like anyone who suddenly loses their job, the former minister's thoughts turned to his family.

At 11.59 p.m., Timothy got the news he was dreading. Tory Justin Tomlinson had held onto Swindon North – but with a significant 3.7 per cent swing to Labour. 'Oh fuck,' he said. The reality of what was happening began to hit home.

*   *   *

For Labour, Swindon North was the moment they started to believe in their dream.

At 1.10 a.m., while senior Tories continued to tell reporters that the exit poll could be wrong, Heneghan called Milne to tell him that there was no chance of the Tories hanging onto their majority. An excited Milne said he would get Corbyn to call Heneghan back immediately.

Karie Murphy, meanwhile, was spotted asleep on the sofa in general secretary Iain McNicol's office. McNicol woke her and told her she might need to speak to Downing Street officials about forming a coalition. Events were moving fast.

When Corbyn rang back, Heneghan ran through the party's findings, according to those who witnessed the exchange.

Had May really lost her majority, Corbyn wanted to know.

'Yes, it's gone,' Heneghan said.

Corbyn gasped. 'That is just tremendous,' he said.

The Labour leader was told there was a 10 per cent chance that his party could finish the night with more seats than the Tories. Corbyn was forced to contemplate the prospect that he could be Prime Minister in the morning.

*   *   *

In Matthew Parker Street, Crosby, Timothy, Hill, Gilbert and Messina watched as results came in fast. At 1.57 a.m., the minister James Wharton lost Stockton South. He had been diverted during the campaign to help candidates in other areas, unaware of the danger he was in.

May's chiefs weighed up what the next day might bring. Fiona Hill stepped outside for another cigarette. Nick Timothy spent time chatting to Chris Wilkins, the strategy director and speech writer who had watched in dismay as his 'change' agenda was sidelined during the campaign. Timothy and Wilkins wondered aloud whether Britain was hours away from discovering what Boris Johnson would look like as Prime Minister.

Timothy was distraught that both his programme for reform and the politician to whom he had given a decade of his working life were in peril. He knew instantly the result would spell the end of his career in Downing Street. 'He just thought, whatever happened to her, that she would need him to go if she was going to carry on,' one of Timothy's friends recalls. 'He came to that conclusion immediately. Obviously, he was distressed for her but also fearful that the whole agenda we'd been driving was potentially now not going to happen.'

Aware how upset his boss was, Timothy also believed May herself should consider stepping down. The world

of politics is brutal at the best of times, even for Westminster bruisers with the thickest skins, and this was
not the best of times. Timothy did not want the woman
he had spent ten years working for, someone who was
his friend as well as his boss, to suffer the vicious wave
of recriminations from her party colleagues that would
inevitably follow. Perhaps, for her own good, she should
go.[280] 'Nick thought she should consider resigning,' one
Tory recalls. 'He wanted to protect her – he just felt it
would be really difficult for her.'[281]

He was not alone in his fears for May's wellbeing.
According to one member of May's senior team, even
her husband, Philip, who was distraught for his wife,
wondered whether she should resign.[282]

*　　*　　*

Timothy wondered if May's time in charge was over –
but he never had a chance to discuss it with her. Events
moved on quickly. May's own count in Maidenhead was
brought forward by an hour, robbing her and her aides
of time to adjust to their new reality. Timothy's attention
turned to what she should say. When he spoke to the
PM, they agreed it was still too early to be sure what
the final result would be and what it would all mean.
So Timothy and Wilkins drafted May a statement that
consisted of a 'holding line' to keep their options open.

A rumour circulating on the fringes of May's Downing Street team claims that she did consider quitting that
night. Some say she confided in her closest friends and
colleagues that she did not know how she could stay on
after presiding over such a disastrous result.

But May herself has denied thinking in this way.
Other senior individuals with strong claims to know the
Prime Minister's true state of mind that night insist she
was clear from the start that she had a duty, however
difficult it would be personally, to provide stability for
the country, and to stop Labour forming a government.
Timothy recalls:

> I don't think she ever thought that she'd have to go but
> I think she knew there might be people who might say
> that. She was just quite clear, from the off, that it was
> her responsibility to stop Corbyn being Prime Minister
> and to give the country stability. When you're the Prime
> Minister, that is your responsibility.[283]

*   *   *

The first public sign of Jeremy Corbyn came at 2.10 a.m.
when he emerged from his front door, alone, to be driven
to his count. As he climbed into the back of the waiting
Special Branch car, a group of supporters gathered outside
his home began cheering and singing 'Oh, Jeremy Corbyn'.

An hour later, he was re-elected Member of Parliament for Islington North, increasing his majority to an
eye-watering 40,086 votes.

At that point in the night, it was not clear who
would – or should – be Prime Minister. Corbyn did not
sugar-coat his message: May had lost her authority to
govern and should resign, he declared.

> The Prime Minister called the election because she
> wanted a mandate. Well the mandate she's got is lost

Conservative seats, lost votes, lost support and lost confidence. I would have thought that's enough to go, actually, and make way for a government that will be truly representative of the people of this country.

* * *

At 3 a.m., the Prime Minister, accompanied by her husband, arrived at the Magnet Leisure Centre in Maidenhead. May and her team went upstairs to a large room with a sofa and a TV, where they could watch other results from around the country being declared as they waited for hers. Members of May's constituency association were there in force, showing their support for the woman who had represented the constituency for the past twenty years. One result from Scotland lightened the grim mood when it appeared on screen. The SNP's leader at Westminster, Angus Robertson, had been ousted by a Tory. 'Well, there's some good news at least,' said May.

When the Prime Minister was called down to the sports hall for the declaration, she found a peculiar sight waiting for her. One of the stranger characters of election night, Lord Buckethead, dressed in a black cape, with something resembling a cylindrical waste-bin on his head, posed with his arms shooting at the sky, in the manner of a triumphant Usain Bolt.

Though there was a swing to Labour, May comfortably held her own seat. Now she needed to hold onto the country. 'At this time, more than anything else, this country needs a period of stability.' If the Conservatives have won the most seats and the most votes, 'then it will be incumbent on us to ensure that we have that period of stability and that is exactly what we will do', she said.

It was far from convincing. May's voice was shaky. The BBC noted how the heavy make-up on her face suggested an attempt to conceal that she had been crying. May thanked Tory voters. The party had put forward a plan for Brexit and to tackle the challenges facing Britain 'in the national interest', she said. 'That is always what I have tried to do in my time as a Member of Parliament and my resolve to do that is the same this morning as it always has been.' Some watching inside CCHQ heard these words and believed the Prime Minister would not last until dawn.

*   *   *

Watching May's speech 180 miles away in Altrincham, Greater Manchester, was the influential chairman of the Conservative Party's backbench 1922 Committee Graham Brady. He is the custodian of the party's leadership election rules, and the conduit for channelling the concerns of backbench MPs. It is to him that MPs must write letters of no confidence if they want to depose their leader.

Brady had been taken aback by the images of May, clearly still shell-shocked at what was happening all around her, and feared she might be about to resign. He picked up his phone to compose a text message to the Prime Minister urging her to stay calm. He wanted to reassure her and said, according to someone who has read the text: 'Don't contemplate doing anything precipitous, you still have the support of colleagues.'

Brady's message, sent at around 3.30 a.m., arrived at the height of May's crisis. If she had doubts about whether she should stay, they would have been most acute at this moment; she was far from Downing Street, her future suddenly uncertain.

*　*　*

Also watching May's speech was the Chancellor, Philip Hammond. He was convinced the Prime Minister's future was at best precarious. Hammond considered which of his colleagues would be best placed to take over, and decided Boris Johnson was the obvious candidate. He passed Johnson a message of support, indicating that if the Foreign Secretary was to put himself forward, he would have his backing.[284]

*　*　*

At around 3.15 a.m., Farron left his home for his own count, confident that he had just done enough to hold the Tories at bay. When the result was finally called, his majority had been cut from 9,000 to 777 votes. Standing in front of his rivals, including a candidate dressed as a fish finger who had changed his name by deed poll to Mr Fish Finger, Farron attacked May for calling the election in the first place. 'Hopefully politicians may learn that calling referendums and general elections to suit your party rather than suiting the country is something to be avoided,' he said.

After his speech at the Kendal Leisure Centre, Farron retreated to a private room with his wife and aides to call party headquarters in London. They listened on speakerphone for the result from Eastbourne, a crucial seat that was among their most ambitious targets. When a huge cheer erupted at the other end of the line, Farron knew they had won it. Beaming with delight, he hopped for joy.

*   *   *

In Conservative campaign HQ, Jim Messina was the lone voice of optimism. According to staff there at the time, he was insisting that the exit poll was wrong and even at 3 a.m. believed the Tories could still defy the odds to win a majority.[285] At 4.20 a.m., the Conservatives learned that Stewart Jackson, a government aide to Brexit Secretary David Davis, had been ousted by 607 votes in Peterborough.

When May returned to Matthew Parker Street at 4.30 a.m., she headed straight into a meeting with Messina, Gilbert, Crosby, Textor, Timothy and Hill. In the quiet of the VIP room, with its sofa, fridge full of soft drinks, and TV, May found her voice. She stared at the men who had designed her campaign, who told her where to go and what to say, and who had led her to think it was all working.

Gilbert, Crosby and Textor all looked white, recalls one of those in the room. Textor offered a few thoughts about what had happened and what she might choose to say. Crosby mumbled, 'Sorry.' Then May expressed her frustration.

'I just don't understand,' she said. 'You've asked me to go round all these seats, I've gone round these seats, you've told me that the numbers were good and feed-back was good – and we've barely won any of them.'

May turned to her own future. 'We've got to make sure Jeremy Corbyn is not the Prime Minister. The country needs certainty and stability, and I must stay.'

May spent forty-five minutes locked away in the small room with her team. The Chief Whip, Gavin Williamson, was getting reports of MPs canvassing colleagues for rival leadership campaigns. The manoeuvrings began as soon as the exit poll results were released. Two men were in the frame to replace her: Boris Johnson and David Davis.

May told her team she wanted urgently to talk to her Brexit Secretary. 'I need to speak to DD,' she said. On the phone a little later, he assured her he would be 'steely' in his support. Johnson sent May a text message, expressing his backing and his sympathies. The Foreign Secretary, who was the subject of fevered speculation during the night, told May to keep her chin up, adding, 'We are with you,' according to witnesses. She was so delighted by the message that she held up her mobile phone and showed it to her advisers in the room.

After discussing the seats still to be declared and the likelihood of a deal with the Democratic Unionist Party, Gilbert and the campaign consultants left May alone with her two chiefs.

They told her these would probably be their final hours together.

'Fi and I had a conversation with her alone about how we thought we would have to stand down at that point,' Timothy recalls.

We just talked about it, we didn't definitively say 'and we are definitely going'. I think we knew that some people would call for it anyway. And I think we thought that it would be better for Theresa to go and have the conversations she needed to have with the party without us. She sort of heard it but didn't say, 'Yes – resign.' It was a part of the conversation.

At 5.15 a.m., three-quarters of an hour after arriving, May stepped out into the war room to address her deflated troops. 'It has been a difficult night but through no fault of anyone here,' a visibly upset Prime Minister told her staff. 'Everyone here has worked incredibly long hours, and I'm thankful for all the work people have put in,' she said. 'The Conservative Party is the best political party in the world. We continue to be the best political party in the world and we live to fight another day.'[286]

Timothy and Hill knew their time was over. Hill had been in tears by the time May spoke. One friend said she was 'desolate and inconsolable' as she left. Timothy was also devastated by the result, and the knowledge of the part he had played in their collective downfall. He left the office and then left London.

CHAPTER 20

HANGING ON

Theresa May arrived back at No. 10 at 6 a.m. on Friday 9 June. She had not slept and was still shell-shocked at the results. Already at work trying to assemble a government was Sir Jeremy Heywood, the Cabinet Secretary, Britain's most senior civil servant. A forceful figure at the heart of the establishment, he wielded great influence in David Cameron's regime and was indispensable to May's. Heywood's priorities were clear: the country needed a government, and it must not be left to the Queen to decide. He discussed the options with the Queen's private secretary, Sir Christopher Geidt. They agreed that even though her situation was difficult, given the numbers, May clearly had an obligation to 'soldier on'.

At 7 a.m., Heywood met May in No. 10. He told her what she later told the country – with 318 MPs, fifty-six more than Corbyn, she was the only person who could hope to form a workable government.[287] Before he could advise the Palace that the Queen should send for the Tory leader, however, he needed to be sure she had the support of her Cabinet to stay in place. It was her job to tell him if she had doubts.

May knew she was in peril. She had called a snap election hoping for a landslide and lost the majority she started with. Her Conservative colleagues were hurt and angry. They wanted sacrificial heads on plates, and some wanted hers. That was not all: potential rivals were considering their options, too. May's focus on the morning after polling day was on survival, from one hour to the next.[288]

Boris Johnson returned to his official residence in London to watch the coverage of the results into the morning. 'Poor Theresa, poor Theresa,' he muttered to aides who were with him. 'I hope she is OK.' Johnson's allies and supporters, meanwhile, called their colleagues and began to plot. Rumours reached David Davis that Johnson was planning a bid. Davis's backers started to consider how to counter Johnson's moves.

In No. 10, May decided it was time for honest conversations. She needed to speak to those senior members of the Cabinet whose support she knew she needed. The Prime Minister wanted her rivals to put their cards on the table. At around 8 a.m., she called Johnson. His text message in the dark hours before dawn had been kind but if she was going to stay on, she needed confirmation of his intentions, especially amid rumours that his supporters were plotting a coup.

'It's not the result we hoped for but I intend to form a government,' she said. 'Can I count on your support or do you intend to stand against me?' Johnson made clear that he would support her. Later, she spoke to Philip Hammond and David Davis. May could continue, for now. Meanwhile, her Chief Whip Gavin Williamson set to work trying to strike a deal with the Democratic Unionist Party's ten MPs, to give May enough votes in the Commons to pass laws.

At 12.20 p.m., the Prime Minister climbed into her official car and sped to Buckingham Palace. The Queen granted her permission for May to try to cobble together the majority she had just lost.

*   *   *

Heywood's team had another overriding concern that morning: Brexit. The financial markets were in turmoil at the shock failure of Britain's Prime Minister to get the majority she needed to form a stable government. With Brexit negotiations due to begin in just ten days' time – as May had repeatedly reminded voters in the run-up to polling day – it was essential for the UK to project an image of strength, or at least competence, at home and across the Channel.

With May's two chief advisers away considering their own futures, the political operation around the Prime Minister largely collapsed. Only JoJo Penn, Stephen Parkinson, the PM's political secretary, and Chris Wilkins remained from May's team of advisers, with Craig Woodhouse, who served as deputy head of press for the Tories, stepping in as her political media adviser. Heywood took charge. He discussed with May what she needed to say to the world when she returned from the Palace. A government must be formed. Europe needed to know that Brexit was still on.

'The civil service were panicked,' one of the PM's team recalls.

The civil service's view was that that was the speech she had to give because that was the message that the

Europeans had to hear the Prime Minister giving. They said, 'You've just got to go out there and give this strong speech and be strong and appear strong because Europe is watching.'[289]

The result was close to catastrophic for May. In a sky blue, high-collared outfit, with her husband Philip beside her, May began:

I have just been to see Her Majesty the Queen, and I will now form a government – a government that can provide certainty and lead Britain forward at this critical time for our country. This government will guide the country through the crucial Brexit talks that begin in just ten days, and deliver on the will of the British people by taking the United Kingdom out of the European Union.

It will work to keep our nation safe and secure by delivering the change that I set out following the appalling attacks in Manchester and London – cracking down on the ideology of Islamist extremism and all those who support it. And giving the police and the authorities the powers they need to keep our country safe.

The government I lead will put fairness and opportunity at the heart of everything we do, so that we fulfil the promise of Brexit together and – over the next five years – build a country in which no one and no community is left behind. A country in which prosperity and opportunity are shared right across this United Kingdom.

What the country needs more than ever is certainty, and having secured the largest number of votes and the greatest number of seats in the general election, it is clear that only the Conservative and Unionist Party has the legitimacy and ability to provide that certainty by commanding a majority in the House of Commons.

As we do, we will continue to work with our friends and allies in the Democratic Unionist Party in particular. Our two parties have enjoyed a strong relationship over many years, and this gives me the confidence to believe that we will be able to work together in the interests of the whole United Kingdom.

This will allow us to come together as a country and channel our energies towards a successful Brexit deal that works for everyone in this country – securing a new partnership with the EU which guarantees our long-term prosperity.

That's what people voted for last June. That's what we will deliver. Now let's get to work.

If the intention was to communicate strength and stability, the outcome was the opposite. Furious Tory MPs and ministers could not believe what they had heard. After a night in which her dreams had been shredded and all their expectations destroyed, May failed even to acknowledge the losses the Tories had suffered. Good colleagues and ministers had been sacrificed at the altar of her ambition and she could not even bring herself to mention her role in their downfall, far less apologise for it, MPs complained.

The mood was so grave that Graham Brady, chairman of the 1922 Committee, was forced to act. He travelled from Manchester to Downing Street for a face-to-face meeting at 2.30 p.m. He told May directly that her statement was disastrous. Colleagues in the party were angry and emotional; they would not put up with it, he said, adding that her speech was the kind that a Prime Minister would give after winning a 100-seat majority, not almost losing power.

The statement had been drafted by a weary Chris Wilkins, the director of strategy who worked so closely with Timothy on all May's most important speeches. He simply wrote the words that the civil service believed would be needed. 'I literally typed up what I was told to type up and I didn't give it any thought,' he says. 'I should have, but my head wasn't really in the right space. You just did what you had to do.'

Later in the day, May invited a television crew back into No. 10, where the PM sounded contrite.

> I am sorry for all those candidates and hard-working party workers who weren't successful, but also particularly sorry for those colleagues who were MPs and ministers, who had contributed so much to our country and who lost their seats – and didn't deserve to lose their seats. As I reflect on the results, I will reflect on what we need to do in the future to take the party forward.

*   *   *

By the afternoon, a gaggle of press photographers and television crews had set up camp outside Nick Timothy's London house. They were trying to doorstep the most controversial man in the government, the powerful chief of staff whose long beard and overwhelming influence on the PM helped earn him the description 'May's Rasputin'. But Nick Timothy wasn't there.

Already out of the capital, somewhere he could find

some peace, Timothy called his boss. He offered his resignation, and May accepted it. She did not try to persuade him to stay. Inevitably, it was an emotional conversation, lasting some time.

'We both knew what we needed to do, so she accepted it,' Timothy says. 'I think we were all sad. We all liked working with one another and I think we worked well together – and we're all friends, so of course it was sad, but it was kind of unavoidable.'

Later, Hill, still distraught at the results, formally resigned too.

Though Timothy was removing himself from the scene, he advised May on two further appointments. Gavin Barwell, the housing minister who had lost his seat hours earlier in Croydon, was talented, popular and loyal, and would make an excellent new chief of staff, especially as she sought to build bridges with her angry MPs. Will Tanner, the deputy head of the Policy Unit, should also be promoted, Timothy said, and given control over the task of developing her agenda for government. The PM took his advice on both.

While Barwell was delighted to take up the new role, Tanner had already come to his own decision. On Monday 12 June, he told May he was leaving. 'You do know what we were about to do, don't you?' she said. But his mind was made up.

GARDENING LEAVE

For Labour, Friday 9 June provided Corbyn with a final chance to dislodge May. John McDonnell was chosen as

the party's chief spokesman for the round of media interviews that morning. As the government wobbled, Labour
strategists were doing all they could to nudge it over the
cliff. The only realistic option for stable government was
for Corbyn to enter No. 10 at the head of a minority
government, McDonnell said. 'I hope she realises today,
very quickly, that she cannot continue,' he told the BBC's
Andrew Neil. 'The Conservative Party needs to recognise it cannot re-enter government in the way it is at the
moment, in its unstable, divided form.' McDonnell said
he hoped the situation would be clarified within days.
'The responsibility is on Theresa May now to stand down
and for the Conservative Party to go away and sort itself
out and let a Labour government take place.'

Corbyn reinforced the message as he arrived at the
Southside building shortly before 9 a.m. 'I think it's pretty
clear who won this election,' he said. But May would not
give up – and in truth Labour did not attempt to force her
out, or to forge its own alliance with other parties. Corbyn's team never made contact with Heywood to seek the
civil service's help with power-sharing talks.

On Saturday 10 June, Corbyn – the man who never
wanted to be Labour leader but had come closer than
anyone imagined possible to entering No. 10 – took himself off to the place where he is happiest: his allotment. 'It's
where he goes to do his thinking,' a colleague explains.[290]

THE '22

While the threat from Labour receded, May remained at
risk of attack from her own side. Some MPs had been

calling for her resignation, still appalled at the terrible campaign and smarting from her disastrous 'victory' speech outside No. 10. Although the departure of her two chiefs of staff had bought her a little time, as Timothy had hoped it would, Downing Street was entirely focused on survival. 'It was a question of making it through the morning, and then the afternoon, hour by hour,' one senior figure involved recalls. 'It was like that all through the weekend.'

With no authority left to make changes to her Cabinet, May telephoned Boris Johnson, David Davis, Amber Rudd and Philip Hammond, the Chancellor with whom she and her team had crossed swords, to confirm them all in their Cabinet positions on Friday afternoon. One Cabinet minister who spoke to May during the reshuffle said she was clearly still 'shell-shocked'.[291] Most other ministers remained at the top table too, though May found room to bring back her old adversary Michael Gove. Nick Timothy had learned earlier that the Brexit-backing Gove had always wanted to take charge of the Department for Environment, Food and Rural Affairs – a crucial area for the EU negotiations. Although Timothy's allies insist he was not involved in the reshuffle, the message reached Gavin Barwell and JoJo Penn, who were working on the ministerial appointments with May.

With the Cabinet decided, May prepared for her toughest test: her backbenchers. On the Monday evening, she had her showdown with the 1922 Committee. Flanked by bodyguards, wearing a black and white jacket, the Prime Minister steeled herself for an onslaught as she opened the heavy wooden door of Committee Room 14, the traditional meeting place for the backbench group.

These were the people who wielded the power now. May gave an assured performance, promising to listen to critics on Brexit and to work to help the thirty-two Tories who had lost their seats to find new roles. The defeated MP Gavin Barwell showed his value as her new chief of staff immediately, earning a cheer from his colleagues in the room. 'I got us into this mess, and I'm going to get us out of it,' May said. Finally, she threw herself upon the mercy of her colleagues. 'I am here as your leader for as long as you want me.'

To MPs in the room, May was transformed. No longer the mechanical, two-dimensional 'Maybot' of the campaign, but a warm and likeable leader who knew how badly her party was hurting – and cared. After the meeting, Heidi Allen, the Conservative MP for South Cambridgeshire, who had previously predicted May would be gone in months, was glowing. 'I saw an incredibly humble woman who knows what she has to do, and that is, be who she is and not what this job had turned her into,' Allen said. 'She has lost her armadillo shell and we have got a leader back.'[292]

Graham Brady, chairman of the 1922 Committee, spoke to his colleagues and reached two conclusions: Tory MPs had no appetite for a leadership contest, and nobody wanted another general election.

CHAPTER 21

SNAPPED

There was a moment in the dark hours before dawn on 9 June when both Theresa May and Jeremy Corbyn believed that Britain could be on the brink of choosing an unreconstructed socialist for Prime Minister. The thought probably terrified them both.

The snap election of 2017 was unique. It came out of the blue, amid the extraordinary upheaval of Brexit and a renewed debate about Scottish independence. The country was not expecting an election and did not want one. Seven weeks later, the fortunes of the two rival leaders were dramatically transformed. The electorate had delivered a hung parliament when everyone expected a handsome Tory win. It was the third shock result in as many years, following the 2015 election and the EU referendum in 2016. Polling day reshaped Britain – or England, at least – as a two-party country, just two years after the demise of the Lib Dem–Tory coalition.

The Conservatives won 42.4 per cent of the votes cast, some 13.7 million in total. They achieved the largest increase in the Tory vote since Margaret Thatcher's victory in 1979. Labour won 40 per cent, with 12.9 million votes, almost wiping out the Tory gains with their biggest increase in support since Attlee in 1945. The Conservatives finished with thirteen fewer seats:

the total of 318 MPs left Theresa May eight short of a
Commons majority. Labour gained thirty seats overall,
taking their tally to 262.

*   *   *

Elections are tumultuous events, spasms of public life in
which democratically run countries make their changes. They are always human stories as well as political
dramas. Inside the campaigns, a few hundred people of
different political stripes work sixteen- or seventeen-hour
days – and a sizeable number then fail and lose their jobs.
Others do not expect to win, and find themselves 'one
more heave' from Downing Street. For the defeated and
the diminished, the exercise carries a heavy personal cost.
If Theresa May, Nick Timothy or Fiona Hill were ever in
doubt about the potential price of a casual dalliance with
democracy, they are not any longer.

Within hours of the extraordinary election night exit
poll, as votes were still being counted, the recriminations began. May's tight circle of trusted aides privately
blamed the party's hired consultants for leaking internal
arguments from the campaign to the papers while the
election was still being fought. When it was over, Tory
staff were told: 'Brief your fucking heads off.' Tory MPs
and defeated candidates had their knives out instantly for Hill and Timothy. Then the all-powerful chiefs
quit. Hill fled the country, too distraught for anything
more than a bland statement. Timothy, however, fought
back. He took aim at Lynton Crosby and Jim Messina,
claiming in *The Spectator* that they had followed the

wrong strategy.[293] Supporters of Crosby retaliated in the pages of the *Evening Standard*, a paper edited by George Osborne, a friend of the Australian's (Osborne kissed Crosby as a forfeit after the surprise 2015 election victory). Crosby had 'begged' May not to call the snap election, in an explosive memo, the paper reported. It was not that simple. As this book reveals, Crosby did draft a memo to point out the risks, but quickly agreed to sign up for the campaign. He had a business to run and the party were offering £4 million for a little under two months' work.[294]

The snap election shredded the reputations of the most senior figures in the government, and cast a shadow over the records of some of the world's most lauded political strategists. It left the country in turmoil on the eve of Brexit negotiations and emboldened Jeremy Corbyn's left-wing, populist Labour Party supporters to believe they were within striking distance of power.

Why did the decision to call an early vote backfire so badly for Theresa May? What were the forces that shaped the contest? Who or what was to blame for the dysfunctional Tory campaign? How did Jeremy Corbyn, ridiculed before the election, manage to win 40 per cent of the vote and emerge almost as enhanced a figure as May was diminished? What does it all mean for the future? The story told in these pages suggests four key features defined the contest and shaped the result: the shock nature of the early election; the context of Brexit and the popular call for change that the referendum embodied; the events of the seven-week campaign; and the character of the two main party leaders themselves.

THE SNAP FACTOR

Springing an election onto the world with no notice was a decision akin to a head teacher at a sleepy primary school volunteering for a full Ofsted inspection – and then refusing to prepare. Perhaps the most obvious but also significant contributory factor to the outcome of the election is the 'snap' nature of the contest itself.

It explains why both the Labour and Tory campaign machines were shambolic for the first few weeks. Candidates had to be selected, campaign strategists had to be hired (for the Tories), laptops bought, cars and battle buses rented, target seats selected, messages developed and leaflets designed, printed and sent. That's all even before the manifestos were written and the televised debates agreed. The fact is, Labour were better prepared than the Tories. For the first time in recent memory, the Labour Party had a war chest of £3.5 million ready to spend – just in case May called an early vote. They also had leaflets designed, which meant they had the money and the content that enabled them to launch a national mailshot of leaflets in the crucial free week before Electoral Commission spending restrictions came into force. The Tories had nothing, even though they called the vote. There was not even enough paper in the country to send Tory leaflets to voters at the start of the campaign.

In the readiness of the main party leaders, there was also a gulf. May had never fought a national campaign of any significance, even for the leadership of her own party. Corbyn, by contrast, has made a career out of campaigning. He had spent the previous two years fighting first to win and then to keep the Labour leadership, in two long and bruising national contests. In this time, he discovered that campaigning, often in front of crowds of thousands, was something he could do – and loved doing. In truth, he has been doing it for most of his life.

The rude awakening extended to the country at large. The electorate did not want an election – or, perhaps more importantly, expect one. While May's personal approval ratings in April reached stratospheric levels of +21, compared to -35 for Corbyn, her chief campaign adviser Lynton Crosby knew that her support base was shallow.[295] People liked what they saw, but they did not know her well. In the months leading up to a long-planned election, such as that in 2015, public opinion polls invariably tighten as the prospect of voting focuses voters' minds. But the public polls before May's shock announcement of 18 April were divorced from the reality of an imminent requirement for voters to choose.

Traditionally, the Tories' biggest advantage has been money. But to say that overlooks the crucial importance of time. Without time to spend the money, and to invest in the technical preparations that the money will buy you, it is useless. The Tories raised £24.8 million to fight the 2017 campaign, almost double what came to Labour.[296] The trouble was there is a good chance that they spent it in the wrong places. Scores of candidates reportedly complained that the data on voters in the areas where they were canvassing was wrong. Time after time, they knocked on doors with Labour posters in the windows to be told that there was no chance of finding a Tory voter hiding inside. Jim Messina, the international election consultant, was responsible for helping identify target voter types. He joined Crosby on Cameron's election-winning

team in August 2013, almost two years before the election. In 2017, there was no time to prepare.

The Labour Party had seen how badly they were
beaten by the sophisticated Conservative digital warfare
operation in 2015 and worked hard to catch up. They
threw more money than ever before at their digital campaign and built a special data programme that was only
just ready in time for the general election – but it was
ready, allowing Labour to compete in the battle of the
Facebook ads. Labour and its loose alliance of third parties – trade unions, campaign groups and, most crucially
of all, Momentum – spread the red message organically
across social media far further and faster than the Tories.
May's aides shunned avenues such as Twitter because
they did not want to ape David Cameron's hyper-active
communications style. They succeeded in not emulating
his electoral success either.

THE AGE OF REVOLUTION

Theresa May called the election because of Brexit. Although neither of the two main parties volunteered to
provide new details on their own Brexit policies, it was
still the essential context for the election. According to
British Election Study data, based on responses from
30,000 people during the campaign, Brexit was by far
the most dominant issue for voters.

As the question of EU membership was now mainstream and in the centre of the national focus, the
two smaller parties who were most passionate about
it – UKIP and the Liberal Democrats – were crushed.

More than half of UKIP voters switched to the Tories, compared with under a fifth who went to Labour. The Conservatives, who had a clear position favouring a so-called hard Brexit (leaving the customs union and single market), became the party of Leave. Less predictably, Labour became the party for voters who had backed Remain in 2016, according to the findings from the BES.

Despite an ambiguous position on the single market, Labour was seen as the best bet for those wanting to keep closer ties with our European neighbours. Not only did they win over a large number of Remainers from the Conservatives, but also from the pro-EU Greens and Lib Dems. Nearly two thirds of 2015 Greens went to Labour, as well as around of a quarter of Liberal Democrats. Overall, more than half of all Remain voters voted for Labour, compared to a quarter for the Conservatives and 15 per cent for the Lib Dems.[297]

Nick Timothy wondered what the Tories could possibly have done to stop Lib Dems and Greens switching to Labour. One answer, it would seem, could be to have adopted a different policy on Brexit. But to Timothy and ultimately to May, the 2016 referendum demanded a clean break from the EU, to implement the will of the 52 per cent who voted to leave. Failing to do so would be a dangerous betrayal that could unleash waves of anti-establishment anger which would be hard to contain. Politically, it would also have made it harder to win over UKIP voters, now a key group in the Tory coalition.

The referendum was also more than simply a national verdict on Europe. May and Timothy saw in Brexit a cry for change from millions of disillusioned voters, ordinary working people who felt the economy was not

working for them – the same people Ed Miliband believed he could help in the run-up to the 2015 election.
Like Miliband, May could see the need to restore trust in
politics and push through economic and social reforms,
with an industrial strategy or energy price caps. Also
like Miliband, possessing this insight did not equate to
possessing the capacity to be the leader of that change.

Some in May's team also believed the Brexit vote was
a verdict on mainstream politics itself. Ben Gummer, the
co-author of May's manifesto, says democracy 'doesn't
matter as much' to societies that have lost touch with
the generations who had to fight for their liberty. When
political parties' election machines then introduce highly
sophisticated targeting techniques as shortcuts to winning, voters 'feel used' and become cynical, he says.[298]

When it counted, May and Timothy – to their deep
regret – allowed the Conservatives to ditch their reforming mission. Instead, they swallowed hard and strapped
themselves to Lynton Crosby's classic right-wing campaign, with its micro-targeted digital advertising and
segmentation of the electorate. Promising stability (not
change), security (not risk) and competence (not chaos),
it was the unfashionable sibling of Cameron's 2015 campaign, delivered with the same rigid message discipline
that focused on contrasting May's 'strong' leadership with
relentless attacks on the 'weak' and dangerous Corbyn.

'All the way through the campaign we just trusted that
they would deliver the numbers,' says Chris Wilkins. 'We
knew quite early on that the campaign was screwing the
brand but we took the view that we had done the deal,
and they would deliver the numbers, and afterwards we
would have to rebuild the brand.'

May is no revolutionary. Perhaps Nick Timothy isn't either.

The one party leader who could be, in June 2017, was Jeremy Corbyn. It's almost impossible to imagine Corbyn agreeing to compromise his values for the sake of a professional tactical campaign to the same extent. His form of politics is one long campaign. When the outlook was desperate, and the party had slumped to a historically bad set of local election results, Corbyn stood up and said: 'Let me be me.' He had the benefit of being the underdog. Labour had run out of options and the only thing left to try was total Corbynism. He was courageous where May was cautious. The Labour election strapline – 'For the many, not the few' – was a statement of values. To some senior Conservatives, the Tory slogan – 'Strong and stable leadership' – was a technocratic description of a process. One Cabinet minister says: 'We didn't have a mission.'

In Scotland, the dynamics were different. Ruth Davidson, the Scottish Tory leader, managed to be both revolutionary and conservative at the same time: she said 'no' to more upheaval in the form of an independence vote, but was the face of the popular opposition to Sturgeon's established SNP administration. Davidson in some ways was the candidate May wanted to be but could not be. Without her success in Scotland, Corbyn could have been in No. 10.

EVENTS

Conventional wisdom holds that nothing much changes in the course of a short, full-time election campaign.

Most voters at most elections have made up their minds well before Parliament is dissolved and little that happens during the campaign itself will shift their views. This time, it was different.

In 2017, it was as if the slumbering electorate had been violently woken by a bucket of ice-cold water and then slapped repeatedly by shocking and unpredictable events. First, Labour's entire manifesto leaked, grabbing the public debate and dominating it for days with talk of taxing the rich and nationalising the railways. Then, the Conservatives published their manifesto and provoked a revolt from the party's heartlands over the so-called dementia tax, causing habitual Labour voters who had warmed to the Prime Minister to think again about just how different Theresa May really was from all the other Tories in the 'nasty party'. Then, the woman who voters had been willing to believe was as strong and stable as she claimed ditched the policy that was causing the row, only four days after hailing it as the answer to the 'giant challenge' of Britain's ageing society.

Hours later, a suicide bomber killed twenty-two people, including children, in Manchester. Four days before the election, eight more civilians were murdered by terrorists in a van and knife rampage in London.

These four major events were pivotal moments in the 2017 contest and would be in any election. During the campaign, more people altered their opinions about the major parties the longer the contest went on. By the end of the campaign, 15 per cent of voters said something had happened in the past few days to make them change their views of the parties, up from 7 per cent in the early part of the campaign.[299] These events destroyed the best plans of the smartest election strategists that money could – and, for the Tories, did – buy. The two terror attacks in particular meant Crosby lost control of the one thing that he knows matters more than anything else: the emotions of the electorate.

At a champagne reception to celebrate his election triumph in 2015, Crosby noted that 'in politics, when reason and emotion collide, emotion invariably wins'. In that campaign, he had successfully harnessed the English electorate's fears of instability and unpredictability. Voters in marginal seats recoiled at the idea of a weak Ed Miliband being pushed around by a dominant Nicola Sturgeon in some kind of coalition. They chose to give Cameron a majority instead.

The terrorist attacks of May and June 2017 triggered outbursts of public grief, fear and anger. Out of respect for the victims, the parties suspended their campaigns, acknowledging that political argument would seem tastelessly cheap in the context of such tragedy.

There was no way to predict how the country at large would respond. Most staffers in both main parties expected May to benefit – looking prime ministerial, taking charge and exposing the weak Corbyn as a 'friend' of terrorists. Instead, the narrative turned quickly to austerity and May's record in the Home Office of overseeing cuts to the police. 'You can't protect the public on the cheap,' Corbyn said. It was hard to argue with the sentiment – and impossible for the Tories to quarrel with the detail. They had cut the police by 20,000 since 2010. If reason alone were enough, the Conservative argument that bobbies on the beat would not have stopped the Manchester bomber – or delivered the intelligence to uncover the terror cell that hit London Bridge – was swept away in a wave of public emotion.

'Social care dominated for days because we didn't respond and didn't take the decisions we had to take,' recalls Jim Messina, President Obama's former deputy chief of staff, who worked on modelling for the Tories. 'We finally managed to wrestle it back to our issues and then suddenly we spent the last week talking about police cuts.'[300]

The question was not just about events, but about how the party leaderships responded to those events.

LEADERSHIP

Theresa May's decision to call a snap election was a giant gamble that the Tories were poorly equipped to win. May, Nick Timothy and Fiona Hill did not know what an election campaign was, they just knew they wanted one. They hired the proven winner, Lynton Crosby. He certainly understood the reality of fighting elections, but he did not know Theresa May. Taken together, this knowledge gap meant neither the Conservative candidate nor the party's powerful consultants knew enough about each other's work to know how to win the snap general election of 2017.

What happened was disastrous. Lynton Crosby ran his campaign, and Nick Timothy wrote a manifesto for an entirely different one.

There was one person in a position to bridge the gulf between the May triumvirate and Crosby's consultants: Stephen Gilbert. As head of campaigning in 2015, and a Tory stalwart for twenty years, he knew and trusted Crosby and had good relations with May, Timothy and Hill. Yet leading a campaign war room was never Gilbert's ambition. He was desperate to persuade Crosby, the charismatic 'Wizard of Oz', to do it instead. When he arrived, Crosby – a natural and proven commander of Tory troops – was happy to oblige, and Gilbert gladly stepped back. Crosby, though, never took on the title of campaign director.

May's co-chiefs of staff, who some claim were closer to being co-Prime Ministers, were distracted. Timothy was writing his manifesto. Hill had to lead the communications team. They thought it would not matter because, in the words of one, 'We believed we were going to win big.' May herself was on the campaign trail but still depended on her aides – and they were not the types to relinquish their influence on the PM's mind, however great their workload had become.[301]

The impact of May's dislocated leadership and the incoherent Tory campaign fed into public perceptions about which leader would make the best Prime Minister and fuelled the dramatic rise in support for Labour. According to British Election Study data, 'the main reason that Labour gained so much in the campaign at the expense of the other parties is the strong performance of Jeremy Corbyn, especially relative to Theresa May'. Corbyn lagged far behind May in leadership ratings at the start of the campaign but had caught up by the end. His leadership substantially closed the gap on the Tories on the question of which party would handle the biggest issues facing the country best, and who would make the best PM.[302]

Corbyn owned every inch of his revolutionary campaign message while May was absent from hers, a timid figure doing as she was told. Her willingness to compromise on her own agenda for change allowed the Tories to toxify themselves.

During the course of writing this book, the authors have found it impossible to establish any single individual who is willing to admit that they were in charge of the Conservative Party's election campaign. To her credit, Theresa May has come closest, though in truth she was not running the operation day to day. Timothy says Gilbert was initially in charge, though Crosby took over when he arrived, while Patrick McLoughlin apparently chaired some campaign meetings. Timothy acknowledges that the structure was 'messy'.[303]

May is of course capable of making big decisions – the caricature of her as an empty vessel who depends on others to get dressed in the morning is unfair. She made the biggest decision of all: to throw herself upon the mercy of the electorate. She paid the price and she has taken responsibility for the discordant and fundamentally flawed campaign her side fought. Those close to the Prime Minister in the new No. 10 say she will not tolerate talk of anyone else taking the blame. It was her call.

Yet many who have worked closely with her describe how she lacks confidence and self-belief. She is habitually cautious, nervous about public appearances, unhappy in the limelight and personally shy, they say.

Liberated from the fear of impending disaster by the fact of an electoral catastrophe, something in May seemed to change in the days after the election. Gone were the chiefs of staff and the pressure of the polls. Gone too was the Maybot; in its place stood a humble and human figure who won over her colleagues in the parliamentary party. At the time of writing, she is still there, working long hours, carefully weighing her options, doing her duty, though her position is certainly not secure.

A senior Tory who was among the most trusted members of May's team says the campaign failed in its first task – to represent the candidate accurately. 'None of us was bold enough with our own feelings,' the Tory says.

> The sadness is that whilst the PM has got an amazing sense of principle about the way she does the business of policy, she does not have confidence in her own political judgement. I suspect in all this, had we all listened more to the PM, had the PM had more faith in her own judgement, we wouldn't be where we are.

NEXT TIME

The next time a sitting Prime Minister considers whether to trigger a snap election, they will think twice. The Brexit referendum has politicised the country. A group of voters who did not previously know where their nearest polling stations were have now found their political bearings and are using them.

Corbyn's extraordinary surge in support blew the political consensus apart in exactly the way he had always promised. Followers of the Westminster orthodoxy had scoffed at his claims. A number of Labour MPs had

gone further than mockery, and resigned in despair, pre-
ferring to go out on their own terms rather than march
headlong into the inevitable slaughter. Instead of carnage, Corbyn delivered a carnival. Thousands packed
football stadiums, spilled onto streets and waited in the
rain, chanting over and again, 'Oh, Jeremy Corbyn'.

In 2015, Ed Miliband's Labour Party tried to play by
the rules of mainstream, moderate Westminster politics
– and went backwards. In 2017, Corbyn broke free of
the rules, and showed they were outdated and useless to
begin with.

The Conservatives relied on micro-targeting segments
of the electorate, getting target voters to turn out; sending 4,000 different Facebook messages to varied shades
of voter types on polling day. Labour still faces challenges if it is to win the next election. But clever Tory
campaign tactics are no match for sheer numbers of
people – not least because the battle for dominance on
social media reflects and amplifies the power of these
people. To Corbynistas sick of the mainstream press and
broadcasters, social media is their socialist media.

*   *   *

On 4 October 2017, May stood on the Conservative
conference stage in Manchester to explain to her party
what had gone wrong. While her speech that day would
be remembered more for the repeated interruptions, first
by a prankster and then by a persistent cough, May's
analysis was clear. 'We did not get the victory we wanted
because our national campaign fell short,' she said. 'It
was too scripted, too presidential, and it allowed the

Labour Party to paint us as the voice of continuity, when the public wanted to hear a message of change.' May took responsibility for the result that had left her in tears, cost her two chiefs their jobs and put the government of the country in doubt.

'I led the campaign,' she said. 'And I am sorry.'

LYNTON CROSBY'S 2017 ELECTION STRATEGIC NOTE – APRIL 2017

ABOUT THIS RESEARCH

C|T|F Partners conducted two pairs of focus groups among soft voters (those undecided how they will vote, or likely to change their mind) from marginal seats in both London and the North West. In addition, we have completed a nationally representative political benchmark poll of n=1000 voters.

SUMMARY

The research shows there is clearly a lot of risk involved with holding an early election – and there is a real need to nail down the 'why' for doing so now. Voters are actively seeking to avoid uncertainty and maintain the status quo, and yet by calling an election the Conservatives are the ones who are creating uncertainty. Therefore, Theresa May must be able to show that by holding an election *now* she is minimising *future* uncertainty and instability.

Furthermore, if an election was held today there is a risk that the Conservative vote share would end up

broadly similar to that the party secured in 2015. And
as earlier research has shown, there is the potential for a
significant number of seats won from the Liberal Democrats in 2015 to return to Tim Farron's party – largely
based on the performance of incumbent MPs compared
to their predecessors.

Theresa May is the most favourably viewed individual tested, while Jeremy Corbyn is the least favourably
viewed. Of all the other Conservative individuals tested,
only Ruth Davidson has a net favourable rating.

There is a strong preference for the Conservatives to
be in government after the next election with Theresa
May as Prime Minister. But there are also exception-
ally high expectations that this will be the outcome of
any election held now. Both quantitatively (in Liberal
Democrat seats) and qualitatively (in Labour seats)
this is leading voters to believe that they can vote for
the best local MP, or not reject their current good local
MP, while still remaining secure in the knowledge that
Jeremy Corbyn will not be Prime Minister. Thus the
Conservatives must urgently work to ensure that any
election is seen through a national prism.

Voters do not want the uncertainty that an election
will cause, in large part because they are worried about
the risk of potential election outcomes – namely a hung
parliament creating chaos over the delivery of Brexit
and Nicola Sturgeon calling the shots, and the spectre of
Jeremy Corbyn as Prime Minister.

Instead voters desire a better future where Brexit is
a success, the economy stays strong, and they maintain
their standard of living. To win this election, the Conservatives must demonstrate how only a vote for them

can provide the leadership and stability needed to secure this better future.

The consequence of not voting Conservative is that Brexit negotiations will stall and fail – either through a hung parliament creating chaos and stasis, or Prime Minister Jeremy Corbyn messing up negotiations with the EU – and that will mean Britain could fall behind other countries, damage the economy, and lead to lower living standards.

WHAT THE CONSERVATIVES MUST DO

1. Be clear why this election is needed *now* – to prevent *future* uncertainty that would hamper Britain's ability to make a success of Brexit, maintain economic competitiveness, and improve voters' standard of living.
2. Ultimately frame the election as a choice between continuity and stability, or chaos and uncertainty.
3. Demonstrate the only way to secure a better future is through strong leadership, backed up by a stable and united party, that voters can trust to make the right decisions.
4. Demonstrate the only way to secure strong leadership (and Theresa May as Prime Minister) with the stable government needed to secure a good deal for the UK and a better future is by voting Conservative.
5. Use Theresa May as the campaign's main communication vehicle – and take every opportunity to contrast her with Jeremy Corbyn.

MANIFESTO PLANS: EMAIL CHAIN BETWEEN MARK TEXTOR AND NICK TIMOTHY

Note: This email exchange shows the emerging Tory manifesto policies at a relatively early point in the election. The policies outlined here were among those deemed to be potentially controversial or difficult to sell to voters.

The messages show Nick Timothy sending details of the potentially contentious policies to Mark Textor, the pollster from CTF. The policies were to be tested in focus groups and polling research before being refined for inclusion in the manifesto, or left out altogether.

From: Mark Textor
Date: 25 April 2017 at 14:04:37 BST
To: Nick Timothy
Cc: Will Tanner
Subject: Re: Is this ok for you?

Yes.

We will present it in a way that these are presented double blind

Tex

From: Nick Timothy

Date: Tuesday, 25 April 2017 1:19 pm

To: Mark Textor

Cc: Will Tanner

Subject: Is this ok for you?

Some of the slightly more controversial ones, with thanks to Will.

Pensioner benefits
Scrap the Winter Fuel Payment for all but the poorest of pensioners at risk of fuel poverty, and instead use the proceeds to fund long-term care for the elderly which at the moment is under-funded.

Triple lock for pensioners
Stick to the 2015 manifesto promise to retain the triple lock for pensions until 2020. This means that the state pension will rise in line with earnings, inflation or at 2.5 per cent, whichever is highest. However, because pensioner poverty has now been largely fixed and pensioner income is now high, we think that from 2020 there is no case for pensioner incomes growing faster than those for families in work. So from 2020 we will move to a double lock, allowing pensions to rise in line with earnings – but with extra safeguards in case inflation is high.

Social care
We will scrap the Winter Fuel Payment for all but the poorest of pensioners, allowing us to put the proceeds into long-term care for the elderly. We will change the rules so people receiving care at home can defer the

costs while they are alive, just as they can already for residential care and guarantee that, no matter how large the cost of care, people will never be left with less than £50,000 in savings and assets after paying for care costs.

For younger people, we will introduce a new social care insurance system, backed by a British sovereign wealth fund, so that everyone – no matter where they live and how much they have earned – can be promised a secure and dignified old age.

Cost of energy review

Independently review the cost of energy in the UK, including costs of different types of energy and the effect of government subsidies and taxes, to make sure that UK costs are as fair, reasonable and low by international standards as possible, while still ensuring a reliable supply and reducing carbon emissions. We will cease future subsidies for renewable energy beyond those we have already committed to.

UK Shared Prosperity Fund

Use the money that comes back to the UK from the EU to create a United Kingdom Shared Prosperity Fund designed purely to invest in the nations and regions of the UK to encourage growth and reduce poverty.

School funding and UIFSMs

Increase the schools teaching budget year on year, funded by changing free school meals for children at primary schools so that they are no longer universal and instead for the poorest pupils only. This is what happened until the last year or so.

Digital Bill of Rights and regulation of cyber agreement

We will introduce a digital bill of rights to protect internet users and their children online and work with other democratic countries to agree an international code on the regulation of cyber space.

International aid reform

Make sure the 0.7% is spent well by working with other countries like the Dutch to reform what counts as aid spending, so that it can be spent on Navy hospital ships, economic development in poor countries, or insuring developing countries against natural disasters. If other countries do not agree, we will legislate to change the rules so we would continue to spend 0.7% of GDP on aid but in a way that makes sense for taxpayers and the people we are trying to help.

Re-training

Introduce a guarantee of re-training for workers in industries and occupations that are in decline, so that people can learn a new skill to support them to transition to another role or business.

Housing

Build many more homes to make housing more affordable and to fix the dysfunctional housing market, prioritising quality housing like terraced homes and mansion blocks in places people want to live.

Maintain the strong protections on the green belt and rebalance housing growth across the whole country, in line with our modern industrial strategy.

Increase the stock of social housing, supporting councils and housing associations to build new short-term social housing which must be sold on each generation, with the profits reinvested in more houses for local people.

NHS
Increase the NHS budget in real terms every year for the next five years and introduce the largest capital investment programme ever in the history of the NHS. Review the way the NHS is run so that all NHS trusts can be like the best ones. In particular review the operation of the NHS internal market to see whether it makes the health service more or less efficient.

Minimum service levels for strikes
Legislate to introduce minimum service levels in transport and other public services including border force staff, prison staff, teachers, doctors and nurses, in the event of a strike.

APPENDIX 3

KEY DATES FOR
2017 ELECTION

8 May 2015 – David Cameron forms the first Conservative majority government since 1992.

20 February 2016 – Cameron sets the date for the EU referendum. A gang of five Cabinet ministers jump ship to Vote Leave.

23 June 2016 – European Union referendum vote.

24 June 2016 – Cameron resigns after UK votes to leave EU by 52 per cent to 48 per cent.

13 July 2016 – May becomes Prime Minister, fires George Osborne and Michael Gove, appoints Boris Johnson Foreign Secretary, Philip Hammond Chancellor, Amber Rudd Home Secretary. David Davis and Liam Fox move into Cabinet from the backbenches.

16 February 2017 – Conservative election away day at Chequers. Lynton Crosby, Patrick McLoughlin, Fiona Hill, Nick Timothy and Chris Wilkins join Theresa May at her official country retreat to review the 2015 campaign and begin to consider 2020.

13 March 2017 – Article 50 Bill passes final parliamentary hurdle.

Week of 20 March 2017 – A delegation of No. 10 aides tells May she should call an early election.

22 March 2017 – Westminster terror attack. Five killed.

29 March 2017 – May triggers Article 50, sending notification letter to EU, formally starting Brexit process.

Week of 9 April 2017 – The Mays go on a five-day walking holiday in Wales.

18 April 2017 – May announces snap election for 8 June. Lynton Crosby, Jim Messina, Stephen Gilbert, Tom Edmonds, Craig Elder and others are brought on board.

11 May 2017 – Labour manifesto leak.

16 May 2017 – Labour manifesto launch in Bradford.

17 May 2017 – Lib Dem manifesto launch in London.

18 May 2017 – Tory manifesto launch in Halifax.

22 May 2017 – PM social care U-turn in Wrexham.

22 May 2017 – Manchester Arena suicide bombing. Twenty-two killed.

25 May 2017 – UKIP manifesto launch in London.

25 May 2017 – NATO summit, Brussels.

26 May 2017 – Corbyn foreign policy and terrorism speech, London.

26 May 2017 – G7 summit, Sicily.

29 May 2017 – *May vs Corbyn: The Battle for No. 10*, Sky/Channel 4.

30 May 2017 – SNP manifesto launch in Perth.

2 June 2017 – BBC *Question Time* special with May and Corbyn.

3 June 2017 – London Bridge attack. Eight killed.

7 June 2017 – Corbyn's homecoming rally Islington.

8 June 2017 – Polling day.

9 June 2017 – May forms minority government. DUP talks begin.

9 June 2017 – Nick Timothy and Fiona Hill quit as May's co-chiefs of staff.

12 June 2017 – May tells Tory MPs she'll get the party out of the 'mess' she has created, at meeting of 1922 Committee.

19 June 2017 – Brexit negotiations begin in Brussels.

21 June 2017 – Queen's Speech.

26 June 2017 – Conservative–DUP 'supply and confidence' deal finally agreed.

29 June 2017 – Queen's Speech passes the Commons.

4 October 2017 – May apologises for general election in her speech to the Tory conference in Manchester.

APPENDIX 4

THE RESULTS

SEATS WON AND LOST

	GE2017 SEATS WON	GE2015 SEATS WON	SEAT GAINS	SEATS LOSSES	SEAT CHANGE (NET)
Conservative	317*	330	+20	-33	-13
Labour	262	232	+36	-6	+30
SNP	35	56	0	-21	-21
Lib Dem	12	8	+8	-4	+4
DUP	10	8	+2	0	+2
Sinn Féin	7	4	+3	0	+3
Plaid Cymru	4	3	+1	0	+1
Green	1	1	0	0	No change
Independent (NI)	1	1	0	0	No change
Speaker	1	1	n/a	n/a	n/a

* Not including the Speaker

VOTES AND VOTES SHARE

	VOTES 2017	VOTE SHARE 2017	PPCS 2017	VOTES 2015	VOTE SHARE 2015	PPCS 2015	VOTES +/-	VOTE SHARE +/-%	PPCS +/-
Conservative*	13,670,989	42.4%	639	11,334,920	36.9%	647	+2,336,069	5.5%	-8
Labour	12,877,869	40.0%	631	9,347,326	30.4%	631	+3,530,543	9.6%	0
Lib Dems	2,371,861	7.4%	629	2,415,888	7.9%	631	-44,027	-0.5%	-2
SNP	977,568	3.0%	59	1,454,436	4.7%	59	-476,868	-1.7%	0
UKIP	594,068	1.8%	378	3,881,129	12.6%	624	-3,287,061	-10.8%	-246
Green	525,665	1.6%	467	1,157,613	3.8%	573	-631,948	-2.2%	-106
DUP	292,316	0.9%	17	184,260	0.6%	16	-108,056	0.3%	1
Sinn Féin	238,915	0.7%	18	176,232	0.6%	18	-62,683	0.1%	0
Plaid Cymru	164,466	0.5%	40	181,694	0.6%	40	-17,228	-0.1%	0
SDLP	95,419	0.3%	18	99,809	0.3%	18	-4,390	0.0%	0
UUP	83,280	0.3%	14	114,935	0.4%	15	-31,655	-0.1%	-1
Alliance	64,553	0.2%	18	61,556	0.2%	18	+2,997	0.0%	0
Ind (NI)	16,148	<0.1%	1	17,689	<0.1%	1	-1,541	0.0%	0
Other parties	95,701	0.3%	189	270,723	0.9%	680	-23,551	-0.1%	-304
Other Independents	151,471	0.5%	187						
	32,204,141	100%	3,304	30,698,210	100%	3,971	n/a	n/a	

PPC: Prospective Parliamentary Candidates

SNP: Scottish National Party

DUP: Democratic Unionist Party

SDLP: Social Democratic & Labour Party

UUP: Ulster Unionist Party

* Including the Speaker

NOTES

1   Private interviews
2   Alasdair Palmer, 'The prime minister ruined by her gruesome twosome', *Sunday Times*, 25 June 2017, accessed 13 October 2017 at: https://www.thetimes.co.uk/article/the-prime-minister-ruined-by-her-grusome-twosome-v9gvg68bc
3   Private interview
4   Private interview
5   Interview, Katie Perrior
6   Private interview
7   Private interview
8   Interview, Katie Perrior
9   Dani Garavelli, 'Insight: Fiona Hill, from Scotsman reporter to Theresa May's right-hand woman', *The Scotsman*, 13 May 2017, accessed 10 October 2017 at: http://www.scotsman.com/news/politics/general-election/insight-fiona-hill-from-scotsman-reporter-to-theresa-may-s-right-hand-woman-1-4445037
10 Tim Ross, 'Michael Gove apologises as Theresa May's adviser quits over row', *Daily Telegraph*, 7 June 2014, accessed 10 October 2017 at: http://www.telegraph.co.uk/news/politics/conservative/10883761/Michael-Gove-apologises-as-Theresa-Mays-adviser-quits-over-row.html
11 See *Why the Tories Won: The Inside Story of the 2015 Election* by Tim Ross (Biteback Publishing, 2015)
12 Nick Timothy, 'What does the Conservative Party offer a working-class kid from Brixton, Birmingham, Bolton or Bradford?', ConservativeHome.com, 22 March 2016, accessed 10 October 2017 at: https://www.conservativehome.com/thecolumnists/2016/03/nick-timothy-what-does-the-conservative-party-offer-a-working-class-kid-from-brixton-birmingham-bolton-or-bradford.html
13 Tim Ross, 'Nick Timothy: end ban on new grammar schools', *Daily Telegraph*, 7 November 2015, accessed 10 October 2017 at: http://www.telegraph.co.uk/education/educationnews/11981856/Nick-Timothy-end-ban-on-new-grammar-schools.html
14 Nick Timothy, 'I've already voted Leave – but these wretched

campaigns show everything that's wrong with British politics', Conserv-ativeHome.com, 14 June 2016, accessed 10 October 2017 at: https://www.conservativehome.com/thecolumnists/2016/06/nick-timothy-ive-already-voted-leave-but-i-cant-wait-to-get-away-from-this-bloody-referendum-campaign.html

15   Nick Timothy, 'What does the Conservative Party offer a working-class kid from Brixton, Birmingham, Bolton or Bradford?', Conservative-Home.com, 22 March 2016, op. cit.

16   Ibid.

17   Interview, Nick Timothy

18   Statement by new PM Theresa May, Downing Street, 13 July 2016, ac-cessed 10 October 2017 at: https://www.gov.uk/government/speeches/statement-from-the-new-prime-minister-theresa-may

19   Interview, Katie Perrior

20   Private interviews

21   Private interview

22   Interview, Katie Perrior

23   Interview, Katie Perrior

24   Private interviews

25   Glen Owen, 'The Great Red Box Rebellion', *Mail on Sunday*, 18 Septem-ber 2016, accessed 26 September 2017 at: http://www.dailymail.co.uk/news/article-3794744/The-Great-Red-Box-Rebellion-Theresa-faces-re-volt-furious-mandarins-feel-sidelined-PM-s-Brummie-Rasputin.html

26   'Code of Conduct for Special Advisers', Cabinet Office, December 2016, accessed 10 October 2017 at: https://www.gov.uk/government/uploads/system/uploads/attachment_data/file/579768/code-of-conduct-special-advisers-dec-2016.pdf

27   Private interview

28   'Working with Ministers: A practical handbook on advising, brief-ing & drafting', Policy Profession/Civil Service Learning, November 2014, accessed 10 October 2017 at: http://www.civilservant.org.uk/library/2015_Working_with_Ministers.pdf

29   Private interviews

30   Private interview

31   Private interview, Cabinet minister

32   Private interview, Cabinet minister

33   Interview, Will Tanner

34   Private interview

35   Private interview

36   Interview, Nick Timothy

37   Interview, Nick Timothy

38   Private interviews

39   Private information

40   Private interviews

41   Private interview

42 Interview, Chris Wilkins

43 Private information

44 Private interview

45 May speech, Lancaster House, 17 January 2017: 'I want to be clear. What I am proposing cannot mean membership of the single market. European leaders have said many times that membership means accepting the "four freedoms" of goods, capital, services and people. And being out of the EU but a member of the single market would mean complying with the EU's rules and regulations that implement those freedoms, without having a vote on what those rules and regulations are. It would mean accepting a role for the European Court of Justice that would see it still having direct legal authority in our country. It would to all intents and purposes mean not leaving the EU at all.'

46 Private interview

47 Interview, Will Tanner

48 Private interview

49 Interview, Chris Wilkins

50 Private interview

51 Interview, Nick Timothy

52 Interview, Jon Lansman

53 Tom McTague, 'Inside account of Labour MPs' attacks on Jeremy Corbyn', Politico, 27 June 2016, accessed 10 October 2017 at: http://www.politico.eu/article/inside-account-of-labour-mps-attacks-on-jeremy-corbyn-shadow-cabinet-resignations-brexit/

54 Interview, Niall Sookoo

55 Private interview

56 Private interview

57 Interview, Jon Lansman

58 Amelia Gentleman, 'MP and wife split over school', *The Guardian*, 13 May 1999, accessed 13 September 2017 at: https://www.theguardian.com/politics/1999/may/13/uk.politicalnews2

59 Interview, Jon Lansman

60 Interview, Niall Sookoo

61 Interview, Jon Lansman

62 Private interview

63 Schedule to the Chequers Estate Act 1917, quoted at: http://www.chilternsaonb.org/uploads/files/AboutTheChilterns/People_and_History/PDFs/Chequers_additional_material.pdf, accessed 13 September 2017

64 Private interviews

65 Private interviews

66 Interview, Lynton Crosby

67 Interview, Chris Wilkins

68 Private interviews

69 Private interviews. Philip May is a popular figure with No. 10 staff, unfailingly polite and friendly. In meetings of the Prime Minister's close

aides, which took place in the Downing Street flat or in their home in Sonning, he would invariably make cups of tea for the team. In private, May relies on him for advice. Another senior Downing Street figure explains: 'The PM had three key advisers: Nick, Fiona and Philip – and Philip was the most important of all.'

70 Private interview
71 Nazia Parveen, '"The walks give clarity": how Wales hike helped PM decide on next step', *The Guardian*, 22 April 2017, accessed 13 September 2017 at: https://www.theguardian.com/politics/2017/apr/22/the-walks-give-clarity-how-wales-hike-helped-pm-decide-on-next-step
72 Private interview
73 Private interviews
74 CTF Partners 2017 Election Strategic Note – April 2017; see Appendix 1
75 Interview, Lynton Crosby
76 Interview, Chris Wilkins
77 Private interviews
78 Private interviews
79 Theresa May speech announcing general election, 18 April 2017, accessed 13 September 2017 at: https://www.conservatives.com/sharethefacts/2017/04/we-need-a-general-election
80 Interview, Katie Perrior
81 Interview, Katie Perrior
82 Private interview
83 Private interview
84 Private interview
85 Interview, Nick Timothy
86 Private information
87 Private interviews
88 Helena Horton, 'Jeremy Corbyn says "I can't name one mistake I've made – there have been too many" and reveals he has hundreds of secret diaries', *Daily Telegraph*, 18 April 2017, accessed 14 September 2017 at: http://www.telegraph.co.uk/news/2017/04/18/jeremy-corbyn-says-cant-name-one-mistake-made-have-many-reveals/
89 Private interview
90 Private interview
91 Private interview
92 Private interview
93 Heneghan left a few months after the election.
94 Interview, Andrew Gwynne
95 Interview Andrew Gwynne
96 Interview Andrew Gwynne
97 Private interview
98 Private interview
99 Private interview
100 Charlie Cooper and Tom McTague, 'Union chief Len McCluskey sets

low bar for Labour', Politico, 16 May 2017, accessed 14 September 2017 at: http://www.politico.eu/article/len-mccluskey-jeremy-corbyn-labour-general-election-2017/

101 Private interview
102 Private interview
103 Private information
104 Interview, Jon Lansman
105 Figure from Momentum
106 The mobilisation of mass support bases – by both the left and the Brexit-backing right, carries risks as well as rewards. During the election, there were signs that some on these political fringes were willing to resort to intimidation and threats in order to further their cause. One senior Tory strategist recalled that candidates were for the first time afraid to put their names and addresses on the electoral roll. In a parliamentary debate shortly after the election, numerous MPs described the abuse they suffered on social media and in emails, as well as in their constituencies. It included vandalism, death threats, rape threats and racism. Twitter trolling is commonplace for journalists reporting politics, too. For the BBC's political editor, Laura Kuenssberg, the intimidation took an even more serious turn, requiring her to have personal security protection while she was out reporting during the election and afterwards.
107 Interview, Lynton Crosby
108 Private interview
109 Interview, Damian Green
110 Private interviews
111 Private interviews
112 See John Curtice, 'Don't be fooled by the local election results – the Tories still face an uphill battle in their bid to crush Labour', *The Independent*, 5 May 2017, accessed 14 September 2017 at: http://www.independent.co.uk/voices/local-election-2017-latest-analysis-john-curtice-tory-landslide-general-election-a7720801.html
113 Private interviews
    This is the list of thirty-nine attack seats that Labour officials added to their campaign on 18 May 2017: Amber Valley, Broxtowe, Corby, Derby North, Erewash, Lincoln, Northampton North, Sherwood, Bedford, Ipswich, Peterborough, Thurrock, Waveney, Croydon Central, Hendon, Carlisle, Blackpool North and Cleveleys, Bolton West, Bury North, Crewe and Nantwich, Warrington South, Weaver Vale, Brighton and Kemptown, Hastings and Rye, Southampton Itchen, Plymouth Moor View, Plymouth Sutton and Devonport, Stroud, Cardiff North, Gower, Vale of Clwyd, Halesowen and Rowley Regis, North Warwickshire, Telford, Calder Valley, Keighley, Morley and Outwood, Pudsey, Sheffield Hallam.
114 Private interview
115 Private interviews
116 Private interviews

117 Private interview

118 See: http://www.electionpolling.co.uk/battleground/targets/labour, accessed 10 October 2017

119 Interview, Sam Tarry

120 Private interview

121 Private interviews

122 Private interview

123 Private interviews

124 Quoted in Jessica Elgot, 'Back me despite Corbyn as May will win, Labour candidate urges voters', *The Guardian*, 2 June 2017, accessed 16 September 2017 at: https://www.theguardian.com/politics/2017/jun/02/back-me-despite-corbyn-as-may-will-win-labour-mp-urges-voters

125 Interview, Lynton Crosby

126 Interview, Lynton Crosby

127 Jon Mellon and Chris Prosser, 'Did people vote for Jeremy Corbyn because they thought he would lose?', British Election Study, 3 August 2017, accessed 16 September 2017 at: http://www.britishelectionstudy.com/bes-findings/did-people-vote-for-jeremy-corbyn-because-they-thought-he-would-lose/#.WabG4neGN5k

128 Interview, Craig Elder

129 Private interviews

130 Private interview

131 Interview, Craig Elder

132 Private interview

133 Private interview

134 Private interview

135 Robert Booth, Martin Belam and Maeve McClenaghan, 'Tory attack ad misrepresents Corbyn views on IRA, says Labour', *The Guardian*, 2 June 2017, accessed 16 September 2017 at: https://www.theguardian.com/politics/2017/jun/02/labour-accuses-tories-of-fake-news-over-video-of-corbyn-ira-comments

136 Mark Bridge, Katie Gibbons and Henry Zeffman, 'Millions of online hits for advert attacking Corbyn', *The Times*, 1 June 2017, accessed 23 September 2017 at: https://www.thetimes.co.uk/article/millions-of-online-hits-for-advert-attacking-corbyn-pbz5kvkm6

137 Private interview

138 Private interview

139 Private interview

140 Private interview

141 Jamie Grierson and Nicola Slawson, 'Corbyn tells anti-austerity demo he's "determined to force new election"', *The Guardian*, 1 July 2017, accessed 16 September 2017 at: https://www.theguardian.com/politics/2017/jul/01/jeremy-corbyn-to-speak-at-london-anti-austerity-march

142 Gavin Barwell interview, BBC *Panorama – Election 2017: What Just Happened?*, first broadcast 12 June 2017

143 Interview, Andrew Cooper

144 Private information

145 Private interview

146 Interview, Nick Timothy

147 Private interview

148 Robert Hutton and Brian Parkin, 'May Says Juncker Clash Shows Brexit Talks Will "Not Be Easy"', Bloomberg, 1 May 2017, accessed 17 September 2017 at: https://www.bloomberg.com/news/articles/2017-05-01/may-says-leak-of-juncker-clash-shows-brexit-talks-will-be-tough

149 Tim Ross, 'Tories See May's "Genius" Attack on EU Giving Her a Boost', Bloomberg News, 4 May 2017, accessed 17 September 2017 at: https://www.bloomberg.com/news/articles/2017-05-04/may-s-genius-attack-on-eu-boosts-her-election-bid-tories-say

   Juncker's chief of staff Martin Selmayr was accused of leaking the account of the Downing Street dinner. Shortly afterwards, German Chancellor Angela Merkel told May that she was appalled by the incident and would demand that Juncker sack his aide, according to a senior official.

150 Department of Health/Ipsos MORI (2010) 'Public attitudes towards care and support', cited in 'Public opinion research on social care funding – A literature review on behalf of the Commission on the Funding of Care and Support', Ipsos MORI, February 2011, accessed 10 October 2017 at: http://webarchive.nationalarchives.gov.uk/20110321134835/http://www.dilnotcommission.dh.gov.uk/files/2011/03/MORI.pdf

151 Private interview

152 https://www.markpack.org.uk/150573/why-conservatives-lost-steve-parker/, accessed 17 September 2017

153 Interview, Andrew Gwynne

154 Private information

155 Private interview

156 Private interview, Cabinet minister

157 Private interview

158 Private interview

159 Private interview

160 In fact, Miliband's 'bacon sandwich moment' occurred in the 2014 European Parliament election campaign, but the image was revived by his opponents during the 2015 general election.

161 Private information

162 Ewen MacAskill, 'The fight of his life: on the road with Jeremy Corbyn', The Guardian, 2 June 2017, accessed 6 October 2017 at: https://www.theguardian.com/politics/2017/jun/02/the-fight-of-his-life-on-the-road-with-jeremy-corbyn. The Labour leader did take a pot of jam onto The One Show but he appeared on his own.

163 Private interviews

164 Private interview

165 Private interview

166 Private interviews

167 Private interview

168 Private interview

169 Private interview. The sparring between Gwynne and Johnson continued after the election. When newly elected MPs gathered back in Westminster, Gwynne got into the lift beside Strangers' Bar on the lower ground floor of the Commons. It was crowded with Tory MPs, on their way up to the first floor for a meeting of the party's backbench 1922 Committee. There was a single, tight space left amid the throng, next to Gwynne. In bounded Johnson. The two men came face to face for the first time since their televised wrestling during the election. 'Hello, Boris,' Gwynne beamed. 'Oh,' said Johnson. 'I think I'll get the stairs.'

170 Private interview

171 Private interview

172 Private interview

173 Private interviews

174 Ewen MacAskill, 'The fight of his life: on the road with Jeremy Corbyn', *The Guardian*, 2 June 2017, op. cit.

175 Private interview

176 Private interview

177 'Peter Willsman reports from Labour's July executive', Left Futures, accessed 10 October 2017 at: http://www.leftfutures.org/2017/07/peter-willsman-reports-from-labours-july-executive/

178 Interview, Lynton Crosby

179 Private interview

180 William Beveridge's 1942 report identified the 'five giant evils' of society: want, ignorance, disease, squalor and idleness. It prepared the ground for the development of the welfare state, including unemployment benefits and the National Health Service. The 'Five Giant Challenges' of the 2017 manifesto were: the need for a strong economy, Brexit and a changing world, enduring social divisions, an ageing society and fast-changing technology.

181 Private interviews

182 Private interview

183 Private interview

184 Private interview

185 Private interview

186 Private interview

187 One source involved in developing the plan recalls: 'In retrospect, appealing to younger voters who were worried about the housing ladder would have been a wonderful policy. But we couldn't find a way to afford it.

'There was lots of agonising about what we could get away with on tax and whether or not we needed to have some kind of tax lock. If we did something like scrapping stamp duty, we would show our intent [to cut taxes] in a very progressive, pro-young people, pro-housing way. It would have been great.

'If you just do it on principal residences, because you wouldn't want to do it on second homes, it creates a £6 billion black hole in the public finances so you need to find it from somewhere. One of the areas we looked at was Capital Gains Tax on property – abolishing stamp duty and replacing it with CGT. Then when you run the numbers, to make it financially sustainable, it would need to be quite a high rate of CGT on very expensive homes. It could have worked. The numbers would have to be around 28 per cent or 30 per cent Capital Gains Tax on properties worth over £500,000, if you wanted to mitigate those at the bottom end of the property ladder.

'In theory it's fine, but it has a big impact on Tory voters. Actually it plays into exactly the same territory that the social care proposal went into, in terms of taking away a load of people's housing wealth. For a country of homeowners, it was deemed too difficult.'

188 Private interview
189 Private interview
190 Private interviews
191 Private interview
192 Private interviews
193 Email, Crosby to Timothy, 16 May 2017
194 Interview, Chris Wilkins
195 Private interview
196 Tim Farron, interview with Press Association, 19 May 2017
197 Private interview
198 Private interview
199 Private interview
200 Private interview
201 Private interview
202 Interview, Chris Wilkins
203 Private information
204 Private interview
205 The draft policy suggested a £50,000 capital floor would be protected. The eventual policy proposed protecting the last £100,000 of an individual's assets from being spent on care fees. The policy outlined in Timothy's email to Textor of 25 April said: 'We will change the rules so people receiving care at home can defer the costs while they are alive, just as they can already for residential care and guarantee that, no matter how large the cost of care, people will never be left with less than £50,000 in savings and assets after paying for care costs.'

The email also outlined a further innovation on social care, which never made it into the manifesto. Had it done so, it's just possible that the eventual row over scrapping the Dilnot cap could have been avoided. The email said: 'For younger people, we will introduce a new social care insurance system, backed by a British sovereign wealth fund, so that everyone – no matter where they live and how much they have earned – can be promised a secure and dignified old age.'

206 See Appendix 2 for the full email
207 Interview, Nick Timothy
208 Interview, Nick Timothy
209 Private interview
210 Private interviews
211 Private interview
212 Private interview
213 Interview, Nick Timothy
214 Private interview
215 Private interview
216 Private interview
217 Private interview
218 Interview, Andrew Gwynne
219 Interview, Andrew Gwynne
220 Private interview
221 Heather Stewart, Robert Booth and Vikram Dodd, 'Theresa May to tackle Donald Trump over Manchester bombing evidence', *The Guardian*, 24 May 2017, accessed 30 September 2017 at: https://www.theguardian.com/uk-news/2017/may/24/theresa-may-to-tackle-donald-trump-over-manchester-bombing-evidence
222 Private interview
223 Private interview
224 Private interview
225 Private interview
226 Private interview
227 Private interview
228 Private interview
229 Private interview
230 Simon Walters and Glen Owen, 'May Goes Nuclear', *Mail on Sunday*, 4 June 2017
231 Private interview
232 Private interview
233 Private interview
234 Private interview
235 Private interview
236 Private interview
237 Private interview
238 Private interview
239 Private information
240 Ryan Lizza, 'The Final Push', *New Yorker*, 29 October 2012, accessed 30 September 2017 at: https://www.newyorker.com/magazine/2012/10/29/the-final-push

241 Private interview
242 Interview, Jim Messina
243 Private interview
244 Private interview
245 Private interview
246 Private interview
247 Private interview
248 Private interview
249 Private interview
250 Private interview
251 Interview, Craig Elder
252 Interview, Tommy Sheppard
253 Private interview
254 Private interview
255 Private interview
256 Private interview
257 Interview, Tommy Sheppard
258 Private interview
259 Peter Geoghegan, 'Brexit plays into old divisions in Northern Ireland', Politico, 22 May 2017, accessed 30 September 2017 at: http://www.politico.eu/article/brexit-plays-into-old-divisions-in-northern-ireland-general-election-democratic-unionist-party-sinn-fein-ulster/
260 Interview, Paul Butters
261 Private information
262 Private interview
263 Private interview
264 Private interview
265 Interview, Patrick O'Flynn
266 Interview, Nigel Farage
267 Joe Murphy, 'Theresa May exclusive interview: "Terrorism is now breeding terrorism", says Prime Minister after London attack', Evening Standard, 5 June 2017, accessed 12 October 2017 at: https://www.standard.co.uk/news/politics/theresa-may-exclusive-interview-terrorism-is-now-breeding-terrorism-says-prime-minister-after-london-a3557011.html
268 Private interview
269 Private interview
270 Interview, Lynton Crosby
271 Private interview
272 Interview, Jim Messina
273 Private interviews
274 Robert Hutton, 'Eight Nerds, a Sealed Room and One Big British Political Secret', Bloomberg News, 8 June 2017, accessed 25 September at: https://www.bloomberg.com/news/articles/2017-06-08/how-the-secret-general-election-2017-exit-poll-is-produced

275 Tim Ross, Svenja O'Donnell and Alex Morales, 'How May's Sure Thing Became a Political Disaster for the Ages', Bloomberg News, 9 June 2017, accessed 30 September 2017 at: https://www.bloomberg.com/news/articles/2017-06-09/how-may-s-sure-thing-became-a-political-disaster-for-the-ages

276 Interview, Nick Timothy. Marr admitted to the authors that he spoke to No. 10 'seconds before the exit poll was announced', but believes Hill already knew the forecast. 'She didn't sound like she was surprised,' he said. Those in the room that night who were briefed on the exit poll insist there was only one leak.

277 Private interview

278 Private interview

279 Theresa May, interview with Emma Barnett for BBC Radio 5 live, 13 July 2017

280 Private interviews

281 Private interview

282 Private interviews. Later, Philip May's fears for his wife's wellbeing would be heightened after the Grenfell Tower fire. She was being blamed personally for the tragedy and pilloried for her response to it, and he confided to friends that he did not think the Prime Minister was coping.

283 Interview, Nick Timothy

284 Private interview. A source close to Hammond explains: 'It was a knee-jerk assessment of the situation. Philip realises Boris has limited appeal and his position as of 4 a.m. on 9 June changed when the PM made it clear she was staying.'

285 Private interviews. One ally of Messina's says he was merely trying to stay positive for a downcast team at CCHQ and did not necessarily believe the Tories would win a majority.

286 Tim Ross, Svenja O'Donnell and Alex Morales, 'How May's Sure Thing Became a Political Disaster for the Ages', Bloomberg News, 9 June 2017, accessed 30 September 2017 at: https://www.bloomberg.com/news/articles/2017-06-09/how-may-s-sure-thing-became-a-political-disaster-for-the-ages

287 Private interview

288 Private interviews

289 Private interview

290 Private interview

291 Private interview, Cabinet minister

292 Anushka Asthana and Jessica Elgot, 'Theresa May buys time with apology to Tory MPs over election "mess"', The Guardian, 12 June 2017, accessed 20 September 2017 at: https://www.theguardian.com/politics/2017/jun/12/theresa-may-apologies-backbenchers-election-mess

293 Nick Timothy, 'Nick Timothy: Where We Went Wrong', The Spectator, 17 June 2017, accessed 10 October 2017 at: https://www.spectator.co.uk/2017/06/nick-timothy-where-we-went-wrong/

294 Private interview. See also Jack Maidment, 'Sir Lynton Crosby's firm "paid £4 million by Conservative Pary for 2017 general election campaign"', *Daily Telegraph*, 8 August 2017, accessed 12 October 2017 at: http://www.telegraph.co.uk/news/2017/08/08/sir-lynton-crosbys-firm-paid-4million-conservative-party-2017/

295 Figures from Opinium in Toby Helm, 'Theresa May's ratings slump in wake of general election – poll', *The Observer*, 2 July 2017, accessed 20 September 2017 at: https://www.theguardian.com/politics/2017/jul/01/over-60-of-voters-view-theresa-may-as-pm-negatively-poll

296 Kate McCann, 'Conservative donors handed Theresa May a record £25 million to fight an election in which she lost 13 seats', *Daily Telegraph*, 24 August 2017, accessed 20 September 2017 at: http://www.telegraph.co.uk/news/2017/08/24/conservative-donors-handed-theresa-may-record-25-million-fight/

297 Ed Fieldhouse and Chris Prosser, 'The Brexit election? The 2017 General Election in ten charts', British Election Study, 1 August 2017, accessed 20 September 2017 at: http://www.britishelectionstudy.com/bes-impact/the-brexit-election-the-2017-general-election-in-ten-charts/#.WcKSC8iGNPY

298 Interview, Ben Gummer

299 Chris Prosser, 'What was it all about? The 2017 election campaign in voters' own words', British Election Study, 2 August 2017, accessed 13 October 2017 at: http://www.britishelectionstudy.com/bes-findings/what-was-it-all-about-the-2017-election-campaign-in-voters-own-words/#.WeCgjGWhSt8

300 Interview, Jim Messina

301 Private interview

302 Ed Fieldhouse and Chris Prosser, 'The Brexit election? The 2017 General Election in ten charts', op. cit.

303 Interview, Nick Timothy

ABOUT THE AUTHORS

TIM ROSS reports on UK politics and Brexit for Bloomberg. Based in Westminster as a political journalist since 2011, he has worked for the *Daily Telegraph* and *Sunday Telegraph* and wrote the acclaimed book on the 2015 election, *Why the Tories Won*. He lives in London with his wife and their two sons.

TOM McTAGUE is Politico's chief UK political correspondent and is based in Parliament. He previously covered British politics for the *Independent on Sunday*, Mail Online and the *Mirror* and frequently appears as a guest commentator on television. Tom grew up in County Durham and now lives in London with his wife and son.